Virgil's English Translators

Edinburgh Critical Studies in Literary Translation
Series Editor: Stuart Gillespie

The series reflects the current vitality of the subject, and will be a magnet for future work. Its remit is not only the phenomenon of translation in itself, but the impact of translation too. It also draws on the increasingly lively fields of reception studies and cultural history. Volumes will focus on Anglophone literary traditions in their foreign relations.

Published Titles

The English Aeneid: *Translations of Virgil, 1555–1646*
Sheldon Brammall

The Many Voices of Lydia Davis: Translation, Rewriting, Intertextuality
Jonathan Evans

Nature Translated: Alexander von Humboldt's Works in Nineteenth-Century Britain
Alison E. Martin

Virgil's English Translators: Civil Wars to Restoration
Ian Calvert

www.edinburghuniversitypress.com/series/ECSLT

Virgil's English Translators
Civil Wars to Restoration

Ian Calvert

EDINBURGH
University Press

Edinburgh University Press is one of the leading university presses in the UK. We publish academic books and journals in our selected subject areas across the humanities and social sciences, combining cutting-edge scholarship with high editorial and production values to produce academic works of lasting importance. For more information visit our website: edinburghuniversitypress.com

© Ian Calvert, 2021, 2023

Edinburgh University Press Ltd
The Tun – Holyrood Road
12(2f) Jackson's Entry
Edinburgh EH8 8PJ

First published in hardback by Edinburgh University Press 2021

Typeset in 10.5/13 Sabon by
Servis Filmsetting Ltd, Stockport, Cheshire

A CIP record for this book is available from the British Library

ISBN 978 1 4744 7564 8 (hardback)
ISBN 978 1 4744 7565 5 (paperback)
ISBN 978 1 4744 7566 2 (webready PDF)
ISBN 978 1 4744 7567 9 (epub)

The right of Ian Calvert to be identified as the author of this work has been asserted in accordance with the Copyright, Designs and Patents Act 1988, and the Copyright and Related Rights Regulations 2003 (SI No. 2498).

Contents

Series Editor's Preface	vi
Acknowledgements	vii
Note on Texts	viii
1. Desired Futures: Sidney Godolphin and Edmund Waller	1
2. Prophetic Elegy: Sir John Denham	26
3. Absent Presence: Abraham Cowley	53
4. Sacred Majesty: John Ogilby	83
5. Hopeful Prince: Sir Richard Fanshawe	111
6. Private Interest: James Harrington	137
7. Future Contingencies: Sir Robert Howard and John Boys	165
Bibliography	187
Index	196

Series Editor's Preface

Translators, Pushkin's 'post-horses of enlightenment', play a central role in every society's reception of other cultures. The study of translation – in theory, in practice and in relation to broader narratives in literary and cultural history – is now a vibrant scholarly field. It is key to current debates on literary canons in an increasingly global world, and on the possibility of World Literature. Edinburgh Critical Studies in Literary Translation addresses translation as a literary and historical phenomenon and is the first monograph series to do so.

Some of these studies engage with the approaches individual authors have taken to translation. Some deal with the impact of particular source texts or of particular translations on the societies in which they were produced. A central concern of the series is with interactions between translation and other forms of creative work and with the part translation can play in forging the identity of individual authors. We are no less interested in the way translation can set directions for literary cultures at large.

There are no constraints on historical period. The emphasis of the series is in the first instance on translations involving the English language, whether in the context of ancient or modern literature. Our scholarly territory straddles the disciplines of English Literature, Classical Studies, Comparative Literature and Modern Languages. Contributors necessarily work at their frontiers, using innovative tools on interdisciplinary topics.

Stuart Gillespie

Acknowledgements

Parts of Chapters 1 and 2 revise and adapt sections from 'Hindsight as Foresight: Virgilian Retrospective Prophecy in *Coopers Hill* and *The Destruction of Troy*', *International Journal of the Classical Tradition*, 26 (2019), 150–74. An earlier draft of Chapter 4 appeared as 'Slanted Histories, Hesperian Fables: Material Form and Royalist Prophecy in John Ogilby's *The Works of Publius Virgilius Maro*', *The Seventeenth Century*, 33 (2018), 533–55.

Stuart Gillespie has, with great patience and forbearance, provided extensive and invaluable advice over the course of this project. He has read drafts of individual chapters with scrupulous care and attention, and the finished book is immeasurably improved as a result. Emily Wilson gave highly useful feedback regarding the shape of the project as a whole. I have benefited, and continue to benefit, from the counsel, expertise and support of David Hopkins and Tom Mason, both of whom read a full draft of the book. Ed Holberton, John McTague, Imogen Peck and Ros Powell very kindly found the time at a busy point in the academic year to read and comment on drafts of individual chapters. Jen Hobbs provided much-needed advice on French caterpillars. Tessie Prakas has been a long-standing interlocutor and has helped me to articulate my ideas. Any remaining errors in what follows are, of course, entirely my own responsibility.

From the earliest to the closing stages of writing this book Lesel Dawson has been both champion and mentor, especially during the times when my future in academia has been both precarious and contingent. I am extremely grateful for her unstinting encouragement and true friendship. My greatest debts are to my parents, to whom this book is dedicated. My career has only been possible thanks to their selfless and heroic support: *hoc opus, hic labor est*.

Ian Calvert

Note on Texts

Classical texts and glossing translations are cited from the most recent edition of the relevant volume in the Loeb Classical Library (which are cited in the Bibliography by author). I have sometimes silently adapted the translations in the interests of greater accuracy, to remove archaic phrasing and diction and/or to represent an interpretative ambiguity. Translations from other texts are my own unless otherwise stated.

Quotations from Virgil have been checked against the editions and commentaries which the authors that I consider across this study directly cite or refer to in their translations. As only some translators indicate which versions of Virgil they consulted, quotations have also been checked against the text in the other editions which were most readily available in the British Isles during the years of their literary activity. Any substantive differences between the Loeb Virgil and these editions are recorded in a footnote.

For the sake of consistency, and because many of the translations cited in this study exist only in seventeenth-century editions, all quotations from the primary texts are in old spelling (the exception is Denham's manuscript *Aeneid*, which I have accessed through a modern-spelling edition). I have, though, normalised the use of i/j and u/v, expanded most contractions, substituted the short s for the long s and amended obvious typographical errors.

Chapter 1

Desired Futures: Sidney Godolphin and Edmund Waller

Introduction

This book is a study of the individuals who translated Virgil into English between the outbreak of civil war in the Stuart kingdoms and the first years of the Restoration. It argues that these translators found in Virgil's poetry a precedent for acknowledging that the uncertainties of their present moment had made possible a number of national futures, some of which were more palatable to their political affinities than others. Some of the translators used Virgil to predict that one of these futures was destined to occur, both for the purposes of lament and of panegyric, but they more usually engaged with Virgil to offer much less deterministic readings of the recent past and the immediate future. Neither Latin nor English has the formal optative mood that other languages use to express wishes and hopes, but this study nonetheless identifies an optative quality in the writings of Virgil's English translators in the middle decades of the seventeenth century. They engaged with Virgil in an attempt to delineate and secure the future they hoped would come to pass but also to anticipate the future they feared would come.

After an introductory section on Sidney Godolphin (1610–43) and Edmund Waller (1606–87), there are individual chapters on Sir John Denham (1614/15–69), Abraham Cowley (1618–67), John Ogilby (1600–76), Sir Richard Fanshawe (1608–66) and James Harrington (1611–77); I also briefly discuss Robert Heath (1620–85), Richard Crashaw (1612/13–49), Henry Vaughan (1621–95) and Sir William Kingsmill (1613–61). By way of conclusion, I consider Sir Robert Howard (1626–98) and John Boys (1621–c.61), whose careers as published Virgilian writers began in the year of the Restoration. These men belonged to a variety of overlapping social and literary networks. They wrote to and about each other, and they read, responded to, borrowed from and imitated each other's works, including their translations from Virgil, which ranged in scope from a few lines to complete renderings of the Virgilian corpus. For several of them, translating Virgil was a foundational act for a literary career. Others had already written texts which engaged with Virgil's poetry to a substantial degree by the time they produced their translations. This book thus seeks to read their translations not only within a canon of seventeenth-century translations of Virgil, but also within the careers of the individual translators themselves.

These translators spent (or claimed to have spent) at least part of the period under consideration as courtiers or in some other form of royal service. Yet such service should not be equated too readily with their political loyalties, which frequently shifted and adapted according to circumstances; royal service and royalism were not necessarily in complete alignment. In addition, recent scholarship has stressed that royalism incorporated a wide variety of attitudes regarding the role of the monarch within the English political system.[1] The translators' careers demonstrate that royalism was a site of contested affinities, where individual factions owed their primary loyalty to different principles and to different members of the Stuart dynasty, including Charles I, his wife Henrietta Maria and his son Charles, Prince of Wales (to avoid confusion with his namesake father, throughout the book I refer to this individual as the Prince when discussing the period prior to his accession as Charles II in 1660). Loyalty to an individual did not necessarily equate to a specific set of beliefs: people could, and did, profess a sense of duty and obligation to Charles I whilst advocating for a republic. Equally, expressions of loyalty to the royalist cause did not prevent critique, or even hostility towards, the king and his family.

The fairly recent labelling of certain royalist principles as constitutional (or parliamentary) royalism, Queen's Party royalism and ultra-loyalism – terms which, along with two other terms of my own coinage, Prince's Party royalism and autocratic republicanism, are delineated more fully in subsequent chapters – illuminate broader affiliations. However, the boundaries between these groupings were permeable, as were those between royalism and other political positions. The works of the translators that form the focus of this book also show that the royalisms of the late 1630s, the civil wars, Interregnum and Restoration had their own distinct preoccupations, ideologies and aims. In addition, royalism was affected by geographical as well by temporal contexts;[2] although the majority of the texts considered here were composed in England their authors drew on their experience of royal service in Ireland, Scotland and continental Europe, not just the Stuarts' southern kingdom.

Virgil's reception in the mid-seventeenth century of course extended beyond direct translation by people with royalist affinities, however broadly defined; his status ensured that writers from across the literary and political spectrum engaged with his poetry. But Virgil proved to be such a conducive site for royalists because he presented the advent of the Principate under Augustus as having established a form of government that was both innovative and a restored, more stable version of a previous order. Augustus' own self-fashioning did something similar, but where Augustus proclaimed himself (however inaccurately) as the restorer of the Roman Republic Virgil's discourse was overtly monarchical. His presentation of Augustus' acquisition of power could be mapped on to the restoration of the form of rule that was the chief desideratum of Virgil's translators throughout the 1640s and 1650s, although his translators often found it necessary to interpolate information and frame their translations through paratexts to make the Virgilian material better reflect their sense of the precise historical moment. The nature of these changes also helps to identify the translators' different opinions on the origins of a monarch's legitimacy, how extensive the monarch's power should be, the identity of the individual or dynasty who should wield that power, and whether or not Virgil himself considered the monarchical aspects of Augustus' rule to be positive and praiseworthy.

Virgil's accounts of Augustus' ascent to imperial power gave rise to an interpretative tradition that was especially influential in the early modern period and which informs this study as a whole: that Virgil used his poetry to advise Augustus on the art of good governance.[3] One of the most significant passages of Virgil's poetry which encourages this reading comes towards the end of the parade of Roman heroes in the Underworld (*A* 6.756–886), to which I return across the remainder of this section. There Aeneas' father Anchises refers to his son as 'Romane' (*A* 6.851; 'Roman') rather than 'Troiane' ('Trojan') when he defines the Roman imperial mission: 'parcere subiectis et debellare superbos' (*A* 6.853; 'spare the vanquished, and crush the proud'). The tradition that Virgil himself recited Book 6 of the *Aeneid* to Augustus (along with Books 2 and 4) also explains why at this moment Aeneas has long been seen as a proxy for Augustus (who claimed Aeneas as an ancestor), and why Anchises has been thought to act as a stand-in for Virgil himself.[4] But contrary to Servius' claim in his commentary on the *Aeneid* that Virgil's intentions in the poem were 'Homerum imitari et Augustum laudare a parentibus' ('to imitate Homer and to praise Augustus through his ancestors') the nature of the relationship between Augustus and Aeneas was not fixed or stable.[5] The connections Virgil forged between Augustus and Aeneas imparted criticism as well as praise.

Many of Virgil's English translators extended the multivalencies of the potential relationship between past and present in Virgil's poetry, as well as the lacunae between the poem's presentation of Augustus and the known realities of his rule, when applying them to rulers from their own time. As we will see, some consciously adopted the role of a Virgilian poet–counsellor; in a further indication of their engagement with the didactic tradition, almost all of the stand-alone translations of individual books from the *Aeneid* that were published in this period correlated with those which Virgil himself was supposed to have recited to Augustus. Other translators were more self-effacing. They presented themselves as providing commentary rather than counsel, and (in a few cases) as royal servants who directed advice towards their sovereign's supporters and not the sovereign himself. Both traditions also informed these translators' broader literary output. In some cases (such as Fanshawe's translations of Battista Guarini's pastoral drama *Il Pastor Fido* and Luís Vaz de Camões' epic *Os Lusíadas*) this was because the original authors of the texts they were translating had themselves drawn on the tradition of the poet as royal counsellor. In others (which include panegyrics by Waller and Howard, Denham's *Coopers Hill*, Cowley's *The Civil War*, Ogilby's Homer translations and Harrington's political tracts) the authors in question made their writings conform to this tradition by presenting or addressing their chosen sovereign as another Aeneas and/or Augustus.

The didactic potential that the translators discussed here found in Virgil sometimes took the form of imposing a clear narrative on the immediate future. In some cases the translators implied that the imagined future in question was in the best interests of that text's addressee. They encouraged their addressee to interpret this counsel as guidance on how they could fulfil their promise and become a great leader of their people, a latter-day Aeneas/Augustus shorn of all the potentially problematic qualities such an association could bring. Other texts, however, provided a much less fixed account. Such passages remained a means of outlining the individual translator's desired political future, but they recognised that it was far from secure.

This connection between counsel and anticipated futures intersected with another strand of Virgil's early modern reception that I return to across this study: his supposed status as the person who had abandoned the Greek-derived term for a poet, *poeta*, and who had resurrected the Roman word *vates* in recognition that it could denote a prophet as well as a poet.[6] Virgil may not, in fact, have been the first person who revived *vates* within a poetic context, and even if he was, he only used it to describe himself on a single occasion (*A* 7.41). It was his contemporaries, particularly Horace, who made more direct use of the associations between poetry and vatic utterances. Yet critics in the early modern period frequently referred to the concept of the poet as *vates* when discussing the value and social role of poetry: Sir Philip Sidney, for example, asserted 'Among the Romans a Poet was called *Vates*, which is as much as a Diviner, Fore-seer, or Prophet . . . so heavenly a title did that excellent people bestow upon this hart-ravishing knowledge.'[7] Such a reading of *vates*, which persisted into the seventeenth century, was informed and sustained by the legacy of Virgil's reception as a poet who had inadvertently or unconsciously foreseen Christ's birth.[8] This book is concerned with the translators in the seventeenth century who capitalised on the dual meaning of *vates* to give a prophetic quality to their translations and imitations of Virgil and the futures that they anticipated both for the Stuart dynasty and the nation as a whole.

The formal, full-dress prophecies of Virgil and his mid-seventeenth century translators, however, were invariably made *post eventum*, that is, they were written after the specific events that they anticipated. The Roman heroes Aeneas encounters in the Underworld are from after Aeneas' own time, but preceded (or, in the case of Augustus, were contemporary with) Virgil's. As Virgil's most extensive *post eventum* prophecies document the establishment of Augustus' personal rule they can suggest a confident teleological reading of Rome's recent and distant past. In such an interpretation, they present the founding of the Roman people and the rise to power by Aeneas' heir Augustus not only as the future that Virgil himself desired, but as inevitable and predestined events. Consequently, in this reading, the *post eventum* prophecies intimate that any attempts to thwart these events were doomed to failure.

My own reading of the prophetic elements in Virgil and his translators, however, is more in line with James J. O'Hara's contention that Virgil was drawn to revive the term *vates* because of its association with illusion, not with certainty or foresight. For O'Hara, Virgilian *post eventum* prophecies provide a version of events which Virgil expected his first readers to have recognised as being knowingly partial and illusory, particularly with regard to the poem's account of Augustus' status as a wise and predestined sovereign.[9] Where I differ from O'Hara is that I hold that the key term which informed the connections between poetry and prophecy for Virgil is not illusion, but contingency. For all its emphasis on fated destiny, Virgil's poetry reflected on the experiences of civil war and recognised that the consequences of that conflict were far from settled and could still manifest in a number of different, but equally possible, alternative outcomes. As Anne Rogerson has argued, the *Aeneid* 'leaves space for consideration of a variety of futures' for both Augustus' Romans and Aeneas' Trojans.[10] The outcome of the civil wars that ultimately came to pass did not necessarily reflect Virgil's own hopes, but even if it did, Virgil's poetry still acknowledged that desired outcomes were not guaranteed, that there could be unintended consequences to any decisions that have been taken, and alternatives to those decisions could always have been made. Many of his English translators who were active in the Interregnum and early Restoration found themselves having close affinities with this sensibility. For the most part they too saw the future as contingent, not predestined.

In this context, it is significant that even Virgil's *post eventum* prophecies which appear most triumphalist contain moments of uncertainty and hesitancy. The parade of Rome's 'future' heroes in the Underworld ends not with Anchises' expression of the Roman imperial mission, but his lament for Marcellus (*A* 6.867–86), who had been Augustus' heir presumptive until his death at the age of nineteen in 23 BC. The passage combines the technique of the *post eventum* prophecy with another, distinctively Virgilian, motif: that of *mors immatura* ('untimely death'). The phrase occurs in the lament by the Italian king Evander for the death in combat of his young son Pallas (*A* 11.166–7), but both Pallas' and Marcellus' deaths form part of a broader pattern of young men's deaths throughout the poem.[11] Such deaths indicate thwarted ambition, lost hopes and unfulfilled potential for the societies to which they belong as well as for the individuals themselves. In Virgil, what may have begun as propaganda can end as elegy. This shift from the triumphant to the mournful outlines Virgil's recognition that, for all the poem's invocations of fated destiny, any attempt he might make to provide a genuine prediction of the future is at the mercy of events that lie outside any individual's control.

Virgil's mid-seventeenth-century English translators also used *post eventum* prophecy for elegiac purposes, not only to commemorate the *mors immatura* of young men who fought in the civil wars, but also in reference to the death of Charles I and the system of government that he represented. Two passages from the *Aeneid* in particular – Pyrrhus' murder of Priam (*A* 2.554–8) and the curse Dido places on Aeneas and his descendants (*A* 4.615–20) – were regularly co-opted by Virgil's translators in this period for this purpose. I also examine the use of these passages, along with other incidences of the *mors immatura* trope, by Virgil and his translators to register anxieties about the future as well as lament past losses.

Virgil's translators were frequently drawn to the way that Virgil's own accounts of the near future could accommodate alternative resolutions. A high number of the passages in Virgil which either took the form of prophecies or represented moments that were adapted to serve prophetic ends were deliberately framed by the translators to offer an open-ended account of the immediate future. By foregrounding this aspect of the text in their translations (or, in certain cases, imitations) of these passages, they were able to emphasise the various potential consequences of watershed political moments. It is not a coincidence that the translators frequently turned to the *Georgics* as source material for these especially indeterminate moments of anticipation, since, as Melissa Schoenberger notes, Virgilian georgic was preoccupied with mutability and contingency.[12] The *Georgics* (pub. 29 BC) were the product of a highly unstable political climate where the person who would later assume the name Augustus had yet to secure his hold on power; the translations from the *Georgics* that were published in the 1650s and early 1660s similarly stressed the future's instability. They also showed an awareness that even over a short period of time texts could acquire new meanings which had the potential to reaffirm or undermine original authorial intentions. A few of the writers considered throughout this book engaged with the concept of the poet as someone who outlined his preferred version of the future via counsel to a sovereign in an attempt to assert a degree of agency over these additional or deferred meanings; other translators suggested these resonances were either inadvertent or the result of the text passing out of the author's control, and that foresight (whether real or actual) brought no benefits to supporters of the Stuarts.

It is important to remember that between 1649 and 1660 there was very little reason to believe that the Stuart monarchy would return to rule in its former kingdoms, even for those who hoped for a restoration of Stuart rule and sought to bring it about. Just as, from our historical perspective, it might seem inevitable that Augustus' reign would be of long duration and the imperial system of government that it inaugurated would last for several centuries, so too can hindsight portray the execution of Charles I, the foundation of the Commonwealth, its subsequent replacement by the Cromwellian Protectorate and its dissolution for the restoration of the monarchy as fixed and inevitable outcomes. Yet the major political events of Augustan Rome and Interregnum England were the result of contingencies rather than a predestined future. Even though Augustus' hold on power seemed more established by the time of the *Aeneid*'s publication in 19 BC than it had when Virgil published the *Georgics*, the longevity of Augustus' reign and the institutes of government that it inaugurated were far from established. A. M. Bowie has observed how Virgil's use of Aeneas as a proxy for Augustus registered this political uncertainty, since the poem included, via a prophecy, the legend that Aeneas' reign in Latium lasted only three years after his defeat of Turnus.[13] By the time Virgil was writing the *Aeneid* Augustus' personal rule had already surpassed this length of time, but the prospect of his reign being brief or suddenly curtailed had not been removed entirely; Augustus experienced recurrent bouts of serious poor health throughout his life, and he had experienced a near-fatal illness in 23 BC, the same year as Marcellus' death. Both events had raised serious doubts about who would succeed Augustus, as well as the prospect that the Principate might expire with him.

Within the seventeenth-century English political context, John Aubrey recollected that the republican doctrine James Harrington advocated at meetings of his Rota Club during the winter of 1659–60, barely six months before the Restoration, 'was very taking, and the more because, as to human foresight, there was no possibility of the King's returne'.[14] As Niall Allsopp has recently discussed, even to call the years between 1649 and 1660 the 'Interregnum' (the period between two kings) is to impose 'a teleological frame, one which we know has a certain ending'.[15] References to an Interregnum occlude historical contingencies and endorse the reading of the republican governments as a historical aberration, but for most of the writers under consideration here this reading of events remained more a desire than an expectation. Even in the early 1660s, as in the 1650s, the most explicitly deterministic readings of recent political events were usually the result of attempts to assert the legitimacy of precarious forms of government. In the immediate aftermath of the Restoration, fears (and, in certain quarters, hopes) remained that Charles II would experience a further period of exile as a monarch without a kingdom, and poems from this period by Stuart loyalists often contained advice on how Charles could avoid this fate. Attempts to read the Restoration as providential and predestined were prompted in part by a desire to overrule the recent past and repurpose the providentialist rhetoric that Parliamentarians, republicans and Cromwellians had deployed to explain the royalist defeats of the 1640s. At the same time, a royalist providentialism sought to draw a veil over contemporary doubts about the longevity of Charles II's reign.

A key contention of this book is that *post eventum* attitudes have affected our sense of the anticipated futures, political commentary, counsel and prophetic utterances that are contained in the works of Virgil's mid-seventeenth-century English translators. Our knowledge of the Restoration Settlement's relative longevity affects our view of the (sometimes triumphalist, but more often melancholic) potential futures for the Stuart dynasty that the writers considered here included in their translations and other literary works. What from a twenty-first-century perspective look like confident assertions of loyalty that would soon be vindicated may represent wishful, or even delusional, thinking; conversely, expressions of changed loyalties that can appear as evidence of time-serving do not fully take into account how total the rout of the royalist cause seemed in the 1650s. Expressions of praise for a head of state, whether a Stuart or a Cromwell, frequently represented attempts to secure a future that poets hoped would come to pass under that individual rather than their sense of present realities.

The fact that hindsight has affected our sense of the mid-seventeenth-century Virgil translations as texts that are worthy of critical attention, as well as sites that contain political commentary and anticipations of the future, has further elided these differences in early modern and more recent perspectives. Previous scholarship on these texts has largely focused on their status as works which contributed to debates regarding the theory and practice of translation, and as predecessors to and source material for Dryden's engagement with Virgil.[16] My discussion does touch at points on questions of aesthetics and theories of translation, and this study ends with a brief discussion of the connections between the texts under consideration and Dryden's Virgil. I am primarily concerned, however, with situating the works of Virgil's mid-seventeenth-century translators more securely within their fraught, contingent historical context and with recuperating their relationship with contemporary political events.

I first do so for the translation of *Aeneid* 4 by Sidney Godolphin and Edmund Waller that was published in 1658 as *The Passion of Dido for Æneas*. In some respects, particularly its authorship, this text is an outlier amongst the Virgil translations discussed in this study. Although *The Passion of Dido for Æneas* is one of the latest translations of Virgil considered here in terms of its publication, it was, for reasons outlined below, in all likelihood one of the first to be written. Its provenance, its relationship to Godolphin's and Waller's other poems and its reception history provide the most useful means of introducing the broader concerns of political engagement which form the major components of discussion across this book.

The Passion of Dido for Æneas

The Passion of Dido for Æneas was the work of two individuals, but it was not a formal collaboration. Robin Sowerby's edition of the poem has given an extensive overview of both men's involvement in the text's composition, but in essence the poem can be divided into three sections with regard to its authorship.[17] The first (lines 1–454) is usually assigned to Godolphin alone.[18] The second (lines 455–588) is thought to be a sufficiently thorough revision of Godolphin's draft that Waller considered it to be his own work. The authorship of the final section remains unclear, but the reference in the preface to the first published edition that '*all but a very little*' of the translation was the work of Godolphin suggests that it too should be attributed to him.[19]

Godolphin's death in 1643 during a skirmish against Parliamentarian forces gives a *terminus ante quem* for his involvement in *The Passion of Dido for Æneas*, and the wider context of his poetic career (considered below) indicates that the earliest draft of the translation likely dates from before the outbreak of civil war. Lines 455–588 are often printed as a stand-alone poem in collections of Waller, sometimes under the title 'Part of the Fourth Book of Virgil Translated, In the Year 1657'. While this suggests that Waller's revision of Godolphin's draft occurred only a year before its publication, this attribution first appeared several decades after Waller's death,[20] which casts doubts on its veracity. There are sufficient continuities between *The Passion of Dido for Æneas* and poems by Waller and Godolphin that can be securely dated to the late 1630s to suggest that Waller's amendments were more or less contemporary with Godolphin's initial composition. By considering the translation alongside Waller's other literary activities it is possible to see that his revisions to *The Passion of Dido for Æneas* politicised a translation by Godolphin that was initially primarily concerned with aesthetic matters.

Godolphin's poems are mostly occasional in nature, and the events they commemorate date the bulk of his literary endeavours to the period in the 1630s when both he and Waller were part of the 'Great Tew Circle', a literary coterie centred around Lucius Cary, 2nd Viscount Falkland, and which took its name from Falkland's Oxfordshire country estate where its members met. Sowerby has discussed the particular interest several members of this circle (who included other translators of Virgil who form the focus of later chapters) had in developing an 'Augustan' aesthetic for English verse. He has defined this aesthetic as an attempt to replicate in English the qualities of Latin at its most refined and polished, both through imitation and direct translation; Virgil was the focus of emulation since his works were held to represent the height of Latin verse.[21] Many members of the Circle were also associated with the 'Sons of Ben', the group of writers who claimed personal acquaintance and/or literary kinship with Ben Jonson. Falkland's contribution to a commemorative volume of poems on Jonson's death refers to Godolphin and Waller in the same verse-line.[22] Both men also contributed poems to this volume, and there is a considerable overlap with the subject matter of their other works in this period.[23] They both contributed commendatory verses to the biblical paraphrases in verse by a different member of Falkland's circle (and, as I discuss shortly, another translator of Virgil), George Sandys,[24] and wrote poems on the death of Lady Cecil, Countess of Northumberland, which circulated in manuscript together. David Norbrook has discussed the fact that Godolphin's and Waller's poems on the death of another aristocratic woman, Anne Cavendish, Lady Rich, appear sequentially in several manuscripts, and that one of these manuscripts gives Godolphin's poem a title that states he was responding directly to Waller's.[25] Godolphin and Waller could, of course, have been prompted to write elegies for these women independently, but it is more likely that they did so on account of their belonging to the same social circle. Lady Cecil died in the same year as Jonson (1637) and Lady Rich died in the same year that Sandys' biblical paraphrases were published (1638). The two men were evidently closely associated with each other during these years.

Although the poetry that Godolphin wrote in English dates from the late 1630s, he made his poetic debut in the early 1620s with two short Latin epigrams. The two epigrams appeared in separate university miscellanies. One marks the death of the antiquarian William Camden, and Godolphin's poem for this collection contains his only direct engagement with Virgil in his writings outside of *The Passion of Dido for Æneas* that I have been able to identify: one line of the poem closely imitates a line from Aeneas' speech on the anniversary of Anchises' death.[26] However, as Godolphin was only fourteen when this poem was published, the borrowing is more an indication of the central place Virgil played in early modern school and university curriculums than any particular affinity Godolphin had for the poet's work at this point.

The other university miscellany to which Godolphin contributed a Latin poem celebrated the return of Charles I (when Prince of Wales) to England following the collapse of the 'Spanish Match', the unsuccessful attempt to secure a marriage between Charles and the daughter of Philip III of Spain, Infanta Maria Anna.[27] Although Godolphin's poem is of no great significance in itself, the event which prompted it can shed light on Waller's involvement in *The Passion of Dido for Æneas*, as well as on that text's connections both to anticipated futures and to royalist political commentary.[28] These connections occur when considering the translation alongside Waller's commemoration of Charles's homeward journey in the wake of his failure to secure the Spanish Match in the poem first published in 1645 as *Of the danger his Majestie (being Prince) escaped at the rode at St. Andere* ('Saint Andere' is an anglicised form of Santander).[29] *Of the danger* validates Warren L. Chernaik's claim that 'the presence of Virgil hovers over much of Waller'.[30] When a storm hits the ship, Waller compares Charles's actions to those of the storm-tossed Aeneas:

> Great *Maro* could no greater tempest faine
> When the loud windes usurping on the maine;
> For angry *Juno* labour'd to destroy
> The hated reliques of confounded Troy:
> His bold *Eneas,* on like billows tost
> In a tall ship, and all his Countries lost:
> Dissolves with fear, and both his hands upheld,
> Proclaimes them happy whom the Greeks had quel'd.[31]

In keeping with Waller's desire to praise Charles, he has him exceeding the Virgilian precedent by showing none of Aeneas' fear, even though the storm he faced was equal to that documented in the *Aeneid*.

There are specific textual, as well as situational, connections between *Of the danger* and *The Passion of Dido for Æneas*, as the line '*Neptunes* smooth face, and cleave the yelding deep' appears in both.[32] The most logical response would be to date *Of the danger* to the time of the event that it records and so make it the source for the couplet's appearance in *The Passion of Dido for Æneas,* but it is unclear which of these poems borrowed from the other. Timothy Raylor has suggested that 'the absence of evidence either that Waller wrote poetry or that he was known as a poet before the middle of the 1630s' means that *Of the danger* was, like the other poems by Waller that commemorate events from the 1620s, composed in the decade after the events in question actually occurred.[33]

Raylor has argued that this group of poems formed part of Waller's attempt to advance a career at court via a faction which was associated with Henrietta Maria, the French princess Charles had married after the failure of the Spanish Match and a shift in royal policy which favoured an alliance with France over Spain.[34] These poems were 'designed specifically to memorialize Charles's heroic deeds in terms designed to appeal to the queen'.[35] This impulse illuminates the moments in *Of the danger* which present Charles as a gallant and courtly lover whose attentions were always directed to his future bride rather than to the Infanta. *Of the danger* records the pair's first meeting as Charles passed through Paris on his way to Spain:

> if any thought anoyes
> The gallant youth, 'tis loves untasted joyes,
> And deare remembrance of that fatall glance,
> For which he lately pawn'd his heart in France:
> Where he had seen a brighter Nimph then she
> That sprung out of his present foe; the Sea.
>
> (lines 99–104)

Waller has recoded the encounter to make it seem that Henrietta Maria was always Charles's romantic objective and preferred bride. Hindsight allows Waller to endow seemingly marginal events from the Spanish Match escapade with a greater significance than they would have had at the time and to transform a foreign policy embarrassment into a triumph. By obscuring the gap between the composition of the poem itself and these events, Waller was able to introduce an element of vindicated or fulfilled prophecy. Whilst not formally a *post eventum* prophecy, the techniques Waller uses in this poem resemble this Virgilian poetic strategy and other anticipations of desired futures that poets included in works that marked royal events between the outbreak of civil war and the Restoration.

The emphasis in *Of the danger* on Charles as a 'gallant youth' is consonant with the broader literary court culture of the 1630s, but it also provides another point of contact between that poem and *The Passion of Dido for Æneas*. Sowerby has claimed that the use of 'gallant' in the latter's account of the Trojans preparing for a hunting expedition to translate 'delecta iuventus' (*A* 4.130; 'a chosen band of youth'), 'encapsulates the spirit informing the whole translation'.[36] An additional example of courtly gallantry in *The Passion of Dido for Æneas* comes in its translation of Iarbas' complaint to Jupiter that Dido 'conubia nostra / reppulit ac dominum Aenean in regna recepit' (*A* 4.213–14; 'has spurned my offers of marriage and welcomed Aeneas into her realm as lord'):

> hath thought her self <u>above</u>
> <u>The prize and merit of our Ardent Love</u>;
> Yet now <u>with joy</u> receives into <u>our</u> Land
> The flying Trojan <u>and his Conquered band</u>.
>
> (lines 219–22)

The underlined phrases indicate where the translation substantially departs from the Virgilian original. The interpolated reference to 'Ardent Love' introduces a degree of emotional affection for Dido on Iarbas' part that is not present in the original. It makes him and Aeneas rivals for her heart as well as the sovereignty of her realm. As Iarbas subsequently refers to himself as the 'scorned Moore' (line 224) he becomes less the leader of a kingdom that poses a threat to Carthage's existence and more of a frustrated lover. At the same time, *The Passion of Dido for Æneas* removes the references to Dido and Aeneas' marriage. There is consequently less emphasis on the transgressive nature of their conduct, and neither of them attaches much shame to their actions. Despite its title, then, and its renewed emphasis on desire, the translation is less passionate than the original. In accordance with this rather genteel approach Godolphin and Waller expunge many of the text's more controversial aspects, including Dido's reference to a priestess's powers of necromancy, 'nocturnosque movet Manis' (*A* 4.490; 'she awakes the ghosts of night'),[37] and Mercury's notoriously misogynistic statement 'varium et mutabile semper / femina' (*A* 4.569–70; 'a woman is ever fickle and changeable'). These similarities in tone and focus on courtly romance, as well as the presence of the same phrases in both poems, suggest that *Of the danger* and *The Passion of Dido for Æneas* were written at around the same time in the 1630s.

Whatever the precise order of composition and relationship between the two poems, it is useful to apply what Raylor says of Charles in *Of the danger* to the protagonists of *The Passion of Dido for Æneas*: 'the marriage of Charles and Henrietta Maria is providentially ordained and . . . therefore Charles's abandonment of the Infanta was both necessary and justified, involving . . . no breach of etiquette or gallantry'.[38] In fact, a chance to add a clearer narrative trajectory and sense of accomplishment to the Spanish Match debacle could well have motivated Waller's use of Godolphin's *Aeneid* 4 translation. Within *The Passion of Dido for Æneas*, the translation of Dido's reference to Aeneas' 'virtus' (*A* 4.3; 'excellence') as 'princely grace' (line 3) can also act as a mutually reinforcing panegyrical association between Charles and Aeneas. However, as this reference forms part of the translation that is usually assigned to Godolphin it is unlikely to have been prompted by a conscious or deliberate desire to praise Charles. Godolphin did move in court circles, but aside from the Latin poem on Charles's return from Spain he wrote only one other poem on royal events.[39] This lack of political engagement in his wider literary output indicates that his motivations in beginning a translation of *Aeneid* 4 were more likely to do with a desire to refine his poetic skills through an adherence to the Augustan aesthetic that was cultivated by Falkland's Great Tew Circle. It was Waller's association with *The Passion of Dido for Æneas* that made it a poem actively concerned with affairs of state, since Waller's engagement with the political and literary culture of the Caroline court brought the translation into contact with his panegyrics. This in turn made 'princely grace' into a more politically engaged phrase and aligned the translation more closely with the tradition of using Aeneas as a mirror for princes. This occurred less through any specific decisions Waller made as a translator or reviser of Godolphin's material than through his status as one of *The Passion of Dido for Æneas*' authors. The shared material of *The Passion of Dido for Æneas* and *Of the danger* elides Aeneas' sojourn in Carthage with Charles's time in Spain in the early 1620s. Whatever *affaire de cœur* either figure, as a gallant young prince, had experienced, their destined brides lay elsewhere. Both poems suggest that Henrietta Maria was the Lavinia, and the Infanta the Dido, to Charles's Aeneas.

The Caroline-era political resonances of *The Passion of Dido for Æneas* and its connections with *post eventum* prophecy were obscured by the two decades that elapsed between its composition in the late 1630s and its first published edition of 1658. Certain material aspects of the published edition, however, suggest that the text remained connected to Stuart panegyric. Each page of the volume contains as a headpiece an ornamental pattern made up of four separate woodblocks, where each is comprised of one of the traditional emblems of the kingdoms for which seventeenth-century English monarchs held or claimed sovereignty: a rose, a thistle, a harp and a fleur-de-lys (for the kingdoms of England, Scotland, Ireland and France respectively), with each individual emblem surmounted by a crown.[40] The same blocks had been used to form an ornamental pattern in, amongst other volumes, Robert Stapylton's 1634 translation of the same book of the *Aeneid*, and appeared as a headpiece on certain pages of the memorial volume to Jonson to which Godolphin and Waller contributed poems.[41] The more immediate precedent for their use in *The Passion of Dido for Æneas* was the 1648 edition of Fanshawe's *Il Pastor Fido* translation, including on the first page of his *Aeneid* 4 translation.[42] Both *The Passion of Dido for Æneas* and Fanshawe's 1648 *Il Pastor Fido* were published by Humphrey Moseley, and although publishers would regularly reuse illustrative and ornamental woodblocks across multiple volumes the use of this pattern in both texts was likely strategic. Moseley was the principal royalist publisher of the Interregnum, and, in addition to having previously published Waller, he later published several of the texts considered across this study.[43] *The Passion of Dido* thus appeared in print as part of a network of texts and translations which contained both implicit and explicit articulations of royalist sentiment.

Yet, for all its echoes of Caroline-era court culture and its publication by the most prominent royalist publisher of the civil wars and Interregnum, it is difficult to see *The Passion of Dido for Æneas* as an expression of reaffirmed loyalty to the Stuarts. As discussed in later chapters, Interregnum-era publications that contain royalist commentary, including those published by Moseley, generally also imply or articulate some form of accommodation to the new political situation, although such positions may have provided cover for their authors' covert royalist intelligence-gathering. Such ambiguity did not inform either Waller's duties or his literary activities in the Interregnum, as in several poems of that period he signalled a transferral of loyalties from the Stuarts to Cromwell. There is consequently a notable tension between *The Passion of Dido for Æneas*' connections with Falkland's status as a royalist martyr, Waller's association in the 1630s with a political faction centred on the Queen, and his later instigation of what Norbrook has termed 'Protectoral Augustanism' to praise Cromwell.[44] Waller praises Cromwell in the same Virgilian terms that he had used to celebrate Charles in his pre-civil-war poetry. In his 1655 poem *A Panegyrick to my Lord Protector*, Waller even draws on precisely the same passage of the *Aeneid* that he had in *Of the danger*:

> Above the Waves as *Neptune* shew'd his Face
> To chide the Winds, and save the *Trojan* Race;
> So has your Highness rais'd above the rest
> Storms of Ambition tossing us represt.[45]

Where Waller uses this passage in *Of the danger* to compare Charles I favourably with Aeneas, the figure enduring and railing against the storm, in *A Panegyrick* Waller grants Cromwell an even greater authority by comparing him to Neptune, the divinity who calms the storm. The Cromwell of *A Panegyrick to my Lord Protector* has a greater power than Virgil's Aeneas and the Charles in *Of the danger*.

Drawing on the same Virgilian passage in poems written two decades apart to praise Charles I and Cromwell has left Waller vulnerable to accusations of time-serving. The appearance in print of the courtly royalist translation of *The Passion of Dido for Æneas* in 1658, the same year that Waller published another poem on Cromwell, this time on his death,[46] also brings the contrast in his declared allegiances before and after the civil wars into sharp relief. Yet, like a number of individuals who moved across political divides, Waller presented himself as someone who remained consistent in his principles and who was compelled to align himself with different factions at different times in order to do so. There was, admittedly, often a degree of cant in such self-fashionings, but this was not always the case.[47] The Virgilian references in Waller's poems also indicate that he was consistent in his advocacy of a monarchical system of government. Where panegyrics like *Of the danger* make use of the tradition of the *post eventum* prophecy to outline a future Waller knew had already happened, the poems to Cromwell as Lord Protector anticipate the future that Waller hoped would come to pass by repeatedly referring to Cromwell as a prince. In these panegyrics he combines prophecy with counsel and applies the panegyrical tropes with which he had previously celebrated the House of Stuart – and which were themselves derived from the descriptions of Augustus in the *Aeneid* – to the anticipated new ruling dynasty of the House of Cromwell.

However Waller's political loyalties in the 1650s were interpreted by his contemporaries, the reception of *The Passion of Dido for Æneas* in that decade demonstrates that the translation attracted a readership from across the political spectrum. In the early 1650s John Ogilby, whose especially fervent brand of royalism is discussed in Chapter 4, revised the Virgil translation he had published in 1649. This revised version of his *Aeneid* 4 is highly indebted to *The Passion of Dido for Æneas*. Like that text, Ogilby's revised *Aeneid* translates 'delecta iuventus' as 'Gallant Youth'.[48] The likelihood that he took the phrase from *The Passion of Dido for Æneas* is increased when this line is compared with its equivalent in the 1649 edition, since there Ogilby had rendered 'delecta iuventus' as 'prime youth'.[49] Ogilby's revised *Aeneid* took not just phrases but whole lines from *The Passion of Dido for Æneas*. He had initially translated 'aut gremio Ascanium, genitoris imagine capta, / detinet, infandum si fallere possit amorem' (*A* 4.84–5; 'she holds Ascanius on her lap, in case she may beguile a passion beyond all utterance') as:

> Or for the father doth his sonne imbrace,
> If so she might her raging love displace.[50]

For the revised *Aeneid* this couplet was substituted by one from *The Passion of Dido for Æneas*:

> Or keeps Ascanius in her Armes, to prove
> If likenesse can delude her restlesse love.[51]
>
> (lines 93–4)

This quotation is not an isolated case, as Ogilby repeatedly took lines from *The Passion of Dido for Æneas* when revising his earlier version of *Aeneid* 4.[52] As Ogilby's revised Virgil was published four years before *The Passion of Dido for Æneas* he must have had access to the text in manuscript: in addition, one point of contact between the two translations preserves a version of a line that is only present in the manuscript copies of *The Passion of Dido for Æneas*.[53] That Ogilby incorporated these references in his revised *Aeneid* indicates that *The Passion of Dido for Æneas* continued to circulate in royalist circles in the Interregnum despite Waller's increasing association with the republican and Protectorate regimes. It is possible, though, that Ogilby saw only the manuscript versions which contained the section of the translation that is attributed solely to Godolphin, as his borrowings from *The Passion of Dido for Æneas* come from lines 1–454.

Godolphin's status as a prominent early martyr for the royalist cause would likely have added to its appeal for Ogilby as he revised his own translation. Shared political affinities with either Godolphin or Waller, however, were not a prerequisite for translators appreciating the literary merits of the translation or using it as source material for their own work. The influence of *The Passion of Dido for Æneas* on the 1659 translation of *Aeneid* 4 by the republican theorist James Harrington provides a clear example of its appeal across political lines. Harrington translates Dido's wish that Aeneas 'cadat ante diem mediaque inhumatus harena' (*A* 4.620; 'die before his time and lie unburied on the middle of the shore'):

> May he be worsted still, want aid, and crave
> In vain, <u>and let the Vulture be his grave</u>.[54]

The equivalent moment in *The Passion of Dido for Æneas* reads:

> Himself at last without a grave expos'd
> <u>A prey to Vultures in no urne inclos'd</u>.
>
> (lines 629–30)

The Passion of Dido for Æneas is the only other English translation to include a reference to vultures at this point, and it is highly unlikely that Harrington included the reference in his own translation independently.[55] Unlike Ogilby, Harrington need only have encountered *The Passion of Dido for Æneas* in print to have incorporated this detail into his *Aeneid*, but his readiness to adopt lines from that text was by no means an endorsement of either of its authors' loyalties.

The Passion of Dido for Æneas points to the aspects of Virgil's reception in the middle decades of the seventeenth century which form the basis of discussion in subsequent chapters. It demonstrates that a temporal gap between a text's composition and publication could prompt several divergent and competing political readings. The textual links between *The Passion of Dido for Æneas* and other poems by Godolphin and Waller reveal the mutual influence between a translator's rendering of Virgil and their other writings. They show that translations which are (or seem to be) concerned purely with aesthetic matters could also be politically engaged or could later become politicised. The Virgilian elements in Waller's works, including his contributions to *The Passion of Dido for Æneas* as well as his poems to Charles I and Cromwell, indicate the political and optative uses of prophetic counsel and anticipated futures. The political aspects of several Interregnum-era Virgilian texts often engage with panegyrical tropes from the Caroline period: in *The Passion of Dido for Æneas* they function as a nostalgic evocation of a lost epoch, but in other texts the same discourse serves a more revisionary purpose to intimate that flagship Stuart policies led to the outbreak of civil war. The translations' political qualities are shaped by the texts' additions, expansions and reworkings of Virgil through the incorporation of contemporary political vocabulary. They also become connected to political commentary by being placed alongside other works by their author(s), by the way the translations are framed through the paratextual materials and the connections these materials themselves had to other royalists and royalist texts. In the case of *The Passion of Dido for Æneas* the key paratextual materials are printer's ornaments, but other texts invite political readings of a translation through their use of title pages, prefaces, 'arguments' and summaries, dedications, scholarly annotations and other authorial marginalia, illustrations, and both the presence and sequencing of other works within the same volume in which the translation in question appears. Borrowings from *The Passion of Dido for Æneas* in other texts provide evidence that translators used the phrases, motifs and techniques of their contemporaries in their own renderings of Virgil. The transmission and reception history of *The Passion of Dido for Æneas* show that translations from Virgil circulated in a number of social and literary networks whose members came from across the political spectrum.

Additional evidence of *The Passion of Dido for Æneas*' ability to appeal to non-royalists is its preservation in the commonplace book of the Parliamentarian poet and translator Lucy Hutchinson. The final section of this chapter discusses the other contents of this commonplace book to shed further light on *The Passion of Dido for Æneas*' circulation during the Interregnum. As the first translation from Virgil by Sir John Denham is amongst these contents, my account also introduces the author whose works form the subject of the following chapter.

Lucy Hutchinson, Virgil and the Great Tew Circle

In addition to *The Passion of Dido for Æneas* Hutchinson's commonplace book contains copies of two other poems by Waller: *To My Lady Morton on New-yeares-day, 1650. At the Louvre in Paris* and *A Panegyrick on My Lord Protector*. This last text, however, was likely transcribed only in order to provide source material for one of Hutchinson's own poems. The work in question simultaneously criticises Cromwell for his drift towards a monarchical style of government and Waller's praise of Cromwell for doing so.[56] Where Hutchinson may have had *A Panegyrick* copied out to ensure that she was able to refute as much of its content as possible in her response, the same impulse cannot have prompted the presence of the other two Waller poems.

Hutchinson's appreciation of their literary merits was not undermined or compromised by their authorship or the royalist sentiments that they contained. The presence in the commonplace book of poems by John Cleveland, a more steadfast Stuart loyalist than Waller, as well as lyrics by the 'Cavalier' poet Thomas Carew, indicates that Hutchinson's literary interests were not confined to the works of those who shared her political ideology.

Hutchinson likely accessed royalist literary texts during the civil wars and Interregnum through her brother, the royalist military commander Sir Allen Apsley. Jerome De Groot has suggested that Apsley is the likeliest source for the other Virgil translation that appears in her commonplace book, Denham's rendering of *Aeneid* 2–6; Denham, De Groot notes, had been Apsley's contemporary at the Inns of Court during the 1630s, and the translation is thought to date from that decade.[57] Another of Denham's contemporaries at the Inns of Court was Viscount Falkland, and by the late 1630s Denham was, along with Godolphin and Waller, a member of Falkland's Great Tew Circle. Since Denham's *Aeneid* 2–6 cannot be dated securely, however, it is unclear whether this translation preceded or followed his own association with Falkland. Sowerby has argued that Denham intended his translation to be a continuation of Sandys' *Aeneid* (1632), and that he began translating the *Aeneid* at Book 2 as Sandys had only proceeded as far as *Aeneid* 1.[58] Sandys' *Aeneid* shares the Augustan aesthetic with which the Great Tew Circle is associated, but it was written and published some years prior to the formation of this Circle. Like Sandys, Denham's interest in Virgil and experience of translating him may have been the prompt for his association with Falkland's Great Tew Circle and not something that emerged as a result of his membership of this coterie.

Denham's translation maintains the Augustan aesthetic of Sandys' *Aeneid*, particularly his use of closed, balanced rhyming couplets. Denham's account of the Greek double agent Sinon contains particularly intricate, highly patterned lines:

> Who first himself then us he did betray,
> At once the taker and at once the prey,
> Firmly prepared and of th' event secured,
> Or of this death or his desire assured.[59]

The linguistic doubling and tricksiness is appropriate to Sinon's character. As a double agent he is both hunter and hunted, and an enemy to both Trojans and Greeks. The embellished linguistic 'turns' that describe Sinon are more usually associated with Ovid than with Virgil, but here Denham emulates certain rhetorical features that are present in the

Aeneid itself.⁶⁰ The majority of the 'turns' that are present in Denham's manuscript *Aeneid* in fact closely correspond to similar features in the Latin. Sinon's later entreaty to the Trojans, 'Preserve thy faith who have preserved thee' (Denham, *Aeneid* 2–6, 2.156), for example, translates 'tu modo promissis maneas servataque serves' (*A* 2.160; 'yourself preserved, preserve your faith in me)'. Irrespective of its date of composition, the fact that this translation was Denham's first literary work suggests a parallel between his *Aeneid* 2–6 and the *Aeneid* 4 of his fellow Tevian, Godolphin. Both Denham and Godolphin saw translating Virgil as the best means of undergoing a poetic apprenticeship and developing a literary aesthetic that had been pioneered by Sandys.

Sandys translated the *Aeneid* not only to develop a new aesthetic standard for English poetry, but also to comment on contemporary political debates regarding Stuart foreign policy.⁶¹ By contrast, in his manuscript *Aeneid* Denham limited his concerns solely to aesthetic matters, so that text is not explicitly political. It was only in the early 1640s, after he is known to have become a member of Falkland's Great Tew Circle, that Denham wrote poems that commented on recent events from a royalist perspective. He did so, however, in an idiom that imitated broadside ballads and other popular forms of verse rather than in accordance with the Augustan aesthetic that underpins his manuscript *Aeneid*.⁶² Denham first combined royalist political commentary with a Virgilian poetics and subject matter in the initial versions of his tragedy *The Sophy* and, more influentially, of his topographical poem *Coopers Hill*, both of which were first published anonymously in 1642.

Denham's engagement with Virgil for the purposes of imparting royalist commentary is the primary focus of the next chapter. It identifies the combination of contemporary political engagement and Virgilian translation that informs Denham's two published translations from the *Aeneid*, *The Destruction of Troy* (1656) and *The Passion of Dido* (1668), both of which substantially rework and reshape passages from his manuscript translation. Before and after the Restoration, Denham translates, imitates and alludes to Virgil in order to lament past royalist travails and strategic miscalculations, express his anxieties regarding the potential ramifications of royal policies, and provide counsel to his sovereign in an attempt to prevent further violence.

Notes

1. See especially Robert Wilcher, *The Writing of Royalism, 1628–1660* (Cambridge, 2001); Jerome De Groot, *Royalist Identities* (Basingstoke,

2004); Jason McElligott and David L. Smith (eds), *Royalists and Royalism during the English Civil Wars* (Cambridge, 2007); Jason McElligott and David L. Smith (eds), *Royalists and Royalism during the Interregnum* (Manchester, 2010).
2. For which see Barry Robertson, *Royalists at War in Scotland and Ireland, 1638–1650* (Farnham, 2014); Geoffrey Smith, *The Cavaliers in Exile, 1640–1660* (Basingstoke, 2003).
3. For this tradition and its origins, see Anna Foy, 'Epic', in *The Oxford Handbook of English Poetry, 1660–1800*, ed. Jack Lynch (Oxford, 2016), pp. 473–94 (476–82); Syrithe Pugh, *Herrick, Fanshawe and the Politics of Intertextuality: Classical Literature and Seventeenth-Century Royalism* (Farnham, 2010), pp. 87–173.
4. See Jan M. Ziolkowski and Michael C. J. Putnam (eds), *The Virgilian Tradition: The First Fifteen Hundred Years* (New Haven, CT, 2008), p. 184.
5. *Servii Grammatici qui feruntur in Vergilii Carmina Commentarii*, ed. Georg Thilo and Hermann Hagen, 3 vols (Leipzig, 1878–1902), vol. 1, p. 4.
6. See J. K. Newman, *The Concept of Vates in Augustan Poetry* (Brussels, 1967), pp. 13–74.
7. Sir Philip Sidney, *An Apologie for Poetrie* (London, 1595), sig. B4r.
8. See Ziolkowski and Putnam (eds), *The Virgilian Tradition*, pp. 487–503.
9. James J. O'Hara, *Death and the Optimistic Prophecy in Vergil's Aeneid* (Princeton, 1990), pp. 176–84.
10. Anne Rogerson, *Virgil's Ascanius: Imagining the Future in the Aeneid* (Cambridge, 2017), p. 191.
11. For which see Timothy M. O'Sullivan, 'Death *ante ora parentum* in Virgil's *Aeneid*', *Transactions of the American Philological Association*, 139 (2009), 447–86.
12. See Melissa Schoenberger, *Cultivating Peace: The Virgilian Georgic in English, 1650–1750* (Lewisburg, PA, 2019).
13. A. M. Bowie, 'The Death of Priam: Allegory and History in the *Aeneid*', *Classical Quarterly*, 40 (1990), 470–81 (p. 481).
14. *Aubrey's Brief Lives*, ed. Oliver Lawson Dick (London, 1949), p. 125.
15. Niall Allsopp, *Poetry and Sovereignty in the English Revolution* (Oxford, 2020), p. 165.
16. See L. Proudfoot, *Dryden's Aeneid and Its Seventeenth Century Predecessors* (Manchester, 1960); Robin Sowerby, *The Augustan Art of Poetry: Augustan Translation of the Classics* (Oxford, 2006); Tanya Caldwell, *Virgil Made English: The Decline of Classical Authority* (Basingstoke, 2008), pp. 25–61; Paul Davis, *Translation and the Poet's Life: The Ethics of Translating in English Culture, 1646–1726* (Oxford, 2008); Arvid Løsnes, '*Arms, and the Man I sing* . . .': *A Preface to Dryden's Æneis* (Newark, DE, 2011); Matthew Reynolds, *The Poetry of Translation: From Chaucer and Petrarch to Homer and Logue* (Oxford, 2011).
17. See *Early Augustan Virgil: Translations by Denham, Godolphin, and Waller*, ed. Robin Sowerby (Lewisburg, PA, 2010) (hereafter Sowerby, *Early Augustan Virgil*), pp. 167–90.
18. Line numbers for *The Passion of Dido for Æneas* are taken from Sowerby, *Early Augustan Virgil*.

19. Edmund Waller and Sidney Godolphin, *The Passion of Dido for Æneas. As it is Incomparably exprest in the Fourth Book of Virgil* (London, 1658), sig. A4r.
20. See Edmund Waller, *Poems, &c. Written upon several Occasions, and to several Persons* (London, 1711), p. 207.
21. See Sowerby, *Augustan Art of Poetry*, p. 2.
22. Brian Duppa (ed.), *Jonsonus Virbius* (London, 1638), pp. 1–9 (8).
23. Duppa (ed.), *Jonsonus Virbius*, pp. 30–1 (Waller); p. 27 (for 37) (Godolphin).
24. George Sandys, *A Paraphrase upon the Divine Poems* (London, 1638), sigs. **2r–***3v (Godolphin), ***r–A1v (Waller).
25. David Norbrook, 'An Unpublished Poem by Sidney Godolphin', *Review of English Studies*, 192 (1997), 498–500 (p. 499).
26. Cf. *A* 5.49–50 and *Camdeni Insignia* (Oxford, 1624), sig. C3v.
27. *Carolus Redux* (Oxford, 1623), sig. F2v.
28. For the commentary on the Spanish Match in an earlier translation of *Aeneid* 4, Sir Dudley Digges's *Dido's Death* (1622), see Sheldon Brammall, *The English Aeneid: Translations of Virgil, 1555–1646* (Edinburgh, 2015), pp. 132–3.
29. *Poems, &c. Written by Mr. Ed. Waller of Beckonsfield, Esquire* (London, 1645), pp. 6–11.
30. Warren L. Chernaik, *The Poetry of Limitation: A Study of Edmund Waller* (London, 1968), p. 92.
31. *Of the danger*, lines 85–92; cf. *A* 1.81–123. Line numbers for Waller's poems other than *The Passion of Dido for Æneas* are taken from *The Poems of Edmund Waller*, ed. George Thorn Drury, 2 vols (London, 1904).
32. *Of the danger*, line 42; *The Passion of Dido for Æneas*, line 588, translating *A* 4.583. For a discussion of how the intertextual relationship this couplet signals is complicated by the fact that it is not originally Waller's coinage, but occurs in Edward Fairfax's *Godfrey of Bulloigne* (1600), see Ian Calvert, 'Augustan Allusion: Quotation and Self-Quotation in Pope's *Odyssey*', *Review of English Studies*, 297 (2019), 869–89 (p. 882).
33. Timothy Raylor, 'The Early Poetic Career of Edmund Waller', *Huntington Library Quarterly*, 69 (2006), 239–66 (p. 244). The other poems in this group are *Of His Majesties receiving the newes of the Duke of Buckingham's death*, *To the King on His Navy* and *To the Queen, occasioned upon sight of her Majesties Picture*.
34. Raylor, 'Early Career', p. 239.
35. Raylor, 'Early Career', p. 246.
36. Sowerby, *Early Augustan Virgil*, p. 177, discussing *The Passion of Dido for Æneas*, line 138.
37. Early modern editions of Virgil have 'ciet' ('calls') for 'movet' ('stirs') here. The greater agency 'ciet' grants to Dido may have been another factor in the decision not to translate the line.
38. Raylor, 'Early Career', p. 249.
39. 'To the King and Queene', in *The Poems of Sidney Godolphin*, ed. William Dighton (Oxford, 1931).
40. The ordering of these images is different on each page, so they do not form a standard pattern across the volume. The typesetter presumably used

whichever individual block was nearest to hand each time to create the motifs.
41. *Dido and Aeneas The Fourth Booke of Virgils Æneis Now Englished By Robert Stapylton Esqr* (London, 1634); Duppa (ed.), *Jonsonus Virbius*, pp. 10, 11, 14, 21, 25, 27, 32.
42. Sir Richard Fanshawe, *Il Pastor Fido The Faithfull Shepheard with an Addition of divers other Poems Concluding with a short Discourse of the Long Civill Warres of Rome. To His Highnesse the Prince of Wales* (London, 1648), pp. 271, 273, 297.
43. For a discussion of Moseley's career in this period, see Lois Potter, *Secret Rites and Secret Writing: Royalist Literature, 1641–1660* (Cambridge, 1989), pp. 19–22.
44. David Norbrook, *Writing the English Republic: Poetry, Rhetoric and Politics, 1627–1660* (Cambridge, 1999), pp. 299–309 (307).
45. Edmund Waller, *A Panegyrick to my Lord Protector* (London, 1655), lines 9–12.
46. Edmund Waller, *Upon the late storme, and of the death of His Highnesse ensuing the same* (London, 1658).
47. I draw here on Andrew Hopper, *Turncoats and Renegadoes: Changing Sides during the English Civil Wars* (Oxford, 2012).
48. John Ogilby, *The Works of Publius Virgilius Maro Translated, adorn'd with Sculpture, and illustrated with Annotations* (London, 1654), p. 266.
49. John Ogilby, *The Works of Publius Virgilius Maro* (London, 1649), sig. ^{2}F8v.
50. Ogilby, *The Works of Publius Virgilius Maro* (1649), sig. ^{2}F7r.
51. Cf. Ogilby, *The Works of Publius Virgilius Maro* (1654), p. 265.
52. See Ogilby, *The Works of Publius Virgilius Maro* (1654), pp. 261, 262, 263, 265; *The Passion of Dido for Æneas*, lines 1–2, 17, 61–2, 99–100 (translating *A* 4.1, 15, 56–7, 90–1).
53. See Ogilby, *The Works of Publius Virgilius Maro* (1654), p. 275 and the variant for *The Passion of Dido for Æneas*, lines 341–4 (translating *A* 4.334–5) recorded in Sowerby, *Early Augustan Virgil*, p. 201.
54. James Harrington, *Virgil's Æneis: The Third, Fourth, Fifth and Sixth Books* (London, 1659), p. 40.
55. A possible prompt for the reference to vultures in *The Passion of Dido for Æneas* comes in the interpolated reference to Aeneas' corpse being consumed by 'birds and beasts' at the equivalent moment of Dido's curse in John Vicars, *The XII Aeneids of Virgil* (London, 1632), p. 113.
56. Published and discussed in David Norbrook, 'Lucy Hutchinson versus Edmund Waller: An Unpublished Reply to Waller's *A Panegyrick to My Lord Protector*', *The Seventeenth Century*, 11 (1996), 61–86; Norbrook discusses the poem further in *Writing the English Republic: Poetry, Rhetoric and Politics, 1627–1660* (Cambridge, 1999), pp. 313–16.
57. See Jerome De Groot, 'John Denham and Lucy Hutchinson's Commonplace Book', *Studies in English Literature*, 48 (2008), 147–63.
58. See Sowerby, *Early Augustan Virgil*, pp. 13, 26–7.
59. Denham, *Aeneid 2–6*, 2.55–8. Denham's *Aeneid 2–6* is cited from Sowerby, *Early Augustan Virgil*.
60. Cf. *A* 2.59–62; 'qui se ignotum venientibus ultro, / hoc ipsum ut strueret

Troiamque aperiret Achivis, / obtulerat, fidens animi atque in utrumque paratus, / seu versare dolos seu certae occumbere morti'; 'To compass this very end and open Troy to the Achaeans, deliberately, stranger though he was, he had placed himself in their path, confident in spirit and ready for either event, either to ply his crafty wiles or to meet certain death.'
61. See Brammall, *The English Aeneid*, pp. 139–45.
62. I refer here to Denham's *To the five Members of the honourable House of Commons*; *A Speech against Peace at the Close Committee*; *A Western wonder*; *A second Western Wonder*.

Chapter 2

Prophetic Elegy: Sir John Denham

Introduction

As we have just seen, Denham's first major engagement with Virgil was his 1630s translation of *Aeneid* 2–6 and was the result of his desire to cultivate a Virgilian literary aesthetic in English poetry. This chapter, however, is concerned with the influence that the civil wars and the Interregnum had on the Virgilian presence in Denham's literary output between the early 1640s and his final collection, *Poems and Translations* (1668). It focuses on Denham's reception of the traditions which held that Virgil's writings contain counsel to a sovereign and moments of prophetic insight. Beginning with a discussion of the translation from *Aeneid* 2 that Denham published in 1656 as *The Destruction of Troy*, it pays particular attention to the details Denham added to the account of Priam's death that occurs in that book in order to amplify his sense of grief at Charles's execution in 1649. As Denham amended the passage in a way that allowed him to censure Charles's conduct during the 1630s and 1640s as well as mourn his death, I connect this passage to Denham's affinities with the principles of the loyalist faction that has been termed constitutional (or parliamentary) royalism.[1] He felt that the monarch should act under the law, that Parliament played a part in the rule of law, and his keen sense of duty to Charles as king and the institution of monarchy in general did not preclude criticising policies that he felt led to the prospect of arbitrary rule. Yet Denham's commemorations of Charles I intimated that both the monarch and Denham himself had compromised their personal integrity during the civil wars; there was a strand of self-castigation, as well as criticism of the king, in Denham's Virgilian texts. Virgil was thus a fitting source for Denham to articulate his sense of loss during this period, since, like Aeneas in *Aeneid* 2, in *The Destruction of Troy* Denham remembered and evaluated his own role within deeply traumatic events from the recent past.

The Destruction of Troy heavily abbreviates Denham's own earlier translation of *Aeneid* 2 as well as the original Virgilian text in order to use Priam's death as a means of evoking Charles's execution. Interpreting the political resonances to *The Destruction of Troy* is, however, made more complicated by the fact that the title page of the first edition occludes the text's status as a literary work that was initially completed prior to the outbreak of civil war but had subsequently been revised in order to commemorate events of the late 1640s. Brendan O Hehir has established that Denham revised his manuscript *Aeneid* in the early 1650s,[2] but on publication the translation was presented solely as a product of the 1630s. This assertion allowed Denham to suggest that *The Destruction of Troy* represented a series of authentically vatic utterances rather than (as was really the case) a work whose author had adapted existing material to make it speak more overtly to contemporary concerns. In presenting *The Destruction of Troy* in this manner Denham repeated a technique which he had already deployed in the 1650s when revising his 1642 edition of *Coopers Hill*. The Interregnum-era editions of *Coopers Hill*, like *The Destruction of Troy*, lay claim to the status of (to adapt the title of another *post eventum* verse prophecy of Charles I's death) a 'Prophetique Elegy'.[3]

The last sections of the chapter outline Denham's adoption of different strategies in his other published translation from Virgil, *The Passion of Dido* (1668), to offer less explicit and more personal reflections on Charles's execution, and Denham's articulation of concerns regarding the Stuart monarchy's attitude towards royal power in his contribution to Katherine Philips's *Horace* (pub. 1669). Where *Horace* differed from Denham's registering of these concerns in his earlier poems is that they responded to the actions of Charles I's son and successor. In *Horace* Denham both commemorated previous travails and nervously anticipated potential dangers that faced the restored Stuart monarchy. Expressing such anxieties allowed Denham to reassert the identity of a Virgilian counsellor-*cum*-prophet that he had fashioned for himself in commemorating Charles I's death first in *Coopers Hill* and again in *The Destruction of Troy*, to which I now turn.

The Destruction of Troy

In the passage of *The Destruction of Troy* (1656) that recounts Priam's death Denham prompts memories of Charles's execution by expanding

Virgil's narrative and capitalising on biographical parallels between the two kings:

> haec finis Priami fatorum; hic exitus illum
> sorte tulit, Troiam incensam et prolapsa videntem
> Pergama, tot quondam populis terrisque superbum
> regnatorem Asiae. iacet ingens litore truncus,
> avulsumque umeris caput et sine nomine corpus.
>
> (*A* 2.554–8)

('Such was the end of Priam's fates; such the death that befell him by fate, seeing Troy in flames and Pergama laid low, he who had once ruled over so many peoples and lands, the proud monarch of Asia. He lies, a huge trunk upon the shore, the head torn from the shoulders and a body without a name'.)

> Thus fell the King, <u>who yet surviv'd the State</u>,
> With such a <u>signal and peculiar</u> Fate,
> Under so vast a ruine <u>not a Grave</u>,
> <u>Nor in such flames a funeral fire to have</u>:
> He, whom such Titles sweld, such Power made proud,
> To whom the Scepters of <u>all</u> *Asia* <u>bow'd</u>,
> On the <u>cold earth</u> lyes <u>this neglected King</u>,
> A headless Carkass, and a nameless <u>Thing</u>.[4]

It is difficult to imagine any reader in the 1650s encountering a description of a beheaded monarch without being reminded of Charles's execution, but the additional material ensures the parallel is even more pointed. Denham removes most of the immediately localising details to promote this reading. He substitutes 'the King' for Priam, and 'so vast a ruine' for the specifics of 'Troiam incensam' and 'prolapsa ... Pergama'. Such alterations correspond with Denham's stated intention in his preface to *The Destruction of Troy* not to approach the Latin text as a '*Fidus Interpres*' (*Destruction*, sig. A3v), but they also make it easier to evoke Charles's death. Other details seem to apply specifically to Charles, particularly the reference to the 'signal and peculiar' fate. Priam was not the first Trojan king who was killed by a Greek who had invaded the city; Priam's own father, Laomedon, was killed by Heracles during the first sack of Troy. Charles I, however, was the first English monarch to be tried and executed.

Even moments in this passage which initially seem to relate more obviously to Priam also comment obliquely on Charles. The only specific geographical detail that Denham retains is '*Asia*'. The natural connection here is to Priam, not Charles, especially because Denham also augments the sense of Priam as an all-powerful Eastern potentate by adding details about the sceptres (which are presumably intended as a shorthand for other rulers) which used to bow down to him. A figurative meaning is uppermost at this point, but the line also implies the concept of total submission. It is here, though, that potential parallels with Charles suggest themselves, since in the 1630s and 1640s some of Charles's detractors had portrayed him as an Oriental despot. Amin Momeni has argued that Denham himself comes close to doing so in his 1642 tragedy *The Sophy*: there Denham comments on the autocratic elements of Charles's 'Personal Rule' in the 1630s via the play's setting in the Persian royal court, even if the Emperor is not intended as a direct proxy for Charles himself.[5] In *The Destruction of Troy*, the censure that comes from aligning Charles with an Asian monarch appears most clearly in the line 'He, whom such Titles sweld, such Power made proud'. 'Proud' here is prompted by 'superbus', which in Virgilian Latin can mean 'excellent' or 'outstanding' but also 'overbearing' or 'arrogant'.[6] The English 'proud' is also a multivalent term, but on this occasion Denham downplays its more positive associations. It appears after 'He, whom such Titles sweld', which has no prompt in the Latin. 'Sweld', like 'proud', could be used approvingly, but its associations are more usually negative. It suggests a misplaced arrogance, and when combined with 'proud' gestures towards an autocratic style of governance. But in *Aeneid* 2 Priam is no tyrant, but an enfeebled old man. The subtle hints towards autocratic rule in *The Destruction of Troy*, then, seem primarily directed at Charles.

Despite these notes of censure many of the additions that Denham incorporates into the passage on Priam's death are, as in *The Destruction of Troy* as a whole, intended to heighten pathos. Translating 'Asia' as 'all *Asia*' not only serves the translation's metre, it also increases the monarch's authority and power and heightens the tragic disparity between Priam's current and former state. The references to the body lying without a grave on the 'cold earth' are similarly effective in this respect. Mentioning the lack of a 'funeral fire' might seem superfluous, but here Denham was likely inspired by the royalists' sense of outrage that Charles was buried without due ceremony: he was not interred in accordance with Anglican funerary rites.[7] Even though Denham is likely gesturing towards Charles's unfulfilled burial rites in 'funeral fire', the phrase recalls ancient pagan funeral practices, not a ceremony conducted in accordance with the Book of Common Prayer. They may, therefore, be primarily attached to Priam, and indicate that Priam is not merely a simple proxy for Charles in this passage.

Charles and Priam thus move in and out of focus in Denham's account of Priam's death, but for Charles to be present in the passage at all seems to be at odds with Denham's claim in his preface that he had not 'offered such violence to his [Virgil's] sense, as to make it seem mine, and not his'

(*Destruction*, sig. A4v). The manipulation of the text instead appears to bring it closer to Denham's statement in the preface to another of his translations, *Cato Major* (pub. 1669), a verse paraphrase of Cicero's prose essay on old age, *De Senectute*. There he claims 'I Can neither call this Piece *Tully's* [Cicero's] nor my own, being much altered from the Original, not only by the change of the Style, but by addition and subtraction.'[8] Nonetheless, Denham's evocation of Charles's death in *The Destruction of Troy* is motivated by a desire to preserve, rather than alter, what he considered the essential aspects of the relevant passage in Virgil's *Aeneid*, and his additions and subtractions form part of this strategy. It was widely known in the early modern period that Virgil had used Priam as a means of gesturing to the recent past: most of the annotated seventeenth-century editions of Virgil gloss Priam's death by quoting or adapting Servius' comment 'Pompei tangit historiam' ('it touches on the history of Pompey').[9] Just as Denham's first readers would have been reminded of Charles's death when reading about the headless body of Priam, so would Virgil's have found in that passage a clear parallel with the death of Pompey, who fled to Egypt by ship after his defeat at the Battle of Pharsalus and was beheaded as he arrived on shore. Evoking Charles's execution at this point of the translation produces a version of the *Aeneid* that accords with Denham's belief that if Virgil 'must needs speak English, it were fit he should speak not onely as a man of this Nation, but as a man of this age' (*Destruction*, sig. A4v); his approach involved finding equivalents for Virgil's own evocation of recent events.

The attempt to have Virgil speak as a man of Denham's own historical moment informs the use of early modern vocabulary in Denham's translations to translate classical cultural and period-specific details; he 'domesticates' rather than 'foreignises' his source text. These terms were, in fact, first popularised within contemporary Anglo-American translation theory by Lawrence Venuti's reading of *The Destruction of Troy*.[10] Venuti has identified points in the translation where Denham 'domesticates' the original: in the account of Priam's palace, 'ianua' ('door') is translated as 'Port-cullis', and 'domus intus et atria longa' ('the house within and the long halls') becomes 'Chambers, Galleries, and Rooms of State'.[11] But in many respects Denham was continuing the 'domestication' that was originally begun by Virgil. Atria were a Roman architectural innovation, and so did not occur in Virgil's (largely Homeric) sources for the layout of Priam's palace. In addition, the 'domesticated' details in *The Destruction of Troy* generally contain little direct political resonance in and of themselves; the Priam passage is the exception rather than the rule in this regard, and even there the political commentary comes more via textual interpolation than domestication.

Where the text primarily gains its political charge is in its organisation and presentation. Priam's death occurs around two-thirds of the way through *Aeneid* 2, and whilst Denham's manuscript *Aeneid* 2 translates the latter section of the book, *The Destruction of Troy* breaks off after Aeneas' description of Priam's headless body. A. M. Bowie has read the temporal and spatial dislocation in the Virgilian passage on the death of Priam – it is not made clear how Priam's body is conveyed from the altar in his palace to the Trojan shore – as a means of 'drawing attention to the sudden irruption of the historical Pompey into the mythical narrative'.[12] Denham's own lightly concealed reference in *The Destruction of Troy* represents a similar, and perhaps even greater, incursion of the historical into the mythical. It gives the impression that the reference proved so disruptive and emotionally affecting that Denham found himself unable to continue the translation. We will see in the following chapter that Denham's friend and contemporary Abraham Cowley used this type of affective strategy in his own Virgilian writings to heighten pathos and a sense of loss (both textual and political),[13] but the material form of *The Destruction of Troy*'s first edition gives no hint that it is only a partial rendering; its subtitle is simply *An Essay upon the Second Book of Virgils Æneis*. All of the other seventeenth-century stand-alone translations of a single book from the *Aeneid* that had been published by 1656 – those by Sir Thomas Wroth (1620), Sir Dudley Digges (1622), George Sandys (1632), Sir Robert Stapylton (1634) and Sir Richard Fanshawe (1648) – had translated the relevant book in its entirety, so Denham's technique was not one readers would have previously encountered.

Denham also obscures the omitted material by changing the argument that provides a plot summary, usually in prose, but sometimes in verse, that features in early modern editions of Virgil and in the majority of seventeenth-century English translations. The standard argument of *Aeneid* 2 describes the book's principal episodes: Sinon's false account of the Trojan horse, the death of Laocoon, Hector's ghost appearing to Aeneas, the death of Priam, Aeneas' escape with his family, the loss of Creusa and Aeneas leading a group of refugees into exile. The argument to *The Destruction of Troy* provides noticeably fewer details:

> The first Book speaking of *Æneas* his voyage by Sea, and how being cast by tempest upon the coast of *Carthage*, he was received by Queen *Dido*, who after the Feast, desires him to make the relation of the destruction of *Troy*, which is the Argument of this Book.[14]

Denham is more concerned with providing a framing narrative for Aeneas' speech than with informing his readers about its contents. The argument also passes over the fact that Aeneas' speech narrates events which occur after Priam's death.

Denham also extensively revised the passages from the manuscript *Aeneid* that he included in the published version. Establishing the precise nature and full extent of Denham's manipulation of his earlier material is, however, no longer possible since the manuscript *Aeneid* contains several lacunae, one of which incorporates the passage on Priam's death.[15] The lines in *The Destruction of Troy* that evoke Charles and the civil wars may have been written in the 1630s and only acquired a newly politicised resonance after 1649. Alternatively, they may represent revisions of this original version that added contemporary parallels, or an entirely new draft of material that Denham had passed over when producing his initial manuscript translation. Robin Sowerby has persuasively argued that Denham's original translation was continuous and that the lacunae in the surviving version (which occur in Book 3 as well as 2) represent gaps of transcription by copyists.[16] Direct comparison between Denham's manuscript *Aeneid* 2 and *The Destruction of Troy* is possible for just over four hundred lines, and only around a third of this total is the same in both versions. The revisions occur across the text rather than being concentrated in individual episodes or passages, which indicates a sustained and systematic overhaul. It is, therefore, likely that Denham had translated the passage that documents Priam's death in the 1630s, even if this version no longer survives. The fact that the text seems to respond to the events of the 1640s with such targeted specificity, however, suggests that the passage represents a revised version of this now lost original.

Although it is a work of the 1650s that revises an unpublished translation from the 1630s, *The Destruction of Troy* claims on its title page only that it was 'Written in the year, 1636'. Denham consequently insinuates that the translation predicted, rather than commemorated, Charles's death through its treatment of Priam's murder. Denham likely wanted to 'foretell' the death of Charles, and use an emended, abbreviated, version of his *Aeneid* 2 translation to do so, as it enabled him to follow the Virgilian precedent of the *post eventum* prophecy. Denham's statement in his *The Progress of Learning* "Twas certainly mysterious, that the Name / Of Prophets and of Poets is the same' (lines 77–8) comes soon after a reference to Virgil; on its first publication in his 1668 *Poems and Translations* it is glossed with the marginal comment 'Vates',[17] which shows he was aware of the connections between Virgil and the tradition of the vatic poet–prophet.

Priam's death, however, is a wholly retrospective part of the narrative and so is not one of the *Aeneid*'s *post eventum* prophecies. Where the passage does function in this manner is in a 'prophecy' of Pompey's death in Lucan's *Pharsalia*, an epic on the civil wars between Julius Caesar and Pompey that was written nearly a century after the *Aeneid*. Near the beginning of the *Pharsalia* Lucan has Apollo speak through an unnamed woman to give an oblique (but easily comprehended) foreshadowing of Pompey's beheaded corpse: 'Hunc ego, fluminea deformis truncus harena / Qui iacet, agnosco' ('that disfigured body lying on the river sands, him I recognise').[18] Lucan's use of 'agnosco' ('I recognise') has a metapoetic quality. He imitates Virgil's account of Priam's headless body to 'foretell' Pompey's death to demonstrate his awareness that Virgil himself had marked Pompey's death in the passage on Priam's murder in *Aeneid* 2. Denham's use of this event in *The Destruction of Troy* as a *post eventum* prophecy suggests that he was aware of Lucan's reception of the passage as well as the Servian interpretative tradition. Lucan's repurposing of the episode in the *Pharsalia* as a *post eventum* prophecy supplied Denham with a precedent for doing the same and for making his own political application. That *The Destruction of Troy* was initially published without any authorial attribution also encourages readers to approach the text as an anonymous vatic utterance and aligns Denham with Lucan's unidentified seer. David Norbrook has outlined the significant role that Lucan played in shaping early modern republicanism.[19] Denham's potential imitation of Lucan in *The Destruction of Troy*, however, indicates that translators of Virgil with royalist sympathies were able to deploy Lucanian techniques which had an ultimately Virgilian origin to reassert their royalism, or at least engender sympathy for Charles I in their readers.

Denham's backdating of *The Destruction of Troy*'s composition had the added benefit of simultaneously drawing attention to and downplaying the clear parallels that the text implies between the deaths of Priam and of Charles. It insinuates that any prophetic qualities that the translation possessed must be inadvertent. Any date prior to the late 1640s would, though, have served this purpose just as well. 1636 has been taken as the year in which Denham completed his original manuscript draft of the poem, but this is based on the circular process of observing that 1636 is the date which appears on *The Destruction of Troy*'s title page, and retrospectively applying this information to its manuscript predecessor. Jerome De Groot has noted that although Denham's *Aeneid* almost certainly does date from the 1630s, there is nothing to establish it as a work of 1636.[20] Asserting a composition date of 1636 was more likely the result of its political resonances than biographical accuracy. 1636 was the year before the St Giles Riots in Edinburgh, the event which is sometimes treated as the start date of the civil wars' first phase.[21] By asserting a composition date of 1636 for *The Destruction of Troy* Denham was able to capitalise on the benefits of hindsight and intimate that the end of Charles's reign was predicted, even if only inadvertently or unconsciously, at its ostensible high-water mark. It was another means of increasing the text's pathos.

The nature of Denham's royalism, and his actions during the Interregnum, suggests another explanation for his decision to publish only part of his earlier translation. Denham's misgivings about Charles's policies and conduct during the civil wars did not prevent him from remaining loyal to him throughout the 1640s, and he may have even acted as a royalist agent and intelligencer throughout the 1650s. The decision not to include the final section of *Aeneid* 2, however, closes off certain potential royalist readings of the book. John Ogilby uses the death of Priam in his own *Aeneid* translation to mourn Charles's execution but finds in the last section of *Aeneid* 2 the opportunity to anticipate a Stuart Restoration under the Prince of Wales as Charles II.[22] It is possible to discern elements of hope in *Aeneid* 2 when reading the book within the context of the whole poem: it occurs after the text's first 'prophecy' regarding Rome's future greatness, so readers of Book 2 know that Aeneas is describing the traumatic birth pangs of the Roman nation's rise to imperial glory. When viewed in isolation, and especially when the final section that has Aeneas leading the Trojan refugees into exile is removed, it is harder to find consolation in the immense suffering that *Aeneid* 2 documents. In *The Destruction of Troy*, Denham suggests through the fall of Troy that the end of the Stuart cause is final and irrevocable. As *Aeneid* 2 has been one of the most widely read books of the poem since antiquity, Denham could assume that readers of *The Destruction of Troy* would know that the narrative does not end with the death of Priam. The absence from *The Destruction of Troy* of *Aeneid* 2's last section ensures that the text acknowledges, but eternally defers, the hopes of a restored monarchy and a new nation.

The absence of *Aeneid* 2's final third in *The Destruction of Troy* could, therefore, have added to potential suspicions regarding Denham's loyalties. It is worth noting in this context that Philip Major has referred to 'a rueful, if misplaced, perception on the part of the royalists' during the 1650s that 'Denham had returned to England to become the de facto poet laureate of the Commonwealth'.[23] By removing the final third of *Aeneid* 2 in *The Destruction of Troy* Denham refrained from exploiting the opportunity that other translators in this period did to reaffirm his royalist principles and anticipate a Stuart Restoration; equally, he did not draw on an alternative reading of the text that allows it to endorse an unwilling, but fatalistic, acceptance of defeat. After Priam's death

Aeneas is told, first by his mother Venus (*A* 2.589–623) and then by the ghost of his wife Creusa (*A* 2.771–95), that Troy was fated to fall, so he should feel no guilt about fleeing the city. Including these details about Troy's overthrow and also inviting readers to see parallels between Charles's and Priam's fates could have acted as a form of consolation to beleaguered royalists by intimating that nothing they could have done would have altered the outcome of the civil wars. Yet Denham may have felt that including such events ran the risk of suggesting a resignation to the status quo on his part that could have played into the hands of the Protectorate's own myth-making. Ending with the death of Charles-as-Priam allowed Denham to focus on mourning past events and avoid confronting the awkward realities of the present. Although Denham did engage with the tradition of the Virgilian poet–counsellor in other poems (an aspect of his writing to which I return shortly), this strand of Virgil's reception is absent from *The Destruction of Troy*. Unlike other Interregnum-era translators of Virgil, Denham does not use his translation to provide advice on how to secure the Stuart Restoration. There are moments of political commentary, but they remain retrospective articulations of how Denham felt certain royal policies had stoked tensions between King and Parliament.

Ending *The Destruction of Troy* at Priam's death prevents Denham from being firmly identified as either a committed loyalist, or as one who had come to terms with the new republican regime, whilst closing off neither of these interpretations entirely. It contains no direct expression of continued loyalties, nor a declaration of changed loyalties. Rather than seeing this as a Machiavellian strategy to remain in favour with both camps, it is more useful to interpret Denham's omission of *Aeneid* 2's final third as a reflection of his own sense of personal agency and culpability in the events that led up to Charles's execution, and as a sign of his failure to become accommodated to the republican regime. Denham did not use the translation as an opportunity to grant a greater sense of inevitability to recent events and so assuage his own sense of wounded honour. In fact, many of the more proleptic additions to the narrative in *The Destruction of Troy*, such as the reference to the Trojans being 'blinded with the power / Of fate', were already present in the earlier manuscript translation.[24] There was also an established precedent for English translations of *Aeneid* 2 to emphasise the fatalistic aspects of the poem: Sheldon Brammall has discussed the means by which Wroth's 1620 translation of *Aeneid* 2, which was also titled *The Destruction of Troy*, 'reinforces the providential closure' of the text.[25] Denham introduces political readings into his *The Destruction of Troy* in order to acknowledge and preserve his sense of unfulfilled duty to Charles and to the royalist cause. Paul Davis's reading of *The Destruction of Troy* as a work which Denham published so he 'could avoid feeling at home in the republican present', and articulate such discomfort to his fellow royalists, is helpful in understanding this use of the text.[26] *The Destruction of Troy* capitalises on the source text's fatalism for exclusively melancholic purposes. It seeks to disquiet, not console, royalist consciences, including Denham's own.

The potentially self-accusatory elements of Denham's translation also inform the title page's claim of a 1636 composition date. It makes Charles's death something that was anticipated, but not necessarily predestined. The asserted composition date raises the question of whether or not Denham felt that he and his fellow royalists had done all they could for their cause. If Charles's death represented only one possible outcome to the events of the 1630s and 1640s, it could have been prevented. Denham's organisation of *The Destruction of Troy* brought the translation closer to the structure of an elegy than is the case either with his manuscript translation or with Virgil's original text. Many classical and early modern elegies shift from lamenting the deceased to finding some consolation in the mourned figure's death, usually by reframing the death as an apotheosis or by granting the deceased the status of a martyr and/or one who has died to prevent the deaths of others. *The Destruction of Troy* charts a frustrated desire to find consolation in Charles's death by translating Virgil. At the conclusion, Charles-as-Priam has been shown to be all too mortal, and his death serves only as a prelude to further deaths.

The strategies and techniques that Denham deployed to encourage readings that aligned *The Destruction of Troy* with his own form of royalism can be summarised as follows: revising a poem that had first been written before the outbreak of civil war to incorporate new, lightly veiled, references to the death of Charles I, addressing Charles's death through a Virgilian intertext and having the published text simultaneously direct attention towards and away from its political application by asserting a false (or at best misleading) date of composition on its title page. As the following section discusses, Denham first developed and deployed all of these strategies when he was revising his other major literary project, the topographical poem *Coopers Hill*, for republication in the 1650s. *Coopers Hill* was the first time that Denham engaged with Virgil for the purposes of supplying political commentary and to commemorate the king's death. As we shall see, however, what is equally significant for illuminating Denham's strategy in *The Destruction of Troy* was Denham's deliberate misrepresentation of the date and status of the versions of *Coopers Hill* that were published in 1653 and 1655.

He has the events they mark, including Charles I's execution, read like genuine moments of prophetic foresight rather than the moments of retrospective commemoration they really were.

Coopers Hill

Where *The Destruction of Troy* mourns Charles via the death of Priam, the editions of *Coopers Hill* that date from the 1650s do so in their central episode of a hunting expedition in Windsor Forest that ends with the killing of a stag. The stag flees from the hunt 'Like a declining Statesman, left forlorne / To his friends pitty, and pursuers scorne'.[27] As several poems of the early 1650s compare Charles I to a hunted deer, the first readers of these editions of *Coopers Hill* could have made the connection between the poem's stag and the king's death without much prompting.[28] Amongst these poems was Denham's 1649 elegy for Henry, Lord Hastings. The poem forms part of the collection *Lachrymæ Musarum* and, like many of the contributions to that volume, it uses Hastings's death as a means of mourning the king:

> But as the Leader of the Herd fell first,
> A Sacrifice to quench the raging thirst
> Of inflam'd Vengeance for past Crimes: so none
> But this white fatted Youngling could atone,
> By his untimely Fate, that impious Smoke
> That sullied Earth, and did Heaven's pity choke.[29]

The status of the 'Leader of the Herd' as a sacrifice that atones for 'past Crimes' indicates that, as in *The Destruction of Troy*, Denham was prepared to criticise Charles as well as mourn him in this poem. Since it acknowledges that Charles's death has not prevented the deaths of other royalists, Denham's contribution to *Lachrymæ Musarum* anticipates *The Destruction of Troy*'s resistance to include the consolation that is found in traditional elegies.

Denham's use of a stag-hunt to mark Charles's death in *Coopers Hill* and *Lachrymæ Musarum* was influenced by the *Aeneid*. Anne Rogerson has noted that the *Aeneid* contains 'a series of stag deaths that portend serious trouble not only for the Trojans' enemies and victims but for the Trojans themselves and their Roman descendants'.[30] The stag-hunt in *Coopers Hill* contains details which reveal that it was specifically influenced by the hunt (and its aftermath) in *Aeneid* 7 (*A* 7.475–640). There the Fury Allecto, acting on Juno's order to foment discord in Latium, has set the hounds that belong to Aeneas' son Ascanius on a stag, and guides Ascanius' aim as he shoots it. The stag belongs to Silvia, the daughter of King Latinus' chief herdsman, Tyrrhus; Silvia's cries on learning that her pet is wounded summon her fellow Italians, who arm themselves and make for Ascanius. The Trojans come to Ascanius' aid, which prompts an outbreak of fighting between these two peoples, leading to the death of an Italian at the hands of a Trojan and, later, the formal declaration of hostilities. This particular stag-hunt precipitates not just serious trouble, but civil war.

There are, of course, notable differences between the events of *Coopers Hill* and of Virgil's *Aeneid* 7. The death of the stag in the *Aeneid* signals the beginning of a civil war, whereas Charles's execution occurred between two distinct phases of the civil wars. The major factor behind this discrepancy is that the first published version of *Coopers Hill*, which appeared in print in the summer of 1642 (hereafter referred to as the 'A' Text) also contains a stag-hunt.[31] Denham revised and significantly expanded this episode for the versions of the poem that were published in the 1650s (hereafter referred to as the 'B' Text) and applied it to a different execution. In the 'A' Text the stag-hunt, and its 'declining Statesman' simile,[32] primarily recalls Charles's reluctant assent to the trial and death in 1641 of his vice regent in Ireland, Thomas Wentworth, 1st Earl of Strafford. In both the 'A' and 'B' Texts the stag is killed by a monarch, but where the 'B' Text of *Coopers Hill* refers to the stag's hunter as 'the King', the equivalent moment in the 'A' Text refers to 'our Charles', which makes his personal involvement in Strafford's death all the more explicit.[33] Whilst Denham repurposed the original political application of this passage in the *Coopers Hill* 'B' Text by making Charles both the hunter and the hunted stag, he did not wholly eradicate this political application to Strafford of the 'A' Text. Charles's joint identity as hunter and hunted in the *Coopers Hill* 'B' Text also suggests the influence of the stag-hunt of *Aeneid* 7 too, as in Virgil's narrative it is difficult to distinguish between Ascanius and the deer.[34] Ascanius is as much preyed on by Allecto as his hounds prey on Silvia's stag, and Denham has Charles, like Sinon in his manuscript *Aeneid* translation discussed in Chapter 1, become both taker and prey.[35]

The *Coopers Hill* 'B' Text obscures its status as a revised version of a previously published poem by highlighting and denying the connections between the stag-hunt passage and the death of Charles I. All editions of the 'B' Text claim that the poem was 'Written in the yeare 1640'. The 1653 edition gives no further information about the circumstances of the poem's composition and transmission, but the more widely disseminated 1655 edition also contains a 'Note to the Reader' signed 'J. B.', whom P. W. Thomas has identified as the royalist author and journalist

Sir John Berkenhead.³⁶ 'J. B.' begins the Note by asserting the edition's claim to represent the true, original edition of the poem, despite the publication of the 'A' Text in 1642 and its republication in 1643 and 1649:

> You have seen this Poem often, and yet never: for, though there have been Five *Impressions*, this now in your hand is the onely true Copie. Those former were all but meer Repetitions of the same false *Transcript*, which stole into Print by the *Author's* long absence from this *Great Town*. I had not patience (having read the *Originall*) to see so Noble a Peece so Savagely handled: Therefore I obtained from the *Author's* owne papers this perfect Edition. You may know this by that excellent Allegory of the *Royall Stag* (which among others was lop't off by the *Transcriber*) skilfully maintain'd without dragging or haling in Words and Metaphors, as the fashion now is with some that cannot write, and cannot but write.³⁷

The 1655 'B' Text thus falsely presents itself as the lost original of the poem rather than as a substantial revision of the 1642 'A' Text. As with *The Destruction of Troy*, the assertion of a false composition date obscures the fact that the 'B' Text of *Coopers Hill* is a poem that discusses the events of the 1640s from the perspective of the 1650s.

Denham's wish to preserve and expand the original political resonances of the stag-hunt passage influenced the way the first editions of the *Coopers Hill* 'B' Text asserted a composition date of 1640 for the poem. It allowed Denham to impose a teleology on the events of the 1640s and to intimate that the end of one phase of the civil wars could be discerned at its beginning. In doing so Denham was replicating the king's own use of hindsight in 1649. Charles 'regarded his acquiescence in the death of Strafford as the moral origin of his own calamity', and publicly expressed his sense of culpability for this event when he himself was on the scaffold.³⁸ Again, this sense of direct responsibility is reflected in the *Coopers Hill* 'B' Text. It informs one of the couplets in the passage of the dying stag that is not present in the 1642 'A' Text. The stag 'With shame remembers, while himselfe was one / Of the same heard, himselfe the same had done', and so the couplet retains a memory of the earlier version of *Coopers Hill* even as it acts as its replacement.³⁹ The engagement with the *Aeneid* 7 stag-hunt in both versions of *Coopers Hill* also indicates that Denham heightened Charles's sense of active participation in Strafford's death. Unlike Virgil's Ascanius, Charles has no supernatural force guiding his hand as he shoots the arrow; the agency is entirely his own. Where Ascanius' hand is described as 'erranti' (*A* 7.498; 'faltering'), Charles's is 'unerring'.⁴⁰ The full resonances of *Coopers Hill*'s stag-hunt passage would only be available to those readers who possessed a fairly extensive familiarity with both the *Aeneid* and the various different incarnations of *Coopers Hill* itself, which suggests that

Denham intended the full extent of the parallels as private reflections, not public statements. In *Coopers Hill*, as in *The Destruction of Troy*, Denham used Virgil to critique Charles's actions from the early 1640s as well as to mourn the executions (including Charles's own) that Charles himself had helped to bring about.

The desire to criticise as well as support Charles through vatic statements can be found even in the earliest published versions of *Coopers Hill*, most clearly in the final verse paragraph of the 1642 'A' Text. In this passage Denham makes a prophecy in the light of his reading of the 1640s alongside examples of ideal kingship (Edward III) and monarchical overreach (principally the reigns of Henry VIII and John).[41] It combines critique with advice rather than elegy, allowing him to engage with the Virgilian role of royal counsellor as well as *vates*:

> Thus Kings by grasping more than they can hold,
> First made their Subjects by oppressions bold,
> And popular sway by forcing Kings to give
> More, then was fit for Subjects to receive,
> Ranne to the same extreame, and one excesse
> Made both by stirring to be greater, lesse.
> Nor any way, but seeking to have more
> Makes either loose, what each possest before.
> Therefore their boundlesse power let Princes draw
> Within the Channell, and the shores of Law,
> And may that Law, which teaches Kings to sway
> Their Scepters, teach their Subjects to obey.[42]

The final couplet (which, as we will see in later chapters, was imitated by several of Denham's Virgilian contemporaries) look both forward and back to imply that Charles was at risk of imitating his predecessors John and Henry VIII, having previously been associated with Edward III to such an extent that the earlier king's reign could be considered 'to foretell, and Prophecie' Charles's own.[43] Denham's choice of comparison with a river overflowing its banks represents the future which Denham hoped would be averted. The conclusion expresses unease at the prospect of royal authority reasserting itself so thoroughly over Parliament that there is the risk of the monarchy exceeding its natural bounds and no longer operating under the 'concept of limited monarchy which ruled under the law' that David L. Smith has identified as a key concept of constitutional royalism.[44] It is only at the final couplet that Denham outlines the version of the future that he hoped would come to pass, which is directed as much to the monarch's subjects as the king himself.

The anxieties and views that inform the conclusion to the 1642 edition of *Coopers Hill* correspond with the attitude towards monarchy that Denham expresses in his occasional poems from the same period. Denham wrote a more formal elegy on Strafford's death as well as marking it in *Coopers Hill*. Many of the commemorative poems on Strafford that were written in the immediate aftermath of his execution present him as someone who nobly sacrificed himself in order to prevent civil war, but Denham's adopts a more equivocal position on the ramifications of his death. The poem thus provides an early example of Denham both invoking and frustrating the conventions of elegy, as well as combining a lament for a royal servant with criticism of Charles's policies. Another elegy by Denham that dates from the early 1640s commemorates Sir George Croke, the judge who had ruled Charles's imposition of the Ship Money levy to be unlawful without the assent of Parliament. In the poem Denham approves of Croke's ruling and praises the judge in suitably nautical language. He refers to Croke's 'proper and resolved course' and calls him 'the first who happily did sound / Unfathomd Royalty and felt the Ground'.[45] Denham did not seem prepared to express such attitudes in print, at least directly: both poems stayed in manuscript throughout the civil wars. The conclusion of the 1642 *Coopers Hill* re-emphasises the ideas that Denham expresses in the Croke elegy about the necessity of curbing royal power and the potential dangers that arise when it is unchecked, but it articulates them more obliquely than in his occasional poems.

The prophecy that concludes the *Coopers Hill* 'A' Text could also have been made only before the royalists had started to experience heavy defeats on the battlefield; it would have already been under strain when the poem was first reissued in 1643. The 1650s 'B' Text reworks the conclusion to amend Denham's earlier inaccurate prophecy in the light of the royalists' subsequent experiences. The 'B' Text conclusion retains the first six lines of its 'A' Text equivalent,[46] but Denham removes the final six lines and replaces them with a passage that is noticeably more apocalyptic:

> When a calme River rais'd with sudden raines,
> Or Snowes dissolv'd, o're flowes th'adjoyning Plaines,
> The Husbandmen with high-rais'd banks secure
> Their greedy hopes, and this he can endure.
> But if with bayes and Dammes they strive to force
> His channell to a new, or narrow course;
> No longer then within his banks he dwels,
> First to a Torrent, then a Deluge swels:
> Stronger, and fiercer by restraint he roares,
> And knows no bound, but makes his power his shores.[47]

The reflection on the nature of monarchical power and the mutually stabilising relationship between a sovereign and his subjects has been replaced with a more general reflection on the unleashing of forces that have been made 'fiercer by restraint'. The passage's ostensible subject is kingship, but unlike the original conclusion to the poem it cannot be anticipating an overbearing royalist backlash. Instead Denham is reflecting upon the Parliamentary and military forces that were made 'by oppression bold' and were unleashed by the outbreak of civil conflict.[48] In a parallel with the stag-hunt passage Charles seems to be both the vehicle and tenor of the text's application, its chaser and its prey.

The conclusion of the 'B' Text also shows Denham drawing on Virgil to 'foretell' the victory of this all-conquering force. There are parallels in the 'B' Text's conclusion with a passage in *The Destruction of Troy* where Aeneas compares the conquering Greek army taking possession of Troy to a river bursting its banks:

> Not with such rage a Swelling Torrent flows
> Above his banks, th'opposing Dams orethrows,
> Depopulates the Fields, the Cattel, Sheep,
> Shepherds, and folds the foaming Surges sweep.
>
> (lines 482–5)

The despondency that informs the *Coopers Hill* 'B' Text and *The Destruction of Troy* is most likely because Denham worked on them in the aftermath of the Battle of Worcester in 1651, when the royalist cause was at one of its lowest ebbs and when Denham himself was under a form of house arrest. The passage would have acquired an even more gloomy application between the first publication of the 'B' Text in 1653 and its reissue in 1655 soon after the failed uprising against Cromwell led by Colonel Penruddock. Thomas Corns has argued it was following this event that 'the fantasies with which the royalist resistance had fed itself' were 'discredited and abandoned', seemingly for good.[49] The retrospective prophecies that Denham provides in the 'B' Text, as well as in *The Destruction of Troy*, seek to override his earlier unsuccessful attempt at offering a genuinely anticipatory prophecy at the conclusion of *Coopers Hill*'s first published edition. The emphasis on lamentation here and in *The Destruction of Troy* also reflects the trajectory of the civil wars. Denham no longer had a sovereign to advise; he could only mourn (and indeed criticise) his king, not provide him with counsel.

As in Denham's earlier attempts at both anticipatory and *post eventum* prophecies, the prophecy that concludes the *Coopers Hill* 'B' Text proved to be inaccurate, thanks to the restoration of the monarchy seven years after its publication. But even if Denham's royalism meant that he was glad to have this 'prophecy' proved wrong, his post-Restoration publications – which include lightly revised printings of *Coopers Hill* and *The Destruction of Troy* as well as the first publication of Denham's other Virgil translation (to which I will turn shortly), some of Denham's occasional poems and a few new compositions – indicate an inability to resolve his sense of unfulfilled duties to the royalist cause, particularly regarding Charles's death. The work Denham published in the aftermath of the Restoration suggests a parallel between himself and Aeneas at the opening of *The Destruction of Troy* recounting his city's fall: in speaking, both men made their 'old wounds bleed anew' (line 4).

Throughout the 1650s Denham showed a readiness to revise his output from the 1630s and 1640s in order to make it seem that he had anticipated subsequent political developments. This provided a precedent for Denham to edit his earlier works after 1660 to make them a better fit for the new political reality of the restored Stuart monarchy. Denham did indeed do as much for certain texts in his *Poems and Translations* of 1668, both in the case of those which appear in print for the first time in that volume and those that had been published previously. Denham's elegy on Strafford, for example, exists in a short manuscript version that focuses on his trial and execution, but the version that appeared in *Poems and Translations* is more expansive and includes a reference both to the Act of Attainder that led to Strafford's execution and the rescinding of that Act in early 1662; it must, then, have been revised after this later event.[50] *Poems and Translations* reprints another early composition, his tragedy *The Sophy*, but in this case Denham subtracts from his earlier source material. The 1668 *Sophy* lacks the passage from the 1642 edition where Prince Mirza calls hunting 'a Princely sport' that 'much resembles warre'.[51] The hunt in question is a stag-hunt, and is clearly in dialogue with the hunt in the *Coopers Hill* 'A' Text. Denham clearly felt unable to apply the stag-hunt of the *Sophy* to a different political context as he had in the different versions of *Coopers Hill*.

Despite this excision of references to hunting elsewhere in the volume, the stag-hunt passage in *Coopers Hill* remains the same in Denham's 1668 *Poems and Translations* as it had in the editions of 1653 and 1655. In fact, Denham made only a handful of very minor textual changes to *Coopers Hill* for its inclusion in the volume. Most of these changes restore 'A' Text material, but he did not restore the 'A' Text's concluding prophecy on royal authority reasserting itself, even when (despite the qualifications contained within that prophecy) it could have been thought politically expedient to do so. The poem contains no recognition of the fundamental change in royalist fortunes in the years that have elapsed between 1655 and 1668. A copy of *Poems and Translations* has survived with further changes to both *Coopers Hill* and *The Destruction of Troy* in Denham's own hand.⁵² Here too the changes are minor. They are limited to the insertion of a short passage into *Coopers Hill* and the amendment of a single typographical error in *The Destruction of Troy*. Taking these final changes into consideration, it is reasonable to assume that we have Denham's last thoughts on the poems, as *Poems and Translations* was published the year before his death. Yet they remain characterised by the royalist sensibilities of the Interregnum, not the Restoration. Denham is practically unique amongst the poets with royalist affiliations who were active in this period in not composing a poem to mark the Restoration. Even in *Poems and Translations* Denham remains noticeably reticent about acknowledging the Restoration in any form. Although the volume opens with a dedicatory epistle to Charles II, and charts Denham's long associations with the royalist cause, it makes no reference to the Restoration itself.

As well as republishing *Coopers Hill* and *The Destruction of Troy*, the 1668 *Poems and Translations* contains Denham's other published Virgil translation, *The Passion of Dido*. As discussed below, this translation reveals Denham's continued need to commemorate Charles not just in the depths of the so-called 'Cavalier winter' when the royalists' fortunes were at their nadir, but nearly a decade into the Stuart Restoration.⁵³

The Passion of Dido

Although it was first published in 1668, the composition of *The Passion of Dido* likely dates from the early 1650s. As already mentioned, at this date Denham was revising *Coopers Hill* and preparing part of his manuscript *Aeneid* for publication as *The Destruction of Troy*. Like *The Destruction of Troy*, *The Passion of Dido* cuts its source material extensively: Denham's manuscript *Aeneid* translates Book 4 in full, but *The Passion of Dido* represents roughly (with sizeable lacunae) only that Book's second half.⁵⁴ The published translation also substantially revises Denham's earlier version: by my calculation, only 21 of the 258 lines that comprise *The Passion of Dido* are taken directly from the manuscript. Many of Denham's revisions, including almost all his expansions and interpolations, heighten sympathy for Dido.

The choice of title corresponds to Sowerby's argument that Denham was primarily interested in including those passages from *Aeneid* 4 that show Dido to be 'a character of strong will who has commanding rhetorical powers' rather than using the translation to provide much in the way of political commentary.⁵⁵ There are only two brief passages which point unequivocally (if obliquely) to the civil wars and their aftermath. Since Denham's manuscript *Aeneid* 4 has survived in its entirety it is possible to see that these moments of political commentary were not present in Denham's 1630s translation but were added in the wake of the abolition of the monarchy. The first of the two incidents occurs in Denham's translation of 'nusquam tuta fides' (*A* 4.373; 'nowhere is faith secure'). In the manuscript *Aeneid* he renders the phrase literally as 'Faith nowhere safe' (Denham, *Aeneid* 2–6, 4.415). The same passage in *The Passion of Dido* becomes:

> The just *Astræa* sure is fled to Hell,
> Nor more in Earth, nor Heaven it self will dwell.
> Oh Faith!
>
> (lines 88–90)[56]

Denham has added an unprompted reference to the myth (which is most familiar from Ovid's *Metamorphoses*) of the goddess of justice Astraea leaving the earth at the end of the Golden Age, signalling the start of a new age that will be characterised by civil strife.[57] Denham changes the traditional version of the myth to make Astraea leave earth for hell rather than heaven. The alteration makes Denham's reference to Astraea distinctive enough in and of itself, but would have been even more unusual at the time of its publication, as it goes against the grain of other references to the Astraea myth in the 1660s. A large number of the literary works that were published to mark the restoration of the monarchy refer to Astraea as having left the country for the duration of the civil wars and Interregnum, but as having returned with the advent of Charles II's reign. Dryden's 1660 panegyric *Astræa Redux* is now the best known of these poems, but it was a standard literary trope in the early years of that decade. By retaining this added reference to the departed Astraea on the translation's publication, Denham subverts Stuart panegyric in a manner which resists the prevailing political sentiments.

A more extensive politicisation of the text occurs when Dido, on the brink of death, curses Aeneas and foretells his fate in such a manner as to recall various royalist travails in the 1640s. As in the translation of 'nusquam tuta fides', comparing the manuscript version of the curse with its equivalent passage in *The Passion of Dido* brings out the contemporary resonances Denham includes to reflect the post-1649 political situation:

> at bello audacis populi vexatus et armis,
> finibus extorris, complexu avulsus Iuli,
> auxilium imploret videatque indigna suorum
> funera; nec, cum se sub leges pacis iniquae

tradiderit, regno aut optata luce fruatur,
sed cadat ante diem mediaque inhumatus harena.

(*A* 4.615–20)

('But may he be harassed in war by the arms of a fearless people, be exiled from his lands, and torn from Iulus' embrace, let him plead for aid and may he see the unworthy deaths of his people; nor yet, when he has submitted to the terms of an unequal peace, may he enjoy his kingship or the life he longs for, but die before his time and lie unburied on the middle of the shore.')

But let him be by fatal war oppressed,
By that audacious people be distressed,
By cruel exile let him be divorced
From loved Ascanius' sight, and be enforced
To implore succor; let him see his men
Devoured by untimely death, and when
Forced to conditions of unequal peace
He shall submit, then let him not possess
His kingdom nor his life, but let him fall
Before his fatal day, his burial
Be in the sand.

(Denham, *Aeneid* 2–6, 4.690–700)

<u>When landed, may he be with arms</u> opprest
By <u>his rebelling</u> people, be distrest
<u>By exile from his Country</u>, be divorc'd
From <u>young</u> *Ascanius* sight, and be enforc'd
To implore <u>Forrein aids, and lose his Friends
To violent and undeserved ends:</u>
When to conditions of unequal Peace
He shall submit, then may he not possess
Kingdom nor Life, <u>and find his Funeral
I'th'Sands, when he before his day shall fall.</u>

(*The Passion of Dido*, lines 191–200)

The shift from 'audacious people' to 'rebelling people' recalibrates the nature of the war that Dido predicts. In Virgil she envisions a war between two peoples, but in referring to a 'rebelling people' Denham evokes memories of the civil wars from a royalist perspective. There is a shared vocabulary and outlook here with the title that Clarendon, like Denham a constitutional royalist and a member of the Great Tew Circle, later gave his account of the civil wars: *The History of the Rebellion and Civil Wars in England*. 'Rebellion' precedes 'Civil Wars' in Clarendon's title in order to underpin his sense that the events of the 1640s and 1650s were an attack against the legitimate political authority.

The rendering of Dido's curse to cast a royalist perspective on the events that preceded Charles's death also informs other changes to Denham's manuscript version. Like many royalists, Denham considered the various treaties that Charles signed (or intimated that he would sign) during the 1640s the terms of an 'unequal Peace'. The reference to Aeneas losing 'his Friends / To violent and undeserved ends' suggests the loss of prominent royalists during and after the battles fought in the civil wars; Denham may even be evoking Strafford's fate as well. His substitution of 'implore Forrein aids' for 'implore succor' potentially draws on the experiences of various royalists, including Denham himself, seeking military and financial support from Europe both before and after Charles's execution. In 1650 Denham was part of a fundraising mission to Poland, and the event occasioned a poem that was first published in *Poems and Translations*, as was another poem on the royalists' fundraising efforts in the same period.[58] Readers who worked their way through the volume sequentially would have encountered *The Passion of Dido* after reading these poems, which would have helped encourage a contemporary application of Dido's curse.

The analogy that *The Passion of Dido* draws between Charles and Aeneas is, as in the parallel between Charles and Priam in *The Destruction of Troy*, not precise or sustained. Charles does not replace Aeneas entirely, and the historical circumstances are not so exact as to allow a complete overlap of their respective experiences. Charles was never 'distrest / By exile from his Country'. Nor, in contrast to a contemporary translation of the same passage from the *Aeneid* that has a similar political purpose, does Denham rework the reference to Aeneas' death 'I'th'Sands' in order to make it a better fit for Charles's own execution.[59] Such a decision is in keeping with Denham's aforementioned desire to retain the 'sense' of the author he translates, at least in the augmented definition of 'sense' denoting the author's overall conceptual approach. As Virgil's commentators since Servius have noted, Dido's curse is another *post eventum* prophecy. As well as 'predicting' the wars in Italy that are precipitated by Ascanius' killing of Silvia's stag, it also 'foretells' events from the established Aeneas legend which are not included in the *Aeneid*, principally the death of Aeneas not long after his marriage to Lavinia. *The Passion of Dido* too exploits this temporal manipulation in order to make another *post eventum* prophecy, albeit regarding the death of Charles I instead of Aeneas.

The connection with Charles in *The Passion of Dido* is not, however, given the same prominence as the equivalent point in *The Destruction of Troy*. Dido's curse in *The Passion of Dido* appears as part of a continuous narrative and so does not form a sudden, abrupt conclusion. The political resonances consequently appear less overtly and are more easily passed over than in Denham's earlier Virgil translation. They have certainly not attracted the same level of commentary as the conclusion to *The Destruction of Troy*; as far as I am aware, I am the first to identify them. The strong possibility that Denham was drawing on his own experiences in this passage suggests that this reflection on Charles's execution and its aftermath is more a private moment of recollection than the public commentary offered in *The Destruction of Troy*. The first edition of *The Passion of Dido* provides no information, either authentic or misleading, regarding its composition date, and it lacks any paratexts that would suggest that the passage contains any prophetic element beyond its initial 'foretelling' of Aeneas' fate; Denham leaves readers to discern its contemporary application for themselves.

Horace

The Passion of Dido represents a further instance of Denham publishing material during the 1660s that he had produced earlier in his career; he appears to have written very little after the Restoration. His most extensive original composition during this period was his contribution (a truncated version of Acts 4.6–7 and 5.1–3) to the translation of Corneille's 1640 tragedy *Horace* that Katherine Philips left unfinished at her death in 1664; Denham seems to have completed it around 1667–8 to allow its performance at Charles II's court. This performance in front of the king illuminates why Denham's contribution to the play expresses the same anxieties concerning royal authority that he had articulated at the beginning of his career as a political poet. *Horace* shows Denham readopting the role of the Virgilian poet–counsellor that informs *Coopers Hill* but is largely absent from his direct translations from the *Aeneid*.

Horace dramatises an episode from Rome's conflict with the neighbouring settlement of Alba during the seventh century BC. The conflict is considered by both sides to be a civil war, since Alba, like Rome, was founded by a descendant of Aeneas. Denham has the Roman knight Valerius lament the consequences of this war: 'in the fatal strife, / How many Sons and Brothers lost their life?'[60] These lines have no equivalent in Corneille,[61] and could not fail to have had a contemporary resonance. Denham also has Valerius express anxieties concerning 'arbitrary power', again with no prompt from Corneille.[62] This was precisely the sort of power that the 1642 edition of *Coopers Hill* advises Charles I against adopting or exploiting. Denham's contributions to Philips's *Horace* thus reassert his status as a constitutional royalist and as a royal counsellor. Denham's last translation shows him expressing the concern that Charles II had the same tendencies towards autocratic rule as his father, but had not learned from the events of the recent past and so was in need of advice that urged him to rule in a non-arbitrary manner.

Other than his completion of Philips's *Horace*, Denham has only one significant composition that post-dates the Restoration. In 1667 he published a commemorative poem on the death of Cowley. In it Denham includes the standard praise of calling a modern poet a latter-day Virgil, and stating that if Virgil were living in seventeenth-century England, he would have written like Cowley. He also moves beyond this conventional praise to suggest that if Virgil were living and writing Latin verse, only Cowley could match and properly evaluate his achievement:

> *Horace* his wit, and *Virgil*'s state,
> He did not steal, but emulate,
> And when he would like them appear,
> Their Garb, but not their Cloaths, did wear . . .
> His English stream so pure did flow,
> As all that saw, and tasted, know.
> But for his Latin vein, so clear,
> Strong, full, and high it doth appear,
> That were immortal *Virgil* here,
> Him, for his judge, he would not fear;
> Of that great Portraicture, so true
> A Copy Pencil never drew.[63]

The following chapter shows that Cowley's translations and imitations of Virgil frequently incorporate prophecies of events that related to the royalist cause throughout the 1640s and 1650s. The only prophecies that proved to be accurate, however, were those which were made retrospectively and that 'foretold' royalist catastrophes instead of triumphs. The prophecies that Cowley included in his English and Latin poetry often drew on the same Virgilian material that Denham translated in *The Destruction of Troy* and *The Passion of Dido*. In a further parallel with Denham's prophecies, they focused on lamenting royalist travails even when they were composed and published after the Restoration.

Notes

1. The most helpful study of this royalist faction remains David L. Smith, *Constitutional Royalism and the Search for Settlement, c.1640–1649* (Cambridge, 1994).
2. See Brendan O Hehir, *Harmony from Discords: A Life of Sir John Denham* (Berkeley, 1968), pp. 101–2.
3. Anthony Sadler, *The Loyall Mourner* (London, 1660), p. 1.
4. Sir John Denham, *The Destruction of Troy, an Essay upon the Second Book of Virgils Æneis. Written in the year, 1636* (London, 1656) (hereafter

Denham, *Destruction*), lines 542–9. Line references are taken from *Early Augustan Virgil: Translations by Denham, Godolphin, and Waller*, ed. Robin Sowerby (Lewisburg, PA, 2010) (hereafter Sowerby, *Early Augustan Virgil*). As in my other chapters, underline indicates where the translations substantially depart from or add to the Virgilian original.

5. Amin Momeni, 'John Denham's *The Sophy* and Anglo-Persian Political Parallels', in *Sir John Denham (1614/15–1669) Reassessed: The State's Poet*, ed. Philip Major (London, 2016), pp. 75–87.
6. See Robert B. Lloyd, 'Superbus in the *Aeneid*', *American Journal of Philology*, 93 (1972), 125–32 (pp. 126–9).
7. See Lois Potter, *Secret Rites and Secret Writing: Royalist Literature, 1641–1660* (Cambridge, 1989), p. 169.
8. Sir John Denham, *Cato Major of Old Age. A Poem* (London, 1669), sig. A1r.
9. See, for example, Thomas Farnaby (ed.), *Publii Virgilii Maronis Opera* (London, 1634), p. 139. I discuss the significance of Farnaby's edition in shaping other translators' approaches to Virgil in later chapters: see pp. 87–9, 173.
10. At Lawrence Venuti, *The Translator's Invisibility: A History of Translation* (London, 1995), pp. 44–65.
11. See Venuti, *The Translator's Invisibility*, pp. 56–7.
12. A. M. Bowie, 'The Death of Priam: Allegory and History in the *Aeneid*', *Classical Quarterly*, 40 (1990), 470–81 (p. 474).
13. See pp. 61–2, 75–6, below.
14. Denham, *Destruction*, sig. B1v; roman/italic fonts reversed.
15. The lacunae are at *A* 2.314–35, 370–419, 491–585 and 788–804.
16. See Sowerby, *Early Augustan Virgil*, pp. 13–14.
17. Sir John Denham, *Poems and Translations, with The Sophy* (London, 1668) (hereafter Denham, *Poems and Translations*), p. 166 (for 176).
18. Lucan, *Pharsalia*, 1.685–6.
19. See David Norbrook, *Writing the English Republic: Poetry, Rhetoric and Politics, 1627–1660* (Cambridge, 1999).
20. Jerome De Groot, 'John Denham and Lucy Hutchinson's Commonplace Book', *Studies in English Literature*, 48 (2008), 147–63 (pp. 154–6).
21. For the role the St Giles riots played in precipitating the first phase of the civil wars, see Robert Wilcher, *The Writing of Royalism, 1628–1660* (Cambridge, 2001), pp. 22–3.
22. I further discuss this part of Ogilby's translation at pp. 92–4, below.
23. 'Introduction', in Philip Major (ed.), *Sir John Denham Reassessed*, pp. 1–11 (5).
24. Denham, *Aeneid 2–6*, 2.229–30, translating *A* 2.244. Denham's manuscript translation of *Aeneid 2–6* is cited from Sowerby, *Early Augustan Virgil*. Denham's sole revision of this line is to change the preposition: 'blinded by the Power / Of Fate' (Denham, *Destruction*, lines 235–6).
25. Sheldon Brammall, *The English Aeneid: Translations of Virgil, 1555–1646* (Edinburgh, 2015), p. 118.
26. Paul Davis, *Translation and the Poet's Life: The Ethics of Translating in English Culture, 1646–1726* (Oxford, 2008), p. 30.

27. Sir John Denham, *Coopers Hill. Written in the yeare 1640. Now Printed from a perfect Copy; And a Corrected Impression* (London, 1653) (hereafter *Coopers Hill* (1653)), p. 14.
28. I go into further details about this group of poems in Ian Calvert, 'Hindsight as Foresight: Virgilian Retrospective Prophecy in *Coopers Hill* and *The Destruction of Troy*', *International Journal of the Classical Tradition*, 26 (2019), 150–74 (pp. 161–4). For an additional example of this trope, see Wilcher, *The Writing of Royalism*, p. 243.
29. *An Elegie on the Death of Lord Hastings*, in Richard Brome (ed.), *Lachrymæ Musarum*, (London, 1649), pp. 40–2 (41).
30. Anne Rogerson, *Virgil's Ascanius: Imagining the Future in the Aeneid* (Cambridge, 2017), pp. 149–50.
31. Here I follow the convention of using the labels that were applied to the various editions of *Coopers Hill* in *Expans'd Hieroglyphicks: A Critical Edition of Sir John Denham's Coopers Hill*, ed. Brendan O Hehir (Berkeley, 1969).
32. At Sir John Denham, *Coopers Hill. A Poëme* (London, 1642) (hereafter *Coopers Hill* (1642)), p. 15.
33. *Coopers Hill* (1653), p. 13; *Coopers Hill* (1642), p. 14.
34. See Rogerson, *Virgil's Ascanius*, pp. 151–2.
35. See pp. 20–1, above.
36. P. W. Thomas, *Sir John Berkenhead 1617–1679: A Royalist Career in Politics and Polemics* (Oxford, 1969), pp. 192–3.
37. Sir John Denham, *Coopers Hill. Written in the yeare 1640. Now Printed from a perfect Copy; And A Corrected Impression* (London, 1655), sigs A2r–B1v; roman/italic fonts reversed.
38. Recorded in Denham, *Expans'd Hieroglyphicks*, ed. O Hehir, p. 155.
39. *Coopers Hill* (1653), p. 14.
40. *Coopers Hill* (1642), p. 16; *Coopers Hill* (1653), p. 16.
41. At *Coopers Hill* (1642), pp. 6–7 (Edward III); pp. 8–10 (Henry VIII); pp. 16–17 (John).
42. *Coopers Hill* (1642), pp. 18–19.
43. *Coopers Hill* (1642), p. 7.
44. Smith, *Constitutional Royalism*, p. 3.
45. *Elegy on the Death of Judge Crooke*, in *The Poetical Works of Sir John Denham*, ed. Theodore Howard Banks, 2nd edn (Hamden, CT, 1969) (hereafter Denham, *Poetical Works*), pp. 156–8.
46. *Coopers Hill* (1642), p. 18; *Coopers Hill* (1653), p. 18.
47. *Coopers Hill* (1653), p. 18.
48. *Coopers Hill* (1653), p. 18.
49. Thomas Corns, *Uncloistered Virtue: English Political Literature, 1640–1660* (Oxford, 1992), p. 255.
50. The full changes are indicated in Denham, *Poetical Works*, p. 153.
51. Sir John Denham, *The Sophy* (London, 1642), p. 11.
52. New Haven, Beinecke Rare Book and Manuscript Library, Osborn MS pb53.
53. For the phrase 'Cavalier winter' to describe the Interregnum, see Earl Miner, *The Cavalier Mode from Jonson to Cotton* (Princeton, 1971).

54. The translation begins at *A* 4.276 and ends at *A* 4.705, cutting 292–5, 301–3, 337–9, 342–4, 388–90, 393–407, 450–76, 478–93, 504–83 and 630–43. Denham also drops individual lines on occasion, for example *A* 4.280, 360, 370, 621, 656.
55. Sowerby, *Early Augustan Virgil*, p. 151.
56. Line numbers for *The Passion of Dido* are taken from Sowerby, *Early Augustan Virgil*.
57. See Ovid, *Metamorphoses*, 1.149–50.
58. See Denham's *On my Lord Croft's and my Journey into Poland, from whence we brought 10000l. for his Majesty by the Decimation of his Scottish Subjects there* and his *On Mr. Tho. Killigrew's return from his Embassie from Venice, and Mr. William Murry's from Scotland*.
59. See pp. 54–6, below.
60. In *Poems By the most deservedly Admired Mrs Katherine Philips* (London, 1669), sig. Tt3v.
61. Cf. Pierre Corneille, *Horace, Tragedie* (Paris, 1641), p. 90.
62. Philips, *Poems*, sig. Tt3v; cf. Corneille, *Horace*, p. 90.
63. *On Mr. Abraham Cowley his death and burial amongst the Ancient Poets*, in Denham, *Poems and Translations*, pp. 89–94 (91–2).

Chapter 3

Absent Presence: Abraham Cowley

Introduction

In Cowley's 1638 Latin stage comedy *Naufragium Joculare* (*The Jolly Shipwreck*) the servant Dinon says of his master's tutor, the pedantic scholar Gnomicus, 'Vix soleas, nisi ex *Virgilio* poscet' ('You can't keep his company without him quoting something out of Virgil').[1] In this respect, Gnomicus represents something of a Cowleian self-portrait. Even though Dinon goes on to say that Gnomicus 'ita poetam abutitur' ('abuses the poet so'; sig. B2v), and a number of other characters try and subvert the portentousness of his Virgilian discourse by applying the quotations to bathetic situations, through Gnomicus' dialogue Cowley demonstrates a formidable knowledge of Virgil and respect for his poetry. Cowley repeated several times in his own voice Gnomicus' belief that Virgil was 'poetarum omnium ... principe' ('the prince of [all] poets'; sig. B2v). For Cowley, Virgil was not just the '*Prince*' of Latin poets, and one '*whose Footsteps I adore*', he was also 'the most judicious and divine *Poet*'.[2] John Aubrey's claim that Cowley 'always had a Virgil in his pocket' so he could consult the *sors Virgiliana* (the practice of randomly selecting a passage from Virgil to act as a form of divination) has not been corroborated, but it chimes with the frequency of Cowley's allusions to Virgil, his critical pronouncements on the poet and the near-sacred status that he granted to Virgil's works.[3]

Whether Aubrey's claim is true or not, Cowley found the concept of Virgil as a source of prophetic insight highly conducive. He was particularly drawn to the passage in the *Aeneid* where the Sibyl, the mouthpiece and prophetess of Apollo, cries 'procul o, procul este, profani' (*A* 6.258; 'away, away, you that are uninitiated'). He imitated it in the prefatory poem to *Naufragium Joculare*, in his English and Latin epics and even in his translation of Horace's *Odes* 3.1.[4] Cowley used the phrase so frequently because it allowed him to present himself as a conduit for Virgilian wisdom and to encourage a reading of his poetry as a series of prophetic utterances: he was a Sibyl to Virgil's Apollo. Aligning himself with the Sibyl granted Cowley a certain privileged status, but also denied him agency. Such self-fashioning correlates to his greater interest across his career in the tradition of the Virgilian poet as *vates* than Virgil's supposed status as a princely poet–counsellor. Cowley frequently portrayed himself as a royal servant, but not as a royal adviser.

The connections between Cowley, Virgilian prophecy and royal service meet in his translation of Dido's curse from *Aeneid* 4. Cowley's authorship of this translation has not been fully verified, and the legends surrounding its composition are likely fanciful, but they offer in miniature the trajectory of Cowley's engagement with Virgilian prophecy throughout his career, and thus introduce the issues that I am concerned with in this chapter. The supposed prompt for the translation aligns with Cowley's repeated, and repeatedly frustrated, attempts to write an unambiguously panegyrical prophecy on the Stuart dynasty, its supporters and the nation as a whole.

Cowley's translation of Dido's curse, like the version by Denham,[5] manipulates Virgil's text to make the passage fit the circumstances of Charles I's execution:

> By a bold people's <u>stubborn</u> arms opprest,
> Forced to forsake the land which he posses't,
> Torn from his dearest sonne, let him <u>in vaine</u>
> Seeke help, and see his friends <u>unjustly</u> slain.
> Let him to base unequal termes submit,
> <u>In hope to save his crown, yet loose both it</u>
> <u>And life at once</u>, untimely let him dy,
> And on an open <u>stage</u> unburied ly.[6]

The most significant changes occur in the references that Dido makes to Aeneas losing his crown and his corpse lying unburied on an 'open stage', when Virgil's Dido refers only to the 'harena', 'shore'. No other translations of this passage have this latter detail. Nor do any early modern commentaries or editions of Virgil suggest this alternative reading. In uses of the phrase 'open stage' that are contemporary with this translation, 'open' serves as a synonym for 'public'; 'Stage' aligns the translation with works like Marvell's 'Horatian Ode' which capitalise on the interchangeable meanings of 'stage' and 'scaffold' in their accounts of Charles's death to present the execution as an act of public theatre. The translation creatively misreads the Latin text to present it as a prediction not of Aeneas' fate, but the fate of Charles I.

This translation of Dido's curse first appears in print in a 1677 collection of lyrics with musical settings by Henry Bowman.[7] The 1679 second edition includes the subtitle 'Collected Out of some of the Select Poems of the Incomparable Mr. *COWLEY*, and Others', but no other details about the individual poems' provenance are provided in either edition.[8] As a result, the text is not even acknowledged as a translation from *Aeneid* 4, let alone a translation with royalist resonances. Nor do the Bowman volumes give any indication of when the text was composed. The other surviving sources for the translation, however, some of which may predate Bowman's collection, explicitly acknowledge its status as a politically engaged text. Unlike Denham's version, the text consequently circulated as a stand-alone translation that was (almost always) framed as an unambiguously prophetic utterance, and as an example of Cowley's habit of consulting the *sors Virgiliana*. Yet this may only have occurred through the involvement of individuals other than Cowley himself. One early manuscript version of the translation comes in the 1679 diary of the Anglican clergyman and royal tutor Edward Lake, in a reference to Charles I's consultation of the

> Sors Virgiliana, which hapned at Oxford in the time of the late war, and whilst the parliament sate there; viz. that his majesty being tired out with businesse and afflictions, resolv'd to recreate himselfe with some young noblemen who were students there, by pricking in Virgill for his fortune, which he did, and lighted upon Dido's curse to Æneas when hee left her . . . Whereat his majesty seem'd much concern'd, but sent it by Mr. Geman [i.e. Jermyn], now Earle of St Alban's, to Mr. Cowley, then student of Christechurch, to translate them into English, with a command not to acquaint him whose Sors it was; which Mr. Cowley did.[9]

The details that Lake gives here would date the translation no earlier than March 1643, when Cowley is known to have arrived in Oxford;[10] other versions place the date of this consultation to 1642 or 1640. The Oxford version is the most widespread, but Aubrey gives an alternative account which asserts that the consultation took place in Paris during the winter of 1648, where Cowley himself suggested to the Prince of Wales that he consult the *sors Virgiliana* as a means of diverting his attention from the King's imminent fate.[11] In both versions, however, Cowley's translation stands as an unwilling prophecy of royalist disaster; they differ only in the degree of inadvertent foresight granted to Cowley. The version of Cowley's translation that places its composition at Oxford is framed, as with Denham's *The Destruction of Troy* (1656), in such a way as to intimate that it foretold the end of the civil wars at its beginning.

The translation is thus connected to the 1640s, but as the passage has been adapted to be such a fitting means of marking Charles I's fate it is more plausible that at some point after 1649 Cowley selected it as the most appropriate passage to translate for this purpose. It represents a set of circumstances that were more hypothetical than actual; it suggests if Cowley (or someone else) had consulted the *sors Virgiliana* as a means of discerning Charles I's fate, Dido's curse was the passage that he would (or should) have alighted upon. As the version of the story set in Paris is the first to be recorded and that which accords Cowley the most agency, it is likely that this account circulated first, and over time the story was backdated to Oxford earlier in the 1640s (where Cowley is merely the translator of the passage rather than the instigator of the consultation) in order to make its premonition all the more uncanny and doom-laden.

The rest of this chapter outlines Cowley's other attempts to foretell a promising future for the Stuart monarchy and his lamentations when these prophecies failed to come to pass. His first attempt at prophecy comes in *The Civil War* (1643). The poem dates from the initial stages of the conflict, when for the royalists victory remained a plausible, as well as the desired, outcome. Cowley's original intention to write a triumphalist prophecy of royalist victory was, however, soon overtaken by the losses and setbacks the royalists experienced, which forced him to abandon the poem altogether. In his next attempt at epic, the *Davideis* (1656), Cowley learned from the experience of writing *The Civil War* and used the poem's fragmentary status for greater political advantage. By drawing attention to its status as an incomplete work, the *Davideis* foretells a more hopeful outcome for the royalists whilst also acknowledging contemporary republican realities. Like the *Davideis*, the passage from *Georgics* 2 that was first published in Cowley's 1663 collection *Verses, Lately Written Upon Several Occasions* offers the potential to be read as a prophecy of the Restoration, but it also recognises that such an event is more desired than predestined. However, as the composition date of the translation is unknown, the translation may be a *post eventum* prophecy in the manner of the vatic elements in Cowley's prose satire *Visions and Prophecies*, his stage comedy *Cutter of Coleman-Street* and the first (two-book) version of his Latin epic poem on plants, the *Duo Libri Plantarum*, all of which were published in the wake of the Restoration but claimed to have been written during the last years of the Protectorate. The chapter ends with a discussion of the overt and formal prophecies in the completed (six-book) version of the *Plantarum* (1668) and why they are primarily concerned with mourning past catastrophes and articulating a sense of national decline. As the subjects of Cowley's prophecies relate to key moments in the royalists' attempt to regain power, it is first necessary to consider the nature of Cowley's royalism before discussing the prophecies' Virgilian form, content and what they suggest the royalists had achieved (and were capable of achieving) at various points between the 1630s and 1660s.

Cowley and Royalism

Cowley was, like the poets discussed in the preceding chapters, a member of Viscount Falkland's literary circle that met at his country estate at Great Tew; Cowley, though, seems to have had a closer personal bond with Falkland than they did. Their connection dates from when Cowley shared accommodation as an undergraduate at Cambridge with an associate of Falkland, Robert Cresswell, who wrote to him recommending Cowley as a poet worthy of his patronage. Falkland is the subject of one of Cowley's earliest political poems: *To the Lord Falkland. For his safe Return from the Northern Expedition against the Scots*. This poem was not published until 1656, but it commemorates events from the late 1630s and most likely dates from this period. Cowley praises Falkland's actions in *To the Lord Falkland*, but this poem does not indicate that he shared the political convictions that prompted Falkland to become a key advocate of constitutional royalism. By contrast, the 1645 prose work *A Letter to a Friend* and the 1648 poem *The Foure Ages of England*, which have both been attributed to Cowley, do express political sentiments that are consonant with Falkland's. The author of the *Letter* claims to have once been sympathetic to the Parliamentary cause but has subsequently become a more committed royalist in the wake of Parliament's actions following the outbreak of civil war. Even if Cowley is its author, and as with the *sors Virgiliana* translation it has not been proved conclusively that this attribution is accurate, he may have heightened or invented any scepticism he felt towards Charles in order to advance the text's status as a work of royalist propaganda; the arguments of a recent convert would be more effective than those of a long-term supporter. *Foure Ages* largely adheres to the principles of constitutional royalism thanks to the passages it takes from *Coopers Hill*, and so the poem reflects Denham's political affiliations rather than those of the author.[12] Cowley's authorship of this text has never been established either: he did acknowledge the existence of *Foure Ages* (specifically, its fourth and final section, 'The Iron Age'), but only to deny that he was its author.[13]

Cowley's royalism is not in doubt, at least during the 1640s, but throughout that decade his royalism was primarily based on available patronage networks instead of a fixed political ideology. Lake's diary entry on Charles, Cowley and the *sors Virgiliana* records that by the early 1640s Cowley had started working for Henry Jermyn, whose principles earlier in his political career had aligned with the constitutional royalists but who subsequently became Henrietta Maria's chamberlain. Jermyn thus played a central role in the royalist faction usually referred to as the 'Queen's Party' or the 'Louvre faction'. Cowley remained in Jermyn's employ and part of the Queen's retinue following her departure from England in 1644, where he was responsible for ciphering and deciphering the correspondence that passed between her and Charles: according to Cowley's biographer Thomas Sprat, this work 'for some years together took up all his days, and two or three nights every week'.[14] These duties would have brought Cowley into contact with Denham, if they had not already met at Oxford (both were resident in the city by the early 1640s) or at Great Tew; it was Denham's responsibility to decipher the messages to Charles from the Queen that Cowley had encrypted. Denham himself later recollected that his flight from England back into Europe in 1647 was precipitated by the discovery of some letters in Cowley's handwriting.[15]

There are some aspects of a work by Cowley during this period that suggest the influence of Queen's Party royalism. Queen's Party royalists were more willing to use foreign armies to reassert royal authority in England and were less prepared to reach some form of settlement with Parliament than were other royalist factions.[16] The Queen's status as a French princess also resulted in accusations, by other royalists as much as by their detractors, that her Party fostered Catholic absolutist sympathies. In his 1643 satire *The Puritan and the Papist* Cowley states that if he had to choose between Puritanism and Catholicism he would opt for the latter. Nonetheless, Cowley also repeatedly asserts throughout *The Puritan and the Papist* that his true loyalties will always lie with the Church of England. Rather than seeing this text as an indication either of a shift in political loyalties or a change in religious sensibilities that made the Queen's Party more congenial to Cowley than the constitutional royalism of his earlier patron Falkland, it seems primarily an indication of the anti-Puritanism that he expresses consistently across his career.

Beyond *The Puritan and the Papist* it is difficult to find any connection to Queen's Party royalism in Cowley's works. The hostility that he shows to the Parliamentarians across much of *The Civil War* (1643) does have more in common with Queen's Party attitudes than the more conciliatory approach of the constitutional royalists, but this may be the result of the poem's intention to serve as propaganda. Many of Cowley's love lyrics in *The Mistress* (pub. 1647) likely date from the time that he spent at Henrietta Maria's exiled court, but there is nothing in the poems themselves that reveals the circumstances of their composition or which endorses the Party's policies. Even when Cowley's poetry does contain encomia to Henrietta Maria, the political values that he advocates in them are at odds with Queen's Party royalism.[17]

This state of affairs is symptomatic of Cowley's experiences between the outbreak of war and the early years of the Restoration. Individual relationships, rather than common ideological ground, were the likeliest cause behind Cowley's movement between the already porous royalist factions. His encomia to the Queen were similarly motivated primarily by a sense of personal obligations. Many of the rewards that were promised to Cowley by both Charles I and Charles II never materialised (a common experience for royalists), but in the early 1660s he was granted a tract of land on an estate that belonged to Henrietta Maria. Even this gift had less to do with Cowley's personal relationship with the Queen herself, and was largely thanks to his long-standing connections to Jermyn and other members of her circle.

This sketch of Cowley's associations and activities in the civil wars and Interregnum conforms to David L. Smith and Jason McElligott's contention that 'Royalists did not conform to a series of discrete stereotypes ... but frequently combined a range of circumstances and experiences within the same personality and career.'[18] But even with this qualification in mind Cowley's loyalties do (at least superficially) appear to have been more mobile than many of the other royalist poets considered in this study. Where Cowley was associated with members of the Queen's Party on either side of the Interregnum, his loyalties during the Interregnum itself are much more opaque. Cowley maintained some contact with Queen's Party royalists after his return to England early in the 1650s, and it is possible that he acted as their agent during this period, but he also was thought to have reached some form of accommodation with the new republican order. In the preface to his 1656 *Poems* Cowley notoriously informs his readers that he has suppressed *The Civil War*, along with 'all such pieces as I wrote during the time of the late troubles', before calling on royalists to do as he claimed to have done: to submit 'to the conditions of the *Conquerour*' and '*march* out of our *Cause*' (sig. (a)4r). But to submit is not always to endorse, and even if Cowley had marched out of one cause (and it is not wholly clear whether he did or not), it does not necessarily follow that he marched into another.

It is frequently easier to delimit Cowley's politics through negatives than positives. His political affinities, like the often fragmentary or uncompleted nature of his writings, are defined through lacunae and absences. This process of interpretation through absence began with Cowley's first attempt at writing a royalist and Virgilian epic, *The Civil War*. As the following section outlines, the Virgilian presence in the poem underlines Cowley's royalism. *The Civil War* also shows Cowley associating Virgil with mournful commemoration, and, as Henry Power has discussed, of using the stylistic features of Virgilian epic as a means of increasing the poem's pathos.[19] *The Civil War* was a significant source for the tone and content of Cowley's subsequent epics, the *Davideis* (1656) and the *Plantarum* (1668), not least because certain sections of it were repurposed in those poems. *The Civil War* also contains the first example of Cowley combining his engagement with Virgil with poetic expressions of shedding tears for the royalist cause, a motif to which he also returned later in his career.

The Civil War

The title of *The Civil War* (1643) suggests that its guiding classical presence will be Lucan rather than Virgil, since the alternative title to Lucan's epic *Pharsalia*, *De Bello Civile*, translates as 'On the Civil War'. The text of Cowley's poem, however, bears out Allan Pritchard's claim that 'none of the classical poets left more easily discernible marks of influence upon *The Civil War* than Virgil'.[20] Cowley opens the poem with a clear allusion to the *Eclogues*. 'What rage does *England* from it selfe divide / More then Seas doe from all the world beside?' (*Civil War* 1.1–2) imitates 'et penitus toto divisos orbe Britannos' (*E* 1.66; 'the Britons, completely cut off from all the world'), albeit via the first lines of Lucan's poem.[21] The imitation signals the status of *The Civil War* as a work that engages with contemporary events from a royalist perspective. Cowley would have been aware that numerous poems which had celebrated the 'Caroline Peace' of the 1630s drew on this line, of which Fanshawe's 'Proclamation' ode is the most celebrated.[22] Its presence in *The Civil War* indicates that Cowley has incorporated and overturned the Virgilian discourse of contemporary Stuart panegyric to represent the disrupted political order that followed the outbreak of civil war.

Cowley heightens this sense of disruption by combining Virgilian and biblical material to identify the parliamentary forces as infernal agents of destruction. Like Denham in *Coopers Hill*, Cowley provides an aetiology for the events of the early 1640s by referring to Juno's summoning of Allecto in *Aeneid* 7 to foment civil war: 'dire *Alecto*, ris'en from *Stygian* strand, / Had scattered *Strife* and *Armes* through all the

Land' (*Civil War* 2.5–6). Cowley portrays the Parliamentarian leaders as Allecto's vessels for spreading this discord and chaos. By later staging an infernal council (*Civil War* 2.365–617), Cowley presents them as agents not only of Allecto, but also of the Devil. They are satanic, as well as chthonic, forces.

Cowley's use of Virgil in *The Civil War* invites a teleological reading of the events the poem documents. The Virgilian references imply that the Parliamentarians will be defeated by the royalists just as Turnus' Italians were defeated by Aeneas' Trojans. The references represent in microcosm what Gerald M. MacLean found to be Cowley's prime motive in writing the poem: the anticipation of the future through a selective reading of the past to demonstrate that 'all previous attempts to subvert the authority of the English crown led relentlessly to the downfall of those involved' and to 'convince us of relentless historical movement toward a divinely ordained royalist victory'.[23] Yet Cowley is forced to admit that his original plan has had to be delayed by the need to mourn the royalist dead:

> Nere faile my prophesing *Muse*, in what shee sings,
> Thy conquest soone fame from my paine shall git;
> Meanwhile a sadder *Vict'ry* calls for it.
>
> (*Civil War* 2.354–6)

The deaths of royalists in the first stages of the conflict did not necessarily undermine the poem's intentions, as Cowley recognised some losses were inevitable. Ultimately, however, the frequency of these deaths and of the battlefield defeats meant that Cowley's original intention was not just delayed, but abandoned.

Cowley mourns the deaths of prominent royalists in notably Virgilian terms. He expresses the desire to grieve for a fellow member of Falkland's Great Tew Circle, Godolphin, but the depth of emotion that Godolphin's death provokes makes this impossible: Cowley wants *The Civil War* to mourn Godolphin 'But *teares* breake off my verse' (*Civil War* 1.430). The intended passage on Godolphin thus becomes one of many absent presences in Cowley's poetry. Here Cowley imitates the Virgilian technique of evoking absent presences in a use of a 'half-line'.[24] 'But *teares* breake off my verse' is metrically incomplete, but 'verse' forms a full rhyme for its predecessor, indicating that the verse-line is deliberately hypometric. Its subject matter and sentiment bring it into contact with the Virgilian trope of *mors immatura*, which Cowley deploys with increasing intensity as *The Civil War* progresses. At points Cowley combines separate Virgilian incidents of the trope: his lament for Charles Cavendish (who had died at the 1643 Battle of

Gainsborough), in addition to being, as Pritchard has noted, 'virtually a translation of Virgil's lines on the death of Pallas' (*A* 11.67–70), contains a reference to Virgil's elegy for another prematurely fallen follower of Aeneas, Euryalus.[25] For Power, the Virgilian allusions in *The Civil War* have an 'undigested quality',[26] but here they serve to indicate (albeit in a fairly heavy-handed manner) that although Gainsborough was a royalist victory the death of Cavendish rendered the success somewhat Pyrrhic.

The section of the poem which stands as its default conclusion is another lament for the *mors immatura* of a young royalist. The pathos is particularly extensive for this part, because its subject is Cowley's friend and patron Falkland. Cowley's sadness at Falkland's death partly manifests as anger, since he calls for reprisals against those who caused his demise:

> Boast not for this; for though't bee sadly true
> That Falklands dead, hee's yet not dead to yow,
> His blood amidst yow in your fights will bee,
> As feirce and powerfull as before was hee.
> The place around with slaughter it will fill
> As if the conqu'ering Spirit were in it still.
>
> (*Civil War* 3.629–34)

There is a parallel here with the prophecy that concludes the 1642 edition of *Coopers Hill*.[27] Both Denham and Cowley anticipate a strong backlash by the royalists. Unlike Denham, though, the sentiment that Cowley expresses at the end of the elegy ensures that the prophecy is cancelled almost at the moment of its utterance. This part of the poem overrides itself, rather than finding itself being overridden by external events. Cowley revises his vengeful response to Falkland's death in order to offer a more appropriate tribute to the values by which Falkland himself lived. He hopes that Falkland will serve as a sacrifice that will help bring the civil wars to an end without any further bloodshed. This hope forms the last lines of the poem that Cowley wrote before tears forced him to break off writing it for good:

> We have offended much, but there has binne
> Whole Hecatombs oft slaughterd for our Sinne.
> Thinke on our sufferings, and sheath then againe;
> Our Sinnes are great, but Falkland too is slaine.
>
> (*Civil War* 3.645–8)

The conciliatory gesture that Cowley makes here adopts an approach that is more consonant with Falkland's own constitutional royalism.

This passage on Falkland's death demonstrates the difficulties that

Cowley faced in incorporating vatic elements into his poetry. As with Denham in the first editions of *Coopers Hill*, Cowley found his first major attempts at predicting future public events in verse were unsuccessful; the 'prophesying Muse' failed him. This did not, however, prevent him from including prophecies in his next Virgilian epic, the *Davideis* (1656). This poem incorporates some passages from *The Civil War*,[28] but its debt to Virgil also comes through its own direct engagement with the *Aeneid*. In his notes Cowley uses Virgilian precedents to gloss, amongst other terms, his use of 'honours' to mean 'beauties', and 'lambent' in reference to flames harmlessly licking an individual's hair as a sign of divine approval.[29] Individual episodes and set pieces in the poem are also indebted to Virgil: the ecphrasis that depicts the story of Lot (*Davideis* 3.199–268), for example, imitates Virgil's account of the frieze on Juno's temple in Carthage (*A* 1.446–93).[30]

The following section, however, is interested in the political, rather than the linguistic or structural, influence of Virgil on the *Davideis*. Cowley incorporates political commentary in the *Davideis* with the knowledge that the contemporary events the poem touches on foreshadow a range of possible near futures. The *Davideis* is less rigidly bound by actual and imagined historical circumstances than *The Civil War*. It thus possesses an openness the earlier poem lacks. This enabled Cowley to publish the poem during the 1650s without having to remove the material it contains which gestured towards 'the late troubles', whilst still implying that royalist tears may yet give way to celebration. Although this material is already present in the text, as are the elements of its narrative that can function as royalist prophecies, my analysis primarily focuses on the way that Cowley frames the poem in the preface to his *Poems* of 1656, and in the commentary that he supplies to the poem itself.

Davideis

In the 1656 *Poems* preface, Cowley claims that he envisaged the *Davideis* as a twelve-book poem in emulation of 'our Master *Virgil*' (sig. (b)2v). He also states that he planned to conclude the *Davideis* 'with that most Poetical and excellent *Elegie* of *Davids* upon the death of *Saul and Jonathan*' rather than 'to carry him quite on to his *Anointing* at *Hebron*' (sig. (b)2v). In the notes to the first book, however, Cowley claims 'this *Poem* was designed no farther than to bring him to his *Inauguration* at *Hebron*' (sig. Dddd1v). In the event, Cowley completed only four of these twelve books, and so the poem ends with David still in exile. The *Davideis* is thus doubly abbreviated, and the lost books function as further absent presences in his writing.

That the *Davideis* was abandoned before it reached the lament for Jonathan, let alone David's coronation, encourages a reading of it as Cowley's resigned farewell to the royalist cause. Cowley's Jonathan owes much to the portrayal of Falkland in *The Civil War*,[31] and the poem is influenced by the melancholy of the *mors immatura* trope even though Jonathan's death lies beyond the events covered in the poem. A defeated mindset certainly informs much of the other material in the *Davideis* that had first formed part of *The Civil War*. Many of the lines and passages from *The Civil War* that Cowley recycles in the *Davideis* appear unaltered, but a few are revised to reflect the post-1649 political situation. One of the most extensive self-borrowings comes in a description of hell (*Davideis* 1.71–100; *Civil War* 2.365–96). The only difference between the two passages is the absence in the *Davideis* of the couplet 'Here Rebell Minds in envious torments ly; / Must here forever Live, forever Dy' (*Civil War* 2.385–6). The *Davideis* passage is thus substantially less royalist than its original version in *The Civil War*. Given his suppression of *The Civil War*, however, only Cowley himself would have known the origins of these lines. Nonetheless, the removal of the couplet functions as a key indicator of how differently the two poems engage with contemporary politics.

Cowley's choice of protagonist in the *Davideis* adds to its air of a compromised or defeated royalism. Mid-seventeenth-century writers applied the Saul and David narrative from the Books of Samuel to a number of political contexts, to the extent that David appeared in both royalist and pro-Cromwellian works during the 1650s.[32] In the *Davideis*, however, David functions as a clear (if ambivalent) proxy for the Prince of Wales. The sense of a defeated, even abandoned, royalism is informed by the poem's triangulation of the Prince, David and Virgil's Aeneas. The *Davideis* includes a direct parallel between David and Aeneas (*Davideis* 3.125–38), but there are also more local allusions. The proem to the *Davideis*, especially the lines 'Much danger first, much toil did he sustain, / Whilst *Saul* and *Hell* crost his strong fate in vain' (*Davideis* 1.5–6), is indebted to Virgil's description of Aeneas' suffering at the hands of Juno in the opening lines to the *Aeneid*: 'quidve dolens regina deum tot volvere casus / insignem pietate virum, tot adire labores / impulerit?' (*A* 1.9–11; 'wherein thwarted in will or wherefore angered, did the queen of the gods compel a man so distinguished in piety to endure such fates, to face so many labours?'). The connections that Cowley frequently draws between David and the

Prince also allow this passage to be read as a means of reflecting on all three individuals' experiences of exile.

The comparison of David's tribulations to Aeneas', along with the subtitle that Cowley gives to the epic, *A Sacred Poem of the Troubles of David*, signals that the poem's emphasis is on suffering and on mourning rather than anticipating future glories, either with regard to David himself or his proxies. There are some formal prophecies in the *Davideis*, but they are generally more concerned with outlining Christian eschatology than with the (putative or actual) fates of the Stuart dynasty. Book 1, for example, concludes with a paraphrase of Balaam's prophecy from Numbers 24: 5–9 (*Davideis* 1.919–39). Other 'prophecies' take their structure from *post eventum* prophecies in the *Aeneid*, but their content from the Bible. *Davideis* 2 contains an episode that is modelled on the Parade of Heroes in *Aeneid* 6, but it provides a catalogue of David's descendants that culminates in a vision of Christ.[33] Even here, though, a melancholic sensibility remains. The *Aeneid*'s own prophecies of Rome's future greatness cast long shadows over the poem, but Virgil's emphasis remains on the hardship and the loss of their closest associates that is experienced by Aeneas, his supporters and his antagonists. The *Davideis* acknowledges that the rewards of David's descendants are even greater than those of Aeneas'. It nonetheless remains highly aware of the cost of securing those rewards, which are even more painful for being so long deferred.

The emphasis the *Davideis* places on loss and mourning, couched in a Virgilian language of suffering, initially suggests that it preserves the sensibility that ends up dominating *The Civil War*. This would seem understandable given the political situation at the time of its publication, but for Cowley merely to refer to David's coronation ensures that, when this reference is combined with the implicit comparisons between David and the Prince (sometimes via Aeneas), it is possible to see the text foretelling an imminent royalist revival. The strategically deployed references to David's coronation re-emphasise the monarchical teleology of his biography and express the hope that royalist lament may still give way to panegyric. Thomas Corns argues, however, that, as with *The Civil War*, political events overtook both its composition and Cowley's hopes for a royalist future. For Corns the *Davideis* is 'a would-be prophetic account of the triumph of the royalist underground' that 'marks another attempt at poetic wishful thinking wrecked on the hard reality of Cromwellian domination'.[34] My contention is that, *pace* Corns, Cowley consciously embeds and draws attention to the elements of wishful thinking that are present in the poem. Cowley deliberately cultivates ambivalent parallels with the contemporary political situation, whilst also hoping he will override his unsuccessful prophecy of a royalist victory in *The Civil War*. The *Davideis* preserves Cowley's royalist affiliations, but thanks to his strategy of leaving the epic incomplete, the poem remains available to both royalist and republican readings. The text's anticipation of the future is both optative and realistic.

The *Davideis*, unlike Denham's *The Destruction of Troy* (1656) and Cowley's own *The Civil War*, uses its fragmentary status to allow the possibility that Cowley's desired outcome of a royalist revival could still come to pass. As we saw in the previous chapter, the absence of the final third of *Aeneid* 2 in *The Destruction of Troy*, when combined with the affinities between the Trojan and British royal families that Denham establishes elsewhere in the translation, allows the text to promise, but ultimately defer, the prospect of a Stuart restoration.[35] The paratextual material of the *Davideis*, published in the same year as the *Destruction of Troy*, provides a reminder that the part of David's life that is the focus of the poem concluded with him becoming king. That open-endedness can be applied to the poem's engagement with contemporary politics from a royalist perspective, but, as in *The Destruction of Troy*, it is noticeable that Cowley's *Davideis* does not make use of the tradition of the Virgilian poet–counsellor to provide advice on how to secure this event. In the *Davideis* the prospect of a Stuart Restoration is implied to be one of the possible futures that face the country, even if that restoration is not imminent and if it represents what Cowley hoped rather than thought would occur.

Yet is equally possible that Cowley intended to draw attention precisely to the lack of the *Davideis*' applicability to the contemporary political situation; the text keeps both an active and a surrendered royalist reading in play. Niall Allsopp's recognition of the emphasis placed on providence in the *Davideis* and other works in the 1656 *Poems*, and Cowley's construction of providence as 'remote and inscrutable, rather than a fount of stable moral authority' is useful in this context.[36] Just as providence had caused the downfall of Charles I, so too could it cause the downfall of his successors, hence Cowley's rhetoric of resignation to events that he felt lay outside of human agency. Thanks to the events of the 1660s, it is the poem's royalist readings that came to the fore during that decade; the poem's first readers in the 1650s would have more likely privileged the aspects of the poem that intimated an acceptance of the new Cromwellian status quo. Cowley's acknowledgement in the preface that he has suppressed his former declarations of royalism encourages the latter reading. Even readers in the 1650s who were alert to the royalist sensibilities of the poem would have recognised that its potential commentary on the possibility of the restoration of the Stuart monarchy represents a future that Cowley wanted to come to pass, but that had very little chance of ever occurring. The Prince could be, like David at the end of *Davideis* 4, caught in a seemingly unending exile, looking back to earlier days and hoping for other, better, days to come. Cowley's technique of creating competing and equally plausible accounts of the near future is in many respects the most Virgilian aspect of the *Davideis*. The poem recognises the contingent nature of the contemporary political situation, which had yet to stabilise, despite the seeming total defeat of the royalist cause.

The emphasis on a contingent future is often more immediately apparent in Virgil's *Georgics* than in his *Aeneid*. It may simply be a coincidence that the *Davideis* in its published form has the same number of books as the *Georgics*, but the parallel helps to bring out Cowley's primary concerns. The same interest in contingency is also present in Cowley's translation from the *Georgics*, his only translation from Virgil whose authorship he acknowledged. This translation was not published until 1663, but its composition is most likely contemporaneous with the publication of the *Davideis*. Although Cowley's *Georgics* initially appears to be apolitical, a detailed comparison with its source text indicates that the translation is informed by contemporary royalist discourse. Cowley also frames the conclusion of his translation in such a manner to suggest that the providential restoration of the monarchy could be close at hand, but, as in the *Davideis*, this event remains something that is wished for rather than confidently foretold or presented as an inevitability.

Georgics

The praise of rural life in the second book of the *Georgics* (G 2.458–540) is one of the most celebrated passages not only in Virgil but in the entire classical canon. Although it had not been translated as a poem in its own right before Cowley's version it was widely known and frequently imitated by English poets during this period, including by Cowley himself in his partial Latin translation of the *Davideis* that was published in his 1656 *Poems*.[37] Cowley's translation forms part of his *Verses, Lately Written Upon Several Occasions* (1663), which contains versions of extracts from Horace, Martial and Claudian that praise the country life. His decision to translate the passage as a stand-alone poem could, then, simply be an apolitical reassertion of certain precepts that by the mid-seventeenth century had become commonplaces, even clichés.

As the *Georgics* passage contains several references to civil war, however, it offers an especial topicality for Cowley and his readers. In the event, Cowley's translation simultaneously exploits and downplays its potential to offer political commentary. Like *The Civil War* and *Davideis*, the poem acquires definition through absences. In this case the absences are the result of Cowley omitting phrases from the original Latin text. Knowledge of these omissions plays a key role in insinuating, and subsequently frustrating, a straightforwardly royalist or republican political reading of the passage. Paul Davis has drawn attention to the 'selective repointing of the original text' in the translations Cowley published in the 1650s and 1660s.[38] Whilst Davis identifies some of Cowley's omissions in the *Georgics* passage, he does not discuss the fact that many of them occur where the poem could easily accommodate parallels with the contemporary political situation. For Virgil, the Italian farmers are fortunate because they are 'procul discordibus armis' (G 2.459; 'far from the clash of arms'). As the *Georgics* were written during the conflict between Octavian and Mark Antony, and published soon after its conclusion, Virgil was primarily referring to civil war. Yet Cowley does not translate 'procul discordibus armis' at all, unless the sentiment inspires his expansive later translation of 'secura quies' (G 2.467; 'free from care') as 'calm and harmless life / Free from the Alarm's of Fear, and storms of Strife'.[39] Even if this couplet is informed by the earlier Latin phrase, and Cowley does frequently move lines from their original position to a different point in his translation, the contemporary resonances are much less targeted and politicised. Similarly, he translates a line which contains one of the more familiar tropes of civil conflict, 'infidos agitans discordia fratres' (G 2.496; 'the strife which leads brother to betray brother'), simply as 'quarrels of the mighty' (Cowley, *Verses*, p. 46), which removes its association with internecine strife and warfare. The only direct reference to warfare in the translation is to 'The Camps of Gowned War' (Cowley, *Verses*, p. 46), that is, the legal contests that are fought in the courts between lawyers, rather than pitched battle between armies. The equivalent passage in Virgil reads 'ferrea iura / insanumque forum aut populi tabularia' (G 2.501–2; 'the iron laws, and the madness of the forum or the public archives'). The only other translation of the lines during this period is by John Ogilby in his wholesale rendering of Virgil. He turns it into a statement that decries those who took up arms against the king: he refers to '*Mad Parliaments, Acts of Commons*' and '*sword-Law*'.[40] This highly presentist and royalist approach is absent from Cowley's version.

Cowley also passes over a chance to acknowledge that his political affiliations had affected his personal circumstances. Virgil refers to those who 'exsilioque domos et dulcia limina mutant / atque alio patriam quaerunt sub sole iacentem' (G 2.511–12; 'change their sweet homes and hearths for exile and seek a country that lies beneath an alien sun'). There is a clear potential here to parallel Cowley's personal experience of foreign exile. But the lines in Cowley's translation form part of a more generically moralising observation about the unnatural actions people are driven to in their quest for financial gain: 'Around the World in search of it they roam, / It makes ev'n their Antipodes their home' (*Verses*, p. 46). Once again there is a conspicuous lack of political or personal application.

The decision to translate the *Georgics* extract in this way has parallels with Cowley's acknowledgement in the 1656 *Poems* preface that he has suppressed his poems on the civil wars. The excisions of the original material in the translation can lend weight to the traditional argument, in large part fuelled by Cowley's own pronouncements, that the poetry he wrote following his return to England from exile in Europe largely avoided making political statements, and that he had exchanged the *vita contemplativa* for the *vita activa*.[41] But it is more beneficial to approach Cowley's *Georgics* translation in the light of James Loxley's and (more recently) Caroline Spearing's reassessment of the function of the rural retirement topos in royalist poetry. They argue that poems which celebrate life away from the centre of political action frequently represent an alternative means of offering political commentary.[42] That this impulse informs Cowley's *Georgics* translation may explain why its setting is more immediately reminiscent of classical Rome than of seventeenth-century England when the other translations in *Verses, Lately Written Upon Several Occasions* anglicise their original landscapes and cultural contexts. The poem implies that, such was the devastation to the countryside during the periods of civil conflict, the idea that farmers would have been 'far from the clash of arms' could not be applied to the English situation. Some of Cowley's other excisions serve a similar purpose. Cowley removes the section that refers to the acclamation of politicians in the public theatre (*G* 2.508–10); readers who were familiar with the original could draw parallels between this absence in the translation and the absence of a formally licensed theatrical culture between 1642 and 1660. Such an approach to the text suggests a further continuation of Cowley's practice in the *Davideis* (1656). The absent presences point at precisely the lack of applicability between aspects of Virgil's original text and Cowley's translations and imitations of Virgil. The translation is concerned with identifying points of departure between Virgil's Italy and Cowley's England.

Unlike in the *Davideis*, though, the inability to apply moments of the *Georgics* translation to a contemporary English context make the poem more royalist than politically ambivalent. The royalism expressed within the translation nonetheless remains that of a defeated supporter of the cause. Fairly detailed knowledge both of the original Latin and Cowley's manipulation of it is required to activate these royalist readings, which suggests that Cowley intended the poem as a more private expression of his political sentiments. The widespread familiarity of the original ensures that at least some of his readers would have known it intimately; they could have recognised unprompted which parts of the original Cowley has manipulated, expanded upon or excised in order to make the translation point away from contemporary politics. It requires a collusion between Cowley and his readers to activate its royalist resonances.

The final section of Cowley's translation, which documents the farmer's return to his ancestral homestead, introduces a potentially prophetic, as well as royalist, element to the text. Richard Thomas has argued that in this section of the poem Virgil is 'unequivocally identifying this figure with the inhabitant of the golden age'.[43] Numerous panegyrists compared the Restoration to the return of the classical Golden Age,[44] and Cowley's translation may capitalise on this connection to serve as an oblique call for the return of the monarchy. This possibility is strengthened by Spearing's observation that in other texts Cowley hails Charles II's return as the return of the Golden Age and compares the task that he faced in 1660 to that of a farmer returning to his homeland in terms that are reminiscent of Virgil's *Georgics*.[45] But what is explicit in those texts is only implicit in the *Georgics* translation.

The potential royalist and prophetic elements of the translation are also compromised by Cowley translating the note of retrospection on which the poem ends. After the account of the farmer's return, the text notes:

> ante etiam sceptrum Dictaei regis et ante
> impia quam caesis gens est epulata iuvencis,
> aureus hanc vitam in terris Saturnus agebat;
> necdum etiam audierant inflari classica, necdum
> impositos duris crepitare incudibus ensis.
>
> (G 2.536–40)

('[this was how life was lived] before the sceptre of the Dictaean [Cretan] king held sway, and before an impious race banqueted on slaughtered bullocks, such was the life golden Saturn lived on earth; while yet none had heard the trumpet sound, none heard the swords to ring, as they were laid on harsh anvils'.)

> Such was the Life that ev'n till now does raise
> The honour of poor *Saturns* golden dayes:

> <u>Before Men born of Earth and buried there,</u>
> <u>Let in the Sea their mortal fate to share.</u>
> <u>Before new wayes of perishing were sought,</u>
> Before unskilful Death on Anvils wrought.
> Before those Beasts which humane Life sustain,
> By Men, unless to the Gods use were slain.
>
> (*Verses*, p. 47)

Cowley adds several details, including how the people seek 'new wayes of perishing' and the reference to seafaring. The latter is particularly telling, since the development of navigation traditionally post-dated the Golden Age. The implication that the Golden Age remains firmly in the past is stronger in the translation than in the original, as is the sense that, whilst its return is deeply desired, there is no real prospect of leaving the present Iron Age of conflict and death. Cowley is in part responding to Virgil's own ambivalence about the prospect of a return of the Golden Age, but in the translation the melancholy also affects the political commentary that comes through the possible identification between the farmer and Charles II. In the manner of Denham's *Destruction of Troy* (and to some extent the *Davideis* as well), the translation offers, but subsequently denies, the prospect of this figure's homecoming and the return of the Golden Age. In this passage there is notably no equivalent of Virgil's description of Jupiter as a king.

Cowley's version of the *Georgics*, like his *Davideis*, contains an implicit desire for the return of the monarchy with the recognition that such an event might never come to pass. These factors make a pre-1660 completion date most likely. No indication of its composition date is provided in the published edition of the poem, and Cowley's removal of any explicit reference to civil war in the translation has parallels not only with his statement in the 1656 *Poems* preface but also with the Act of Indemnity and Oblivion that was passed in the early months of Charles II's reign. This Act legally 'forgot' the events of the previous two decades and acted as though the civil wars had never occurred, but could not help preserving memories of those events in the course of their official oblivion. Cowley's translation, which contains potent absent presences for readers familiar with the original text, could reflect both Restoration-era tensions and the royalist setbacks of the 1650s.

Even when his usual emphasis on pathos and melancholy is taken into consideration it would have been highly unusual, not to say perverse, for Cowley to compose a translation after 1660 which offers the restoration of the monarchy only as a possibility. In the immediate aftermath of the Restoration, Cowley in fact published some of his earlier works in a manner that is reminiscent of Denham's strategy from the 1650s: he asserted (or invented) a temporal gap between composition and publication in order to imply that the work in question had prophetic qualities. As the following section outlines, in *The Visions and Prophecies Concerning England, Scotland, and Ireland* (1660), *Cutter of Coleman-Street* (perf. 1661, pub. 1663) and *Duo Libri Plantarum* (1662) Cowley presents hindsight as foresight. Yet the event that Cowley 'foretells' in these texts is not Charles I's execution, but Charles II's coronation. What is merely desired in the *Georgics* translation becomes a formal, if retrospective, prophetic utterance.

Visions and Prophecies; Cutter of Coleman-Street; Duo Libri Plantarum

Cowley writes *Visions and Prophecies* in the persona of a fictional supporter of Cromwell, Ezekiel Grebner. The text includes references to several events of the 1650s before concluding with a prophecy that is clearly intended to 'foretell' the restoration of the monarchy under Charles II. In the introduction to the collection Cowley (as Grebner) draws attention to the accuracy of the text's predictions by claiming that 'Both the Book and this Preface were written in the time of the late little Protector RICHARD',[46] that is, between 1658 and 1659. Even at the tail end of Richard Cromwell's brief Protectorate the restoration of the monarchy was by no means inevitable or widely anticipated. *Visions and Prophecies* is not a lengthy text, and Thomason's copy of it is dated 'November 1660'.[47] As it would have been in Cowley's interests to publish the book as close as possible to Charles II's return to England in May 1660 to emphasise its status as a genuinely prophetic text, it likely foretold events that had already come to pass by the time of its composition as well as its publication.

Visions and Prophecies was reissued in 1661 as *A Vision, Concerning his late Pretended Highnesse, Cromwell, the Wicked*. This edition contained a new advertisement, not written in the persona of Grebner, which claims that the printed text represents 'a small piece of that which was his original Design'.[48] Once again, a text by Cowley becomes defined by its absent presences. The advertisement claims:

> by the extraordinary Mercy of God, (for which we had no pretence of Merit, nor the least glympse of Hope) in the suddain Restoration of Reason, and Right, and Happinesse to us, it became not onely unnecessary, but unseasonable and impertinent to prosecute the work.[49]

Where the initial intention of *The Civil War* as a royalist epic was outpaced by events, and the prospect of a Stuart restoration was mooted as a desired but unlikely outcome in the *Davideis* (and possibly in the *Georgics* translation too), the 'predictions' of extended Cromwellian rule that are present in *Visions and Prophecies* have had to be curtailed as a result of the Restoration. Cowley has, once again, been forced to break off his verses. Unlike in his *The Civil War*, however, tears are being shed by the royalists' opponents, not the royalists themselves. Although Cowley himself celebrates the Restoration in a verse panegyric, in *Visions and Prophecies* he nonetheless places himself in the position of a mourner, as he had in his earlier texts that saw into the future.

A similar strategy of including a prophecy in a text that likely post-dates the events it foretells occurs in Cowley's drama *Cutter of Coleman-Street* (perf. 1661, pub. 1663). The play revises *The Guardian*, which Cowley had written as an undergraduate to honour a royal visitation to Cambridge in early 1642. The setting of *The Guardian* was contemporary with its presentation, but Cowley sets *Cutter* in 1658, rather than in 1642 or 1661. Cowley's work on *Cutter* has consequently been dated to the late 1650s, and as he appears to have been involved in Davenant's attempts to revive the tradition of public stage performances that were happening around this time it may reflect an attempt to revise his existing theatrical output to fit these new circumstances.[50] Stefania Crowther has nevertheless established that Cowley's alterations reflected the performance conditions of the London stage after 1660, particularly in the greater prominence given to female roles.[51] A post-1660 composition date for the play also helps to situate the references to the royalists' travails of the 1640s it contains. Part of the plot concerns a royalist's attempts to regain his family estates that had been confiscated during the war by marrying the widow of the Puritan into whose possession the land had passed. More significantly, setting the play in 1658 allows Cowley to 'predict' the Restoration. The character Lucia harangues one of the Puritans in the play:

> Go cursed race, which stick your loathsome crimes
> Upon the Honorable Cause and Party;
> And to the Noble Loyal Sufferers,
> A worser suffering add of Hate and Infamy.
> Go to the Robbers and the Patricides,
> And fix your Spots upon their Painted Vizards,
> Not on the Native face of Innocence,
> 'Tis you retard that Industry by which
> Our Country would recover from this sickness;
> Which, whilst it fears th' eruption of such Ulcers,
> Keeps a Disease tormenting it within,
> But if kind Heav'n please to restore our Health,

> When once the great Physician shall return,
> He quickly will I hope restore our Beauty.
> (*Cutter of Coleman-Street*, pp. 13–14)

This speech has no equivalent in *The Guardian*, and so must have been written to reflect the changed state of the royalists' fortunes. Virgilian in its status as a *post eventum* prophecy, if not in its content, Lucia's speech in *Cutter* acknowledges that by the early 1660s royalist hopes had become reality. It is still, though, a noticeably contingent prophecy, since the Restoration and the return of the 'great Physician' remains a matter of if, rather than when. Nor, in keeping with Cowley's Interregnum-era prophecies of the Restoration and his sense of himself as a royal servant rather than a royal counsellor, is there any sense of how this event will come about. Cowley has Lucia express his own sense of providence as an unpredictable, inscrutable force.

The ambiguity of setting and subject matter that is found in *Visions and Prophecies* and *Cutter* characterises Cowley's *Duo Libri Plantarum* (1662), which subsequently serve as the first two books of the complete, six-book *Plantarum* of 1668. In the *Duo Libri Plantarum*, Spearing argues, 'Cowley asks the reader to consider the work as the product of the late Interregnum despite its Restoration publication';[52] as I have already suggested, a similar strategy may also inform his *Georgics* translation. The *Duo Libri Plantarum* was written, like the *Georgics*, after Cowley is supposed to have retired from public life to study natural philosophy. But, in a further example of declarations of rural retirement masking political engagement, the completed *Plantarum* of 1668 contains extensive implicit and explicit moments of political commentary.

Sex Libri Plantarum

In the 1668 *Plantarum* Cowley adopts the Virgilian technique of incorporating a formal and extensive *post eventum* prophecy of recent events. The time of the poem's composition meant that Cowley had the opportunity to reverse the pattern of his previous epics and have Virgilian elegy give way to panegyric. The *Plantarum* does suggest that this reversal has indeed occurred, but Cowley consciously undermines the apparent triumphalism of the poem's 'prophetic' statements regarding the fate of the Stuart dynasty. The *Plantarum* sees Cowley combining anticipatory and retrospective prophecy for the purposes of making initially triumphalist and hopeful statements become melancholic and to signal the shedding of tears. As with the *Davideis* and his *Georgics* translation, this was the result of a conscious decision by Cowley, rather than events outpacing the poem's composition as had been the case in *The Civil War*.

Cowley's interests in Virgil, prophecy and royalism coalesce in Book 6 of the *Plantarum*. The narrative moves away from the poem's ostensible botanical subject matter to commemorate recent political events. This account is not presented, however, as a retrospective narrative: where Books 1–2 lack a specific temporal and geographical setting, and Books 3–5 take place in 1660 (first in Oxford, then the banks of the Thames, before moving to the Fortunate Isles in the mid-Atlantic), Book 6 is set in the Forest of Dean during the 1630s. There the Dryad of the Oak 'foretells' events from before the outbreak of civil war to the aftermath of the monarchy's restoration. The Dryad's prophecy is Virgilian in content and form as well as in technique. Her description of the inhabitants of pre-civil-war England, 'Fortunatorum nimium bona si sua nossent',[53] closely follows the opening line of the *Georgics* passage that he translated a few years earlier: 'O fortunatos nimium, sua si bona norint' (*G* 2.458; 'O farmers, happy beyond measure, could they but know their blessings'). Cowley's shift of tense to the pluperfect in his imitation adds to the rueful melancholia: the happiness referred to lies in the past, not the present. The use of the pluperfect also indicates that this state of happiness had come to a definitive end, which helps this part of the poem to articulate a sense of frustrated or thwarted possibilities.

As in his previous works, Cowley uses absent presences in the *Plantarum* both to represent overwhelming emotion and the onset of tears as well as thwarted possibilities. When the 'prophecy' of civil wars reaches Charles's death, the Dryad is unable to give an account of the execution itself. This prompts the imitation of a Virgilian half-line:[54]

> Video productum carcere *Regem*
> *Pegmate in excelso*, suaque ante palatia, in arce
> Imperii summam, populo spectante Dieque,
> Carnificisque manu —
> Substitit hic, gemitusque imam radice petitus.[55]

('I see the King led out from his prison cell onto the high stage, and before his palace, the lofty seat of power, with the people and God watching, with the hand of the executioner — Here she stopped, and let out a groan from the very depths of her roots.')

The Dryad's speech also causes all the assembled tree-spirits to weep for the death of the king. As in the passage on Godolphin in *The Civil War*, words have been forced to give way to tears. Where, as discussed earlier in the chapter, the Virgilian imitations in *The Civil War* are somewhat undigested, those in the *Plantarum* show a more active degree of engagement with Virgil. Cowley reworks and adapts Virgilian stylistic features and sentiments rather than incorporate them more or less wholesale into his own writings.

When the Dryad resumes her prophecy, she describes the state of the country in the wake of the regicide in terms that recall Charles's own fate. Cowley has both the king and the country represent each other:

> Tum vero innumeris confossa *Britannia* telis,
> Et *Capite abscisso*, proprioque in sanguine mersa,
> Non agnoscendum iacet atque informe *Cadaver*,
> *Immanis* sine Mente, Animaque & Nomine *Truncus*.[56]

> ('Then, truly, was Britain pierced with innumerable weapons, the head torn off, and plunged in her own blood, there lies an unrecognisable and deformed corpse, a great trunk without a mind, a soul, or name.')

Cowley's Latin here adapts the same passage in *Aeneid* 2 that recounts the death of Priam at the hands of Pyrrhus which Denham used to mourn Charles I in *The Destruction of Troy*. The use of 'sine Mente, Animaque & Nomine *Truncus*' is well suited to the comparison that Cowley makes between the body politic and a felled oak tree, but it is also indebted to the description of Priam's corpse as 'ingens ... truncus ... sine nomine corpus' (*A* 2.557–8; 'a great trunk ... a body without a name'). Cowley's 'proprioque in sanguine mersa' ('plunged in her own blood') also seems indebted to the description of Pyrrhus dragging Priam to his ancestral altar 'multo lapsantem sanguine nati' (*A* 2.551; 'slipping in his son's streaming blood'). Furthermore, the passage demonstrates Cowley's awareness that Virgil's Priam had been used as a means of commemorating the deaths of other significant political figures. There is a parallel here with Cowley's own 'prophecy' of Charles's death in his *sors Virgiliana* translation. The execution happens '*Pegmate in excelso*' ('on a high stage'), and this term derives from a word with very few recorded instances in classical Latin to denote 'A piece of wooden machinery in the theatre'.[57] Its meaning is exclusively theatrical and links to the reference to the 'open stage' in his rendering of Dido's curse.

After its initial emphasis on trauma and suffering, the Dryad's prophecy ostensibly changes its focus to imperial glory by foreseeing the growth of British naval power under the restored Stuart dynasty. Cowley again couches this in recognisably Virgilian terms. The Dryad, 'foreseeing' the rivalry between the Dutch and the English as naval powers, rebukes the Dutch: 'Et tamen audetis (Spes Ambitionis inepta!) / Imperium pelagi vobis promittere totum' ('And you even dare (a vain, empty hope!) to presume that the entire *imperium* of the sea is promised to you').⁵⁸ Cowley takes 'Imperium pelagi' from Neptune's rebuke to the four winds in the *Aeneid*. Neptune tells them to remind their king, Aeolus (who had released the winds following a request by Juno), about the bounds placed on the authority of Aeolus' own king, Jupiter: 'Non illi imperium pelagi saevumque tridentem, / sed mihi sorte datum' (*A* 1.138–9; 'not to him, but to me, were given by lot the *imperium* of the sea and the harsh trident'). 'Imperium pelagi' thus acts as a shorthand for possessing maritime supremacy, and the implication in the *Plantarum* is that the Dutch are acting as an Aeolus to the English Neptune. This connection between the English and the god of the sea is well established by this stage of the poem, as the Dryad had previously drawn a parallel between the three Stuart kingdoms and the three forks of Neptune's trident.⁵⁹

The *Plantarum* reasserts this account of naval power over the Dutch by ending the 'prophecy' with an account of the 1665 Battle of Lowestoft.⁶⁰ Cowley intimates that this battle represents the bestowing of *imperium* on Charles II and his fleet. This part of Cowley's poem is reminiscent of the 'Advice to a Painter' series of poems (1665–7) and Dryden's *Annus Mirabilis* (1667), which are concerned with celebrating the growth of British naval power and the development of a commercial maritime empire. The use of *imperium* in Virgil, Cowley and these other writers also allowed them to engage with the concept of *translatio imperii*, the westward movement of empire. For Virgil, *imperium* shifts from Troy to Rome, but for Dryden and the 'Advice' poets the centre of *imperium* has shifted westward once again, from Rome to London. Edward Young later engaged with the same principle by calling his 1730 verse panegyric on British naval power *Imperium Pelagi*. Maggie Kilgour has discussed Cowley's engagement with the *translatio imperii* tradition elsewhere in the *Plantarum*, as the 'Dryad herself is descended from an oak on Dodona brought over by the Trojan Brutus',⁶¹ the legendary founder of Britain, great-grandson of Aeneas and (in the British tradition) the true heir to Trojan *imperium*. According to Cowley the descendants of Brutus' oaks will be felled to build the ships that will secure Britain's naval dominance over their European rivals and carry them to the New World. But even in his claim of Britain's imperial rise Cowley focuses on the human cost of the victory. He preserves the attention on death and suffering that informs the earlier sections of the prophecy that are dedicated to the civil wars and Interregnum.

Cowley's anxieties about British imperial power are compounded by the fact that the Dryad's prophecy is the second of two extensive prophecies in the *Plantarum*. Book 5 concludes with a prophecy by Apollo in which Cowley genuinely does attempt to anticipate the future. From a British perspective, this prophecy undermines the more hopeful later account that is given by the Dryad of the Oak. Cowley has Apollo say 'cadet *Europe*' ('Europe will fall'),[62] on account of its insatiable lust for New World gold. As a consequence of Europe's fall, 'Ingenium, Pietas, Artes, ac bellica virtus' ('Genius, Piety, the Arts, and warlike virtue'), as well as many of its people, will flee to the New World and there establish 'regna illustria' ('illustrious kingdoms').[63] It is to this mixed population, of refugees from Europe (as opposed to the earlier waves of its colonisers) and the indigenous people of the New World that the great empire is promised. There are clear parallels here between the mixing of Trojans and Italians to form the Roman race that Jupiter 'foresees' in the final book of the *Aeneid* (A 12.791–842). These inhabitants of the New World are those who are, despite what Cowley suggests later in the poem about the growth of British naval *imperium*, the true heirs to Troy. Cowley's prophecies in the *Plantarum* do not explicitly consider the eclipse of Britain by America, but they do anticipate the end of a British imperial power even at the moment of its ostensible foundation. Even in his most apparently panegyrical work, Cowley uses a Virgilian *post eventum* prophecy to meditate on the losses that lie ahead in the future as well as those which occurred in the past.

In many respects Cowley's *Plantarum* is closer not to the hopeful, even triumphalist, attitude of Dryden's *Annus Mirabilis* or Young's *Imperium Pelagi*, but to later and more melancholic poems of *translatio imperii* like John Dyer's *Ruins of Rome* (1740) and Anna Letitia Barbauld's *Eighteen Hundred and Eleven* (1812). These poets present Britain as a nation which will possess *imperium* only temporarily, and predict that it will one day pass westwards again. For Barbauld, this event had either already occurred or was on the point of occurring: towards the end of her poem, the 'Genius', the spirit of liberty, culture and learning, 'turns from Europe's desolated shores' to Spanish America 'And swears – Thy world, Columbus, shall be free'.[64] The sequencing of the *Plantarum*'s prophecies suggests that the same thought had occurred to Cowley. The *Plantarum* foresees a *translatio imperii* to America and suggests that the felling of the Dryad's fellow oaks to become ships that will carry Brutus' descendants to the New World is an indication, not that Britain has secured *imperium*, but that British possession of *imperium* is already being, and may well already have been, lost.

In the *Plantarum* Cowley revisits his earlier epic on the civil wars to foretell the future, but unlike in *The Civil War* Cowley deliberately predicts disaster. The setbacks the navy experienced between the Battle of Lowestoft and the *Plantarum*'s publication in 1668, which included the humiliating Dutch raid on the fleet at Chatham, would already have undermined the poem's claims of Stuart naval *imperium*. When the Cowley of the Restoration period does look to the future he sees only a brief period of glory before a decline and fall. Even after 1660, Virgil ultimately remained for Cowley the poet of elegy, not of panegyric; Cowley's Virgilian tears anticipate future difficulties as well as lamenting past traumas. To some extent Cowley anticipates the approach to Virgil as the poet of 'sunt lacrimae rerum' (*A* 1.462; 'there are the tears of things') that, as T. W. Harrison has discussed, was such a significant strand of Virgil's English reception in the eighteenth century.[65] Unlike this strand of Virgil's reception, however, the tears Cowley sheds in his Virgilian writing are still primarily focused on political issues rather than a broader sense of human suffering.

The *Plantarum* demonstrates that even after the Restoration Cowley uses Virgil to anticipate the future of the royalist cause as well to commemorate fallen royalists. The same impulse also informed the writings of John Ogilby, which form the focus of the following chapter. The future that Ogilby imagines for the royalists both before and after the Restoration, however, is much more glorious and expressed more confidently than those outlined in the *Plantarum* and the other texts considered thus far. Ogilby translates Virgil to assert his continued loyalty to the royalist cause, but these declarations were noticeably less ambivalent than those of Denham or Cowley. Ogilby's forthright expressions of royalist sympathies stem from his association with a more absolutist strand of royalism than the constitutional royalism of Denham and the mobile but moderate loyalism of Cowley. Ogilby's translations repeatedly present the Stuart Restoration as an inevitability.

Notes

1. Abraham Cowley, *Naufragium Joculare Comædia* (London, 1638), sig. B2v; translations are taken from '*Naufragium Joculare* (1638): A Hypertext Critical Edition', ed. Dana Sutton, in *The Philological Museum* (2001/2), www.philological.bham.ac.uk/cowley/
2. *Poems Written by A. Cowley* (London, 1656) (hereafter Cowley, *Poems*), sig. Eeee1r; Abraham Cowley, *Cutter of Coleman-Street* (London, 1663), sig. a1r; Cowley, *Poems*, sig. Pppp3r. See also the similar comments on Virgil in *The Works of Mr Abraham Cowley* (London, 1668) (hereafter Cowley, *Works*), sig. ²N2v.
3. *Aubrey's Brief Lives*, ed. Oliver Lawson Dick (London, 1949), p. 75.
4. *Naufragium Joculare*, sig. A2r; *Abraham Cowley: The Civil War*, ed. Allan Pritchard (Toronto, 1973), 2.97; *Abrahami Couleii Angli, Poemata Latina* (London, 1668) (hereafter *Poemata Latina*), pp. 74, 240.
5. As discussed on pp. 54–6, above.

6. Cited in *Aubrey's Brief Lives*, pp. 75–6. As in my other chapters, underline indicates where the translations substantially depart from or add to the Virgilian original.
7. Henry Bowman, *Songs for 1, 2, & 3 Voyces* (Oxford, 1677), pp. 43–4.
8. Henry Bowman, *Songs, for One, Two, & Three Voyces to the Thorow-Bass* (Oxford, 1679).
9. *Diary of Dr. Edward Lake*, ed. George Percy Elliot (London, 1846), p. 25.
10. See Arthur H. Nethercot, *Abraham Cowley: The Muse's Hannibal* (Oxford, 1931), p. 78. I draw on this volume for the biographical information on Cowley that occurs across this chapter.
11. See *Aubrey's Brief Lives*, p. 75.
12. Cf. 'And can there be no temperate Region knowne / Betwixt the *Frigid*, and the *Torrid-Zone*? ... For what's the King with a full pow'r to sway, / When there are left no Subjects to obey?' (Abraham Cowley(?), *The Foure Ages of England: Or, The Iron Age. With Other Select Poems* (London, 1648), pp. 53–5) and 'Is there no temperate Region can be knowne, / Betwixt their frigid, and our Torrid Zone? ... And may that Law, which teaches Kings to sway / Their Scepters, teach their Subjects to obey' (Sir John Denham, *Coopers Hill* (London, 1642), pp. 10, 19).
13. See Cowley, *Poems*, sigs. (a)1r– (a)2v.
14. Cowley, *Works*, sig. a1r.
15. See Sir John Denham, *Poems and Translations, with the Sophy* (London, 1668), sig. A3v.
16. I draw here on Lucy Moore, *Lady Fanshawe's Receipt Book: The Life and Times of a Civil War Heroine* (London, 2017), p. 85.
17. See Joshua Scodel, *Excess and the Mean in Early Modern English Literature* (Princeton, 2002), pp. 136–8.
18. Jason McElligott and David L. Smith (eds), *Royalists and Royalism during the Interregnum* (Manchester, 2010), p. 6.
19. See Henry Power, '"Teares breake off my Verse": The Virgilian Incompleteness of Abraham Cowley's *The Civil War*', *Translation and Literature*, 16 (2007), 141–59 (p. 143).
20. Cowley, *Civil War*, ed. Pritchard, p. 39.
21. The Lucanian presence in Cowley's text is discussed in Power, 'Teares', pp. 150–1.
22. I discuss Fanshawe's 'Proclamation' ode on pp. 112–13, below.
23. Gerald M. MacLean, *Time's Witness: Historical Representation in English Poetry, 1603–1660* (Madison, WI, 1990), pp. 193, 202.
24. I draw here on Power, 'Teares', pp. 143–9.
25. Cowley, *Civil War*, ed. Pritchard, p. 40, discussing 2.139–56 (2.151–4).
26. Power, 'Teares', p. 153.
27. For which see p. 40, above.
28. For full details of the relationship between the two poems, see Cowley, *Civil War*, ed. Pritchard, pp. 52–5.
29. 'Honors': see Cowley, *Poems*, sig. Iiii1v; 'Lambent': see Cowley, *Poems*, sig. Pppp3v.
30. Discussed in Sue Starke, '"The Eternal Now": Virgilian Echoes and Miltonic Premonitions in Cowley's *Davideis*', *Christianity and Literature*,

55 (2006), 195–219. Line numbers for the *Davideis* are taken from *A Critical Edition of Abraham Cowley's Davideis*, ed. Gayle Shadduck (New York, 1987).
31. See Cowley, *Civil War*, ed. Pritchard, pp. 53–4.
32. See Philip Hardie, 'Abraham Cowley, *Davideis. Sacri poematis operis imperfecti liber unus*', in *Neo-Latin Poetry in the British Isles*, ed. L. B. T. Houghton and Gesine Manuwald (London, 2012), pp. 69–86; Niall Allsopp, *Poetry and Sovereignty in the English Revolution* (Oxford, 2020), p. 126.
33. Cf. *Davideis* 2.461–786 and *A* 6.756–886.
34. Thomas Corns, *Uncloistered Virtue: English Political Literature, 1640–1660* (Oxford, 1992), pp. 267–8.
35. See pp. 31–2, 34–6, above.
36. Allsopp, *Poetry and Sovereignty*, p. 6.
37. Hardie, 'Abraham Cowley', p. 81 discusses how *Davideidos Liber Primus* line 1028 rewrites *G* 2.458.
38. Paul Davis, *Translation and the Poet's Life: The Ethics of Translating in English Culture, 1646–1726* (Oxford, 2008), p. 104.
39. Abraham Cowley, *Verses, Lately Written Upon Several Occasions* (London, 1663) (hereafter Cowley, *Verses*), p. 44.
40. John Ogilby, *The Works of Publius Virgilius Maro* (London, 1649), sig. F5r. Ogilby's expressions of royalist sentiment in his Virgil translations are discussed at greater length in the next chapter.
41. See Cowley, *Poems*, sig. (a)4v.
42. See James Loxley, *Royalism and Poetry in the English Civil Wars: The Drawn Sword* (Basingstoke, 1997), pp. 192–241; Caroline Spearing, 'The Fruits of Retirement: Political Engagement in the *Plantarum Libri Sex*', in *Royalists and Royalism in 17th-Century Literature: Exploring Abraham Cowley*, ed. Philip Major (Abingdon, 2020), pp. 180–201.
43. *Georgics*, ed. Richard Thomas, 2 vols (Cambridge, 1988), vol. 1, p. 260.
44. As discussed on p. 45, above.
45. See Caroline Spearing, *Abraham Cowley's Plantarum Libri Sex: A Cavalier Poet and the Classical Canon* (unpublished doctoral thesis, King's College London, 2017), p. 163.
46. Abraham Cowley, *The Visions and Prophecies Concerning England, Scotland, and Ireland* (London, 1660), sig. A5v; roman/italic fonts reversed.
47. I draw here on information provided in the entry for *Visions and Prophecies* in *English Short Title Catalogue* (http://estc.bl.uk).
48. Abraham Cowley, *A Vision, Concerning his late Pretended Highnesse, Cromwell, the Wicked* (London, 1661), sig. A4r; roman/italic fonts reversed.
49. Cowley, *A Vision*, sigs A3v–A3r; roman/italic fonts reversed.
50. See Allsopp, *Poetry and Sovereignty*, p. 152.
51. See Stefania Crowther, '"An Old and Unfashionable Building": Cowley's Dramatic Writing and Rewriting', in *Exploring Abraham Cowley*, ed. Major, pp. 229–50.
52. Spearing, *Abraham Cowley's Plantarum Libri Sex*, p. 50.
53. *Poemata Latina*, p. 316 [*Sex Libri Plantarum* 6.67]. Line numbers for the *Plantarum* are taken from '*De Plantis Libri Sex* (1668): A Hypertext

Critical Edition', ed. Dana Sutton, in *The Philological Museum* (2006/7), www.philological.bham.ac.uk/plants/
54. Others occur at *Poemata Latina*, pp. 223, 282, 342 [*Sex Libri Plantarum* 4.529, 5.586, 6.629].
55. *Poemata Latina*, p. 346 [*Sex Libri Plantarum* 6.734–8].
56. *Poemata Latina*, p. 347 [*Sex Libri Plantarum* 6.748–51].
57. Charlton T. Lewis and Charles Short, *A Latin Dictionary* (London, 1879), s.v. 'pegma' 2b.
58. *Poemata Latina*, p. 360 [*Sex Libri Plantarum* 6.1133–4].
59. *Poemata Latina*, p. 360 [*Sex Libri Plantatum* 6.1125].
60. *Poemata Latina*, pp. 360–4 [*Sex Libri Plantarum* 6.1126–226].
61. Maggie Kilgour, 'Cowley's Epic Experiments', in *Exploring Abraham Cowley*, ed. Major, pp. 99–123 (108).
62. *Poemata Latina*, p. 311 [*Sex Libri Plantarum* 5.1186].
63. *Poemata Latina*, p. 312 [*Sex Libri Plantarum* 5.1190–1].
64. *Eighteen Hundred and Eleven*, lines 322, 34, in *The Poems of Anna Letitia Barbauld*, ed. William McCarthy and Elizabeth Kraft (Athens, GA, 1994).
65. See T. W. Harrison, 'English Vergil: The *Aeneid* in the XVIII Century', *Philologica Pragensia*, 10 (1967), 1–11, 80–91.

Chapter 4

Sacred Majesty: John Ogilby

Introduction

Ogilby began his *The Works of Publius Virgilius Maro*, the first complete rendering of the Virgilian corpus into English, after a career which included periods as a sequin-maker, dancing-master, soldier, naval officer and theatrical impresario. The precise dates of the translation's composition are not known, but certain references in the text indicate that it is largely a product of the mid-1640s. The reference to '*covenanting Brethren*' in the account of the giants' war against Jupiter in *Georgics* 1, for example, which translates 'coniuratos ... fratres' (*G* 1.280; 'the brethren who have sworn an oath'), makes more sense as a reference to the allegiances of those who had sworn the Solemn League and Covenant between 1643 and 1647 than later in the decade.[1] Virgil's giants rebel against monarchical rule, so the connection Ogilby encourages between them and the Covenanters suggests that to take up arms against a monarch is to be an agent of chaos and destruction.[2] In August 1643 the Covenanters aligned with the English Parliament against the monarchy but reversed this allegiance in December 1647, so this particular passage of Ogilby's Virgil must have been written between these two dates. His reference to the Covenanters supports Alan Ereira's claim that Ogilby completed the Virgil translation by 1647, although it was only entered in the Stationer's Register in October 1648 and was not published until 1649.[3] It also challenges Tanya Caldwell's claim that Ogilby's Virgil is 'noticeably devoid of political implications'.[4] Ogilby's references to political events embed royalist sentiments into the translation.

Although Ogilby had likely finished the project by 1647 he rewrote at least one passage of his Virgil translation in the year of its publication. Like Denham and Cowley, Ogilby adapted the *Aeneid*'s account of

Priam's death to commemorate the execution of Charles I. His version was, in fact, the first to appear in print of the numerous texts which made the parallel between Charles and Priam:

> So finish'd *Priams* fates, and thus he dide,
> Seeing *Ilium* burn, whose proud Commands did sway
> So many potent Realms in *Asia*.
> Now on the strand his <u>sacred</u> bodie lies
> Headlesse without a name <u>or obsequies</u>.[5]

Ogilby's interpolation of the body lying without obsequies is likely prompted by Charles I's lack of Anglican funeral rites at his burial.[6] The specificity of this reference, and its status as an addition to the narrative, indicates that the passage had not simply acquired new resonances between its composition and publication, but that it was revised to make the contemporary parallel more explicit. Unlike the translations and imitations of this passage by Denham and Cowley, however, Ogilby does not attempt to grant it prophetic status; it functions purely as political commentary and royalist lament.

Other details that Ogilby includes in the Priam passage reveal how his royalism differed from that of the other writers so far discussed in this study. Only Ogilby states that Priam's body is '*sacred*', indicating he shared the belief in a divinely sanctioned monarchy that was such a feature of the early Stuart kings' own myth-making. Its appearance in a passage that was clearly intended to prompt memories of Charles I shows that Ogilby's royalism conformed to the 'belief in absolute monarchy supported by the doctrine of the Divinity of Kings' that Syrithe Pugh has outlined as the hallmark of ultra-loyalist attitudes.[7] This strand of royalism was significantly more hard-line than either the Queen's Party royalism or the constitutional royalism considered in earlier chapters. The emphasis on the divinity of kings that informs Ogilby's use of '*sacred bodie*' is not limited to the passage on Priam – Ogilby's equation of the giants/Covenanters against the Olympians/Stuarts in the *Georgics* also reveals the same attitude – but its use here grants the corpse sacred status in death as well as life. This aligns the translation with the views not just of the ultra-loyalists, but also those who were sufficiently committed in their royalism to think of the executed Charles as a martyr; Ogilby himself uses this term to describe Charles in a (now lost) epic poem on the civil wars, *Carolies*.[8] *The Works of Publius Virgilius Maro* shapes Virgil in Ogilby's own image as an unequivocal supporter of absolutist, divinely sanctioned monarchical rule.

This chapter demonstrates the strategies Ogilby employed in his translation of Virgil to assert his belief that overthrowing a sacred monarch threatens the natural order. It argues that in *The Works of Publius Virgilius Maro* Ogilby adapted parts of Virgil's text and manipulated the volume's paratextual material and typography to situate the translation within an explicitly ultra-loyalist framework. It also examines Ogilby's use of Virgil to predict (and later celebrate) the Stuart restoration under Charles II. Where the prophetic elements in Denham are generally *post eventum* and 'foretell' setbacks to the royalist cause, and in Cowley's Interregnum-era publications the monarchy's return represents just one of several possible futures, Ogilby's ultra-loyalism allowed him to anticipate a royalist triumph with complete confidence. Like Cowley, Ogilby was interested in attributing the outcome of events to providence, but Ogilby's conception of providence lacks the elements of inscrutability and ambiguity that are present in Cowley's formulation.[9] For Ogilby, providence was firmly on the side of the Stuart Restoration. His emphasis on this event as an inevitability ensured that his prophecies of the Restoration in the 1649 Virgil served largely as propagandistic encomia. Ogilby's translation also contains some moments of counsel, but they are directed to supporters of the monarch rather than the monarch himself. When Ogilby revised his Virgil translation for republication in 1654 he often reframed these moments of prophetic counsel, but elsewhere in the text he introduced creative misreadings to reassert the belief that the Restoration was both providential and imminent. The Homer translations that Ogilby began in the latter years of the Interregnum also frame the *Iliad* and *Odyssey* along ultra-loyalist and providentialist lines, which he achieved by deploying the same strategies that he had developed in his Virgil; Ogilby's Homer even incorporated lines from his Virgil translation on occasion. This chapter concludes by focusing on a further instance of self-quotation: the lines from Virgil that Ogilby included in the '*Speeches, Emblemes, Mottoes, and Inscriptions*' that the City of London commissioned him to write for the triumphal arches Charles encountered on the royal progress that formed part of his coronation ceremony.[10] The Virgilian presence in Ogilby's contribution to the coronation festivities celebrated the return of the monarchy and vindicated the conviction that this event would come to pass which he had first articulated in his 1649 Virgil translation.

The Works of Publius Virgilius Maro (1649)

Ogilby's translation followed the standard practice of early modern Virgil editions by prefacing each individual poem in the *Eclogues* and the books of the *Georgics* and *Aeneid* with an argument that summarises its contents. Many of the arguments in Ogilby's edition are fairly neutral, but others, such as the argument for *Eclogue* 1, contain explicit political commentary:

Sad Melibæus *banished declares*
Those miseries attend on civill Wars,
But happy Tityrus, *the safe defence*
People enjoy, under a setled Prince.[11]

As the poem's subject matter is the experience of being dispossessed by the events of a civil war it would be very difficult in this period to produce a translation of it that was devoid of political implications, and here the sentiments are clearly royalist. Annabel Patterson has suggested that the argument would 'inevitably shape a reader's first impressions' of the poem it introduces,[12] but its influence is not confined just to *Eclogue* 1. As the first passage that readers of the volume encounter (after a brief dedicatory preface to William Seymour, Earl of Hertford, whose royalist credentials were such that he was one of the pall-bearers at Charles I's funeral) it also suggests that the translation as a whole will be informed by its royalist sentiments.

Where the events referred to in the argument to *Eclogue* 1 are sufficiently generic that its composition could date from any point in the 1640s, the argument to *Eclogue* 5 may represent, like the passage on Priam's death, a section that Ogilby redrafted in 1649 in the wake of Charles's execution:

Since Kings *as* common Fathers *cherish all,*
Subjects *like* children *should lament their fall;*
But learned men of grief should have more sense,
When violent death seizes a gracious Prince.[13]

This argument appears to have evoked recent events from a royalist perspective too overtly and in too targeted a manner. When *The Works of Publius Virgilius Maro* was reprinted in 1650 this was the only argument to be revised. The new version downplays a potential contemporary application to foreground a classical one instead:

Poor Swains mourn Cæsars *losse, husbandmen may*
At Princes Obsequies their sorrow pay;
And it concerns them, when the death of Kings
Oft murrains, rots, and mighty famine brings.[14]

This version removes the reference to a king's '*violent death*', and is much closer both to the events of *Eclogue* 5 and to the standard arguments of that poem which appear in contemporary Latin and English editions. They recount that in *Eclogue* 5 the shepherds Menalcas and Mopsus mourn the death of their friend Daphnis, and that Daphnis has been thought to represent someone from Virgil's own time who is usually (but not exclusively) identified as Julius Caesar.[15] Even Ogilby's revised version, though, encourages readers to find a parallel between Daphnis/Caesar and Charles I, while retaining its predecessor's emphasis on monarchy as a guarantor of order.

Other passages in Ogilby's translation also stress the connection between monarchical rule and the preservation of social order by drawing attention to the calamitous social collapse that follows the loss of a king. In *Georgics* 4 Ogilby applies this principle to bees:

rege incolumi mens omnibus una est;
amisso rupere fidem, constructaque mella
diripuere ipsae et crates solvere favorum.

(G 4.212–14)

('while the king is safe, all are of one mind; when he is lost, faith is destroyed, and themselves break up the honey they have reared and tear up the structure of their honeycomb'.)

Whilst their King <u>lives</u>, they all agree in one,
But dead, the <u>publick</u> faith is overthrown.
They make the <u>Commonwealth</u> a spoyle, and rend
Their waxen Realms, <u>his life did all defend</u>.[16]

In contrasting the once harmonious royal '*Realms*' with the spoiled '*Commonwealth*' Ogilby evokes the declaration of England as a Commonwealth in 1649. As with the passage on Priam and the argument to *Eclogue* 5, then, these lines likely represent material that was revised in the wake of Charles's death.

The 1649 edition of Ogilby's Virgil prints all the lines which express royalist attitudes that I have so far cited in italics. Their use in the volume's arguments corresponds to standard seventeenth-century typographical practice, but the italicisation of lines within the translation itself must represent a deliberate choice by Ogilby. There is only one brief example of this practice in English translations of Virgil prior to Ogilby's,[17] but several early modern Latin editions of Virgil draw attention to certain lines and phrases by printing them in a different typeface to the majority of the text. The sizeable overlap (around 50 per cent) between the lines that Ogilby italicises and those that Thomas Farnaby treats in a similar manner in his 1634 *Publii Virgilii Maronis Opera*, as well as the wide circulation of this edition in the British Isles during this period, suggests that Farnaby was the primary inspiration for Ogilby's practice.

Farnaby was a royalist, and was even imprisoned during the civil wars on account of his loyalism, but the lines he singles out in his edition are not related to his political convictions and instead serve a purely didactic, ethical purpose.[18] The italicised lines in Ogilby's 1649 *Works of Publius Virgilius Maro* also frequently represent moralising *sententiae*. There are, in fact, more examples of italicised lines that function in this way than those which can be read purely as expressions of royalism. Several of them, nonetheless, remain open to royalist interpretation.[19] That the overlap between Ogilby's italicised lines and those which are given the equivalent treatment in Farnaby's Virgil is considerable, but not total, indicates that Ogilby's volume adapts Farnaby's practice in order to express ultra-loyalist sentiment in the guise of offering moral instruction.

Some of the italicised *sententiae* place Ogilby in the guise of a Virgilian counsellor. It is, at least, difficult not to hear Ogilby addressing other royalists in lines like Aeneas' exhortation '*Live, and preserve yourselves for better chance*' and the politician Drances' statement at the Latian council '*In war no safety*'.[20] The attitude that informs these lines may seem to be at odds with Ogilby's ultra-loyalism, and potentially reflects both the seeming collapse of the royalists' military hopes in 1644–6 and the change in Ogilby's personal circumstances in this period. He spent the first phase of the civil wars in Ireland but subsequently moved to London, where he remained for the duration of the Interregnum. There he became associated with a network of poets with royalist sympathies called the Order of the Black Riband.[21] Other members of this Order included Thomas Stanley, Edward Sherburne (both of whom were themselves significant and prolific translators of classical texts), Robert Herrick and James Shirley. Ogilby had first met Shirley in Dublin in the 1630s when he was the Master of Revels at Strafford's viceregal court and Shirley its principal dramatist, so Shirley may well have been Ogilby's first point of access to the Order.

The Order adopted a more quietist attitude than some of their fellow royalists towards the political situation of the late 1640s and early Interregnum. Their approach seems to have focused on hoping for better times whilst, if not actively approving, then at least accepting the present situation. In that respect, their attitude was reminiscent not only of Ogilby's Aeneas telling his men to live and preserve themselves for better chance, but also of the advice Aeneas' helmsman Palinurus gives the Trojans in *Aeneid* 5. He states 'superat quoniam Fortuna, sequamur, / quoque vocat, vertamus iter' (*A* 5.22–3; 'since Fortune is the victor over us, let us follow and turn our course wherever she calls'). Ogilby's translation of these lines reads 'In vaine we strive, nor make we any way; / Therefore since fortune conquers, let's obey', and so imparts an attitude which could easily be co-opted for the purposes of royalist quietism.[22] This couplet, however, represents one of the occasions where Ogilby does not italicise a line that Farnaby felt merited special attention, which suggests that Ogilby did not wish to allot it a similar status in his translation. It seems intended purely as a rendering of the original text and does not encourage any contemporary application.

Unlike his fellow members of the Order of the Black Riband, and indeed other royalists, Ogilby did not equate quietism either with retirement or a resigned accommodation to the status quo. Even the attitudes that he expresses in his italicised lines which initially suggest a defeated royalist mindset, such as '*In war no safety*', in fact indicate a conviction that the Restoration is destined to happen. His brand of quietism was not in conflict with his ultra-loyalism, but emerged from it. He felt there was no need to rise up against the new regime and risk further acts of war, as no human act could either precipitate or delay the fated return of Stuart monarchy under Charles II. Ogilby's views represent a more confident incarnation of the Black Riband royalism which advocated that Stuart loyalists should bide their time and await the restoration.

Several italicised lines in Ogilby's translation reassert his conviction that the restoration would soon take place. The overarching royalist framework of the translation that he establishes through the argument to *Eclogue* 1 and the responses to specific events of the 1640s from a royalist perspective that are found across the volume encourage a royalist interpretation for statements that might otherwise read like examples of generalised truths, such as '*Labour returns in circle to the Swaine, / And years revolve in their own steps again*' and '*Such change workes length of time*'.[23] These lines present restoration and change, and hence the revival of the monarchy's fortunes, as an inevitable, natural process. Whilst the connection with royalism is generally implicit at these moments, certain *sententiae* do deploy terms that contain noticeable royalist resonances to point the parallel. In *Aeneid* 11, for example, Turnus tells his beleaguered forces:

multa dies variique labor mutabilis aevi
rettulit in melius, multos alterna revisens
lusit et in solido rursus Fortuna locavit.

(*A* 11.425–7)

('the passing of the days and the changing labour of shifting time changes things for the better, many people changeable Fortune has mocked, then once more set up on solid ground again'.)

Ogilby's Turnus states:

> *The various work of time and many days,*
> *Often affairs from worse to better raise,*
> *Fortune reviewing those she hath <u>cast down</u>,*
> *Sporting restores again <u>unto their crown</u>.*[24]

Ogilby was not the first English translator of Virgil to refer to the trappings of royalty when translating this passage. John Vicars's 1632 *Aeneid* has Turnus say 'Fortune re-smiles on them / Whom she before threw from a diadem'.[25] Vicars's attitude towards monarchy was at distinct odds with those of the royalists, however, so the interpolated reference to 'diadem' here is purely metaphorical and does not represent an expression of political sentiment.[26] Within the context of the late 1640s Ogilby's use of 'crown', by contrast, can only have been intended to intimate a royalist revival.

The royalism of Ogilby's *Works of Publius Virgilius Maro* reverses the authorial intentions behind the other epic text from the 1640s so far considered in this study, Cowley's *The Civil War* (1643). Cowley's poem was occasioned by a desire to establish the inevitability of royalist victory in the conflict, but he quickly found himself unable to write in this mode, due to events on the battlefield overtaking its composition; the military defeats of the royalists meant that triumphalist prophecy had to give way to elegy. In Ogilby's 1649 Virgil translation, which draws on a much greater span of the 1640s than *The Civil War* and was published in the year of the king's execution, this process was inverted so that elegy gives way to triumphalist prophecy. The following section considers the strategies Ogilby used to reassert this trajectory in the edition of the translation that he published in 1654. Whilst the 1654 Virgil does contain evidence of a shift in Ogilby's overall priorities, the text still anticipates a revival of the monarchy under the Prince of Wales as Charles II, despite its appearance the year after Cromwell's installation as Lord Protector.

The Works of Publius Virgilius Maro (1654)

Ogilby's 1654 *Works of Publius Virgilius Maro* substantially revised the text of the 1649 edition. Considering the revisions alongside the original versions often gives the impression that Ogilby was attempting to downplay or mute the earlier edition's royalism: the individual who can 'repair this ruin'd Age' is described as a 'Prince' in the 1649 translation of *Georgics* 1, but a 'Young Man' at the equivalent point in the 1654 edition.[27] Changes of this type, though, are largely motivated by Ogilby's intention to make the 1654 Virgil the most scholarly and comprehensive edition of Virgil that was available in English rather than a desire to diminish the translation's expressions of royalist sentiment. Changing '*Prince*' to 'Young Man' reflects that fact that in the *Georgics* Virgil himself refers only to 'iuvenem' (*G* 1.500; 'youth'). Rather than removing its royalist elements, the substitution reframes the line's political affinities to make its point more subtly. Ogilby would have expected his readers to see 'Young Man' as a reference to the Prince, just as Virgil's readers were encouraged to see Augustus (still known as Octavian at the time of the *Georgics*' publication) as the 'iuvenem' who will bring civil conflict to an end. In addition, although the practice of italicising certain words or lines with royalist overtones was dropped for the revised edition, the 1654 Virgil retains the majority of the royalist adaptations of the Latin in the 1649 edition, including those discussed in the previous section.

A similar dynamic between the wish to display scholarly credentials and maintain the translation's status as a royalist text informs the most substantial addition to the 1654 Virgil: Ogilby's marginal commentary. The note appended to the line 'Since all with Sequestrations are opprest' (which translates *E* 1.11–12; 'undique totis / usque adeo turbatur agris'; 'such unrest is there on all sides in the land') clearly uses the past to comment on the present:

> Though in literal construction the word [Sequestrations] will not square with the original, yet, since by *turbatur agris* is meant the Civil distractions that follow'd the Defeat of the Brutian and Cassian Party, in which Sequestrations were frequent and violent, the Version may very well by rational consequence be admitted.[28]

Ogilby is ostensibly speaking in purely historical terms by referring to the land confiscation programme that occurred during and after the Roman civil wars, but he is clearly expecting his readers to recall the Sequestration Committee that from 1643 onwards had been confiscating land from royalists. He had encouraged the parallel at the same moment in his 1649 Virgil, from which the line is imported without change, since there '*Sequestrations*' is the first word in the main body of the translation that appears in italics.[29]

The pointed discussion of sequestrations in the 1654 commentary is, however, more the exception than the rule. Ogilby's commentary regularly historicises the Virgilian original, but in a manner that reduces any opportunities to encourage a royalist reading of the text. Scholarship is included in the edition as an end in itself, not as a vehicle for royalism.

Ogilby makes very few references (veiled or otherwise) to contemporary or even post-classical events in the commentary: the only exception is his comparison between the battles of Actium and Lepanto.[30] Nor, outside of *Eclogue* 1, does Ogilby deploy the usual early modern typological strategy of presenting the historical events to which the commentary refers as foreshadowing more recent happenings. Again, a desire for accuracy and comprehensiveness, not royalist equivocation, is the primary factor behind this change.

Where Ogilby does make a more overtly political, rather than scholarly, intervention in the edition is in his inclusion of one hundred engravings (or 'sculptures'). Those that depict Aeneas provide undeniably royalist statements by portraying him with the same style of facial hair that the Prince had grown by the late 1640s. The volume was published by subscription, and each illustration is also dedicated to one of its subscribers. Ereira's analysis has established that many of the subscribers had connections to the 1650s royalist underground and that some of them had already lost their lives in the royalist cause by the time of the edition's publication;[31] if they had read and recognised Ogilby's counsel against fomenting further rebellion in the 1649 translation, they had not heeded it. In including these images, which he subsequently reused in his 1658 Latin edition of Virgil and rededicated to their original subscribers, Ogilby continued his strategy of making political statements through illustration that he had first developed in his 1651 *The Fables of Æsop*. Early modern editions of Aesop frequently include illustrations recycled from earlier volumes, but Ogilby commissioned new images to make his Aesop indicate his royalist affinities. The engraving that accompanies the fable 'Of the Fox and the Lyon' is especially striking in this regard, as the lion wears a crown modelled on the St Edward's Crown that Charles I wore at his coronation.[32] The presence in the 1654 Virgil of engravings that make similarly overt royalist statements, the dedication of these engravings to known loyalists and the presentation in them of the Prince as a latter-day Aeneas corresponds to Matthew Jenkinson's claim that 'Stuart-Augustan survivalism' characterises the volume.[33] They imply that the royalists, like the Trojans, will experience a homecoming after a period of privation and exile.

In the 1654 Virgil, then, as in its predecessor, Ogilby anticipates a royalist revival. In fact, this volume offers a more confident prediction of the royalist cause's ultimate triumph than the previous edition does. Such an impulse not only takes the form of overt statements of royalist intent but also more subtle textual changes. It prompts a minor, but telling, alteration in *Aeneid* 2, where Aeneas tells Dido how he was guided on his journey from Troy by the morning star:

> iamque iugis summae surgebat Lucifer Idae
> ducebatque diem, Danaique obsessa tenebant
> limina portarum, nec spes opis ulla dabatur.
> cessi et sublato montis genitore petivi.
>
> (*A* 2.801–4)

('And now above Ida's topmost ridges the day star was rising, and brought in the morning, and the Greeks held the blockaded gates, nor was there any hope of help for us. I conceded defeat and, with my father on my shoulders, made for the mountain.')

The equivalent passage in the 1649 Virgil reads:

> When the day starre from high brow'd *Ida* rise
> Ushering the morn, our gates the enemies
> Kept with strong guards: no hope left, I retire
> And take the hills, bearing my aged sire.
>
> (Ogilby, *Works* (1649), sig. ²E2v)

Ogilby revised the lines to:

> When *Hesperus* from high-brow'd *Ida* rose,
> Ushering the Day, our Gates beset with Foes,
> Nor hope of succour, I the Mountain take,
> Bearing my aged Father on my back.
>
> (*Works* (1654), p. 228)

Arvid Løsnes calls Ogilby's use of Hesperus in the 1654 edition 'an obvious error', since Hesperus is the evening star.[34] Ogilby knew, however, that the morning and evening star are the same planet (Venus), since his marginal commentary cites a line from Seneca's *Hippolytus* that says as much.[35] Despite this knowledge, at all other points in both editions when Virgil uses either 'Lucifer' or 'Hesperus' Ogilby renders the term accordingly. Løsnes also passes over the fact that Ogilby's use of '*Hesperus*' in 1654 must have been deliberate, since the equivalent passage in the 1649 Virgil refers to 'the day starre'.

Substituting 'Hesperus' for 'the day starre' allows Ogilby to offer a greater degree of hope to the Trojans by anticipating their final destination. Ogilby's note on a different passage refers to the legend, first recorded in Servius, that '*Aeneas*, from the first hour of his setting forth from *Troy*, saw every day the Star of *Venus* [Lucifer/ Hesperus], till he came to *Laurentium*; where seeing it no more, he knew that was the destin'd Ground' (*Works* (1654), p. 181). The term that Virgil uses in *Aeneid* 2 for this territory is not Laurentium, but 'terram Hesperiam' (*A* 2.781; 'the Hesperian land'), which Ogilby renders as '*Hesperia*' in both of his translations.[36] Virgil establishes the connection between Hesperia and Italy earlier in the *Aeneid*:

> est locus, Hesperiam Grai cognomine dicunt,
> terra antiqua, potens armis atque ubere glaebae;
> Oenotri coluere viri, nunc fama minores
> Italiam dixisse ducis de nomine gentem.
> hic cursus fuit . . .
>
> (*A* 1.530–4)

('there is a place, named Hesperia by Greeks, an ancient land, powerful in war and rich in soil, colonised by the Oenotrians; now the story is that their descendants call the land Italy after the name of their leader. This was where our journey lay . . .')

The star's appearance acts as one of several assertions that Aeneas makes in his speech to Dido regarding his destiny as the heir to Troy and the founder of the Roman nation. Ogilby's substitution renders explicit what is latent in Virgil's text.

The royalist associations of Hesperus enable Ogilby to transfer this reminder of a promised final destination from Aeneas' Trojans to the House of Stuart. Hesperus was visible in the noonday sky on the day the Prince was born, and encomiastic works that were addressed to him throughout his life referred to this event as a sign of the divine favour he enjoyed.[37] Ogilby's use of '*Hesperus*' is not an error, but the deployment of a royalist shibboleth to imply the ultimate future triumph of the Stuart cause. Where the 1649 Virgil largely anticipates a Stuart restoration by steering lines that could be held to contain general moral truths in a royalist direction and italicising them to give them greater emphasis, the 1654 edition takes elements from the royalist literary culture of the 1630s in order to act as a reminder of what once had been and to assert what would soon be again.

Ogilby himself asserts (albeit retrospectively) the vatic element of his 1654 Virgil by referring to Hesperus in the dedication to his next major literary project, a translation of the *Iliad* which was published in 1660. In the dedication to Charles II he states:

> May that great God who sent a Star to wait on your Nativity (seen at Noon to the Astonishment of the Beholders, and though long since vanished, yet still remembred and look'd upon as an Omen of your future happiness) be the constant Light and Conduct of all your Actions.[38]

Jack Lynch has argued that this dedicatory epistle places Ogilby's *Iliad* within an explicitly royalist framework and foreshadows how Homer is 'brusquely conscripted to serve with the Royalists' in the translation itself.[39] Ogilby's stated belief earlier in the epistle that Homer was 'a most constant Assertor of the Divine right of *Princes* and Monarchical Government' certainly gives the reader a Homer in Ogilby's own ultra-loyalist mode.⁴⁰ As with his Virgil, the *Iliad* translation asserts that any attempts to overturn such a monarchy are destined to fail. In his *Iliads*, like the Virgil editions of 1649 and 1654, Ogilby primarily engages with the tradition of the poet as *vates*, but includes occasional moments of counsel for his fellow royalists. Such counsel also indicates both that Ogilby's *Iliads* is largely a product of the Interregnum and that the sense of vindicated royalism that it contains is proleptic rather than retrospective.

Homer his Iliads

Ogilby likely began work on his *Iliad* soon after the publication of his revised Virgil, as an entry for the translation appears in the Stationer's Register on 18 April 1656.⁴¹ Certain passages in the text reaffirm the counsel against fomenting armed uprisings that is present in his Virgil, but in a manner which seems more closely to reflect the period when republican rule seemed securely established than the febrile atmosphere of the late 1640s and early 1650s. During a council of the gods Zeus asks 'Shall we deplored War, and deadly Feud / Stir up againe? Or happy peace conclude?' (*Iliads*, p. 92). Homer's Zeus, by contrast, asks 'ἤ ῥ' αὖτις πόλεμόν τε κακὸν καὶ φύλοπιν αἰνὴν / ὄρσομεν, ἦ φιλότητα μετ' ἀμφοτέροισι βάλωμεν' (*Iliad* 4.15–16; 'whether we shall again rouse evil war and the dread din of battle, or place friendship between the armies'). Ogilby's reference to the desire to secure a 'happy peace' is a potentially jarring term for a royalist to use in the context of the Interregnum. The attitude is, in fact, reminiscent of the strand of de factoist thought that was adapted by a number of royalists in the 1650s, but is most frequently associated with Davenant and Hobbes.⁴² De factoist thinking advocated accommodation to whoever held supreme power and offered the prospect of social stability. However, rather than aligning Ogilby's attitudes with the defeated royalism of Davenant and Hobbes, Zeus's speech likely reflected Ogilby's anxieties about provoking further conflict that had been exacerbated (and vindicated) by the failure of the royalist revolts of the mid-1650s. As we have already seen, Ogilby found such uprisings to be valueless, on account of his belief in the providential return of the monarchy that would be secured by divine rather than human agency.

Ogilby's confidence in the return of the Stuart monarchy ensures that on the whole his *Iliad* displays its ultra-loyalist attitudes openly and confidently. His commentary for the *Iliad* in fact contains a far greater degree of partisanship than the commentary for his 1654 Virgil, since it consistently asserts the sacredness of monarchy as an uncontested fact. In other areas, however, the *Iliad* exploits techniques, as well as attitudes, that Ogilby had developed in his Virgil to assert the legitimacy of monarchy and its superiority over all other forms of government. Like the 1654 Virgil, the *Iliad* contains a number of engravings, each of which was dedicated to a subscriber. The majority of the Homer subscribers were, as for the 1654 Virgil, prominent royalists, and some individuals subscribed to both volumes.[43]

Ogilby also encourages a loyalist interpretation of Homer through his use of terms that have notably royalist resonances. By rendering 'Τρώων ἱπποδάμων' (*Iliad* 2.230; 6.461; 'horse-taming Trojans') as 'Cavaliers' (*Iliads*, p. 40; p. 156) Ogilby plays on the fact that the term could be taken simply as an equivalent for 'horse-taming'. 'Cavalier' literally means 'horse rider', but its royalist implications are clear. One of the most significant connections between Ogilby's diction and an assertion of royal authority and legitimacy comes in his account of the Olympian council that opens *Iliad* 4. Ogilby translates 'Οἱ δὲ θεοὶ πὰρ Ζηνὶ καθήμενοι ἠγορόωντο / χρυσέῳ ἐν δαπέδῳ' (*Iliad* 4.1–2; 'Now the gods, seated by the side of Zeus, were holding assembly on the golden floor') as 'Meane while Great *Jove*, and all the Gods in State, / On Golden Thrones in Heavens Star-chamber sate' (*Iliads*, p. 91). He also refers to 'Heavens Star-chamber' in Book 20 (*Iliads*, p. 426), where, in a description of the same locale, the phrase translates 'αἰθούσησιν' (*Iliad* 20.11; 'colonnades'). On both occasions Ogilby can only have used the term to provoke memories of the Court of Star Chamber. In the 1630s Charles frequently used this Court to silence opposition to royal policies, so for his detractors it became a symbol of royal overreach. Ogilby's more positive approach towards the Star Chamber may have been informed by his personal experience as well as his ideas about the nature of royal power. Katherine S. Van Eerde has established that Ogilby appealed to the Chamber in 1633 for redress following his assault by some naval officers.[44] The outcome of the appeal has not come down to us, but this may have been the occasion when Ogilby came into contact with Strafford, who as a Privy Counsellor was a member of the Chamber. It may, then, have been through the Chamber that Ogilby had secured employment as Strafford's impresario. Irrespective of his own connection to the Star Chamber, Ogilby's use of the term in his *Iliad* categorically re-emphasises his belief in sacred monarchy.

The ultra-loyalist nature of Ogilby's royalism might explain the four-year gap between its entry in the Stationer's Register and its publication.

Ogilby might have felt the need to delay the appearance of his more emphatically royalist translation than his Virgil until the political circumstances had changed in the royalists' favour. If so, it remains a sign of the strength of his belief that he was prepared to dedicate such time and effort to translating the *Iliad* in this manner under the assumption that the times would change to correspond with its attitude towards monarchy.

Many of the statements regarding the divine mandate for royal authority in Ogilby's *Iliads* are spoken by Odysseus. To some extent this reflects aspects of the Homeric Odysseus, who draws an explicit connection between kings on earth and the king of Olympus:

> θυμὸς δὲ μέγας ἐστὶ διοτρεφέων βασιλήων,
> τιμὴ δ' ἐκ Διός ἐστι, φιλεῖ δέ ἑ μητίετα Ζεύς.
>
> (*Iliad* 2.196–7)

('Proud is the heart of kings, nurtured by Zeus; for their honour is from Zeus, and Zeus, god of counsel, loves them.')

Ogilby's translation of these lines preserves the sentiment but also includes an additional statement on the consequences that this divine mandate for kings has for their subjects:

> Those who by *Jov's* Commission <u>Scepters sway,</u>
> <u>Subjects must fear, must honour, and obey.</u>
>
> (*Iliads*, p. 38)

This couplet shares the references to sceptres and the sway/obey rhyme in the concluding couplet to the 1642 edition of Denham's *Coopers Hill*: 'And may that Law, which teaches Kings to sway / Their Scepters, teach their Subjects to obey'.[45] It is a sign of the differences between Denham's constitutional royalism and Ogilby's ultra-loyalism that the ultimate authority for Ogilby is divinity rather than the law, and that Denham's 'may' has been replaced by 'must'. For Ogilby's Odysseus, subjects should fear, honour and obey their king as they would their God. Ogilby has the Greeks endorse Odysseus' approach: following Thersites' contretemps with Odysseus, Homer's Greeks say only 'οὔ θήν μιν πάλιν αὖτις ἀνήσει θυμὸς ἀγήνωρ / νεικείειν βασιλῆας ὀνειδείοις ἐπέεσσιν' (*Iliad* 2.276–7; 'Never again, I think, will his [Thersites'] proud spirit set him on to rail at kings with reviling words'). Ogilby's Greeks, by contrast, say that Thersites

> No more will suffer, <u>thus with vain dispute</u>,
> In contumelious Language to upbraid
> <u>The Sacred Majesty of</u> Kings.
>
> (*Iliads*, p. 42)

The belief that monarchy is sacred and that any dispute is ultimately in vain receives an emphasis in the translation that is not present in the original.

The attitudes that Odysseus articulates in *Iliads* anticipate his function in Ogilby's later translation of the *Odyssey*. There Odysseus does not just espouse ultra-loyalist attitudes regarding sacred monarchy, he capitalises on his divine favour and divine right to rule to reclaim his kingdom from the suitors who have usurped him. Odysseus has the status of a proxy for Charles II in the translation that Aeneas has in Ogilby's Virgil. In fact, Ogilby often connects Charles II to Odysseus via Aeneas, a technique that parallels the triangulation of the Prince, David and Aeneas in Cowley's *Davideis* (1656) that we saw in Chapter 3.[46] Furthermore, Ogilby links parts of his *Odyssey* to the expressions of royalist affiliation that appear in his *Aeneid*. Ogilby's commentary frequently cites the relevant Latin lines, and his translation of those lines from his 1654 edition, to support the points of contact between Homeric and Virgilian epic.[47] The following section identifies times when Ogilby incorporates quotations from his Virgil into the text of his *Odyssey* translation. Unlike the more scholarly observations in his commentary, however, these moments of Virgilian reminiscence act as private reassertions of Ogilby's ultra-loyalism.

Homer his Odysses

Ogilby's *Odysses* (1665) blurs the boundaries between Odysseus, Aeneas and Charles II to assert that the latter is a divinely favoured monarch. In *Odyssey* 5 Odysseus sails from Calypso's island to Scheria by taking as his guide the constellation now known variously as the Plough and the Big Dipper. Ogilby translates the Homeric name of this constellation, 'ἄμαξαν' (*Odyssey* 5.273; 'the wagon'), as '*Charles* his Wain' (*Odysses*, p. 70). This term for the constellation long predated the seventeenth century – the original Charles to whom it referred was Charlemagne – but it had acquired a new relevance during the reign of Charles I. In the 1620s and 1630s numerous poets had capitalised on the connection it offered between the reigning monarch and heavenly authority.[48] The use of '*Charles* his Wain' for the constellation in *Odysses* parallels Ogilby's earlier royalist application in the 1654 *Aeneid* of Hesperus guiding Aeneas on his journey to Italy as a means of foreshadowing the Restoration. In addition, at the Restoration itself several writers equated Charles's Wain with Hesperus: just as Hesperus was visible on the day of Charles II's birth, so was Charles's Wain supposed to have been visible during the daytime as Charles entered London as king.[49]

Ogilby finds additional connections between Aeneas, Odysseus and Charles II once Odysseus has arrived on Scheria. When he is asked by Queen Arete to tell her of his travels, Homer's Odysseus replies:

> "ἀργαλέον, βασίλεια, διηνεκέως ἀγορεῦσαι
> κήδε', ἐπεί μοι πολλὰ δόσαν θεοὶ οὐρανίωνες·
> τοῦτο δέ τοι ἐρέω ὅ μ' ἀνείρεαι ἠδὲ μεταλλᾷς."
>
> (*Odyssey* 7.241–3)

('"Hard it would be, my queen, to tell to the end the tale of my woes, since the heavenly gods have given me many. But this will I tell you, of which you ask and inquire."')

Ogilby's translation reads:

>   Impossible almost,
> Great Queen, it is my sufferings to relate,
> So many were impos'd on me by Fate.
> Though my Soul shrink at what my Tongue must say,
> And flies the sad remembrance, I obey.
>
> (*Odysses*, p. 93)

Ogilby's substitution of 'Fate' for 'the heavenly gods' makes the passage more Virgilian than Homeric, but this may simply be the result of 'Fate' providing a convenient rhyme for 'relate' in the previous line. A more deliberate connection to Virgilian epic comes in the final couplet. An addition to the Homeric text which acts as an emotional intensifier, it quotes the response of Ogilby's Aeneas when Dido asks him to speak of his experiences between leaving Troy and arriving at Carthage:

> But since you earnest are to know our Fate,
> And that I *Troy*'s Destruction should relate;
> Though my Soul shrink, at what my Tongue must say,
> And flyes the sad remembrance, I obey.
>
> (*Works* (1654), p. 198)[50]

The 'sad remembrance' here can include Charles II's experiences of exile, as well as those of Odysseus and Aeneas.

Ogilby's other Virgilian interpolations in *Odysses* act as mournful commemorations of royalist suffering. In *Odyssey* 24 the departed spirits of Penelope's suitors arrive in the Underworld and are asked the cause of their deaths:

> ἦ ὕμμ' ἐν νήεσσι Ποσειδάων ἐδάμασσεν,
> ὄρσας ἀργαλέους ἀνέμους καὶ κύματα μακρά;

ἦ πού ἀνάρσιοι ἄνδρες ἐδηλήσαντ' ἐπὶ χέρσου
βοῦς περιταμνομένους ἠδ' οἰῶν πώεα καλά,
ἠὲ περὶ πτόλιος μαχεούμενοι ἠδὲ γυναικῶν;

(*Odyssey* 24.109–13)

('Did Poseidon overcome you on board your ships, when he had roused cruel winds and high waves? Or did hostile men do you harm on land, while you were cutting off their cattle and fine flocks of sheep, or while they fought in defence of their city and their women?')

Whether did *Neptune* them with storms engage,
And swallow'd 'mongst rough Billows in his Rage?
<u>Or by Prophane at th' Altars lost their Lives,</u>
Or fighting for their Country, and their Wives?

(*Odysses*, p. 354)

I can find no precedent in early modern translations, editions or commentaries of the *Odyssey* that would cause Ogilby to substitute a reference to the suitors' dying in front of altars instead of stealing livestock. It is likely that at this moment of the text Ogilby is thinking of Priam's death in *Aeneid* 2. This is not to suggest that he invites the same comparison with Charles I here as he does in that passage from the *Aeneid*. In *Odysseys*, as in his other translations, Ogilby does not draw extended parallels between specific individuals and characters from the epic. The text contains royalist moments, but it is not a sustained royalist allegory. Nonetheless, the unprompted reference here suggests that, like other Virgilian royalists, this passage from the *Aeneid* continued to haunt Ogilby long after he first used it to mark Charles I's execution.

Where Ogilby does incorporate explicit reminiscences of Charles I's death into *Odysses* is in its brief references to the House of Atreus. He refers to Agamemnon's murderer Aegisthus as a 'Regicide' (pp. 9; p. 31), at points when the only term Homer uses to denote Aegisthus is 'δολόμητιν' (*Odyssey* 1.300; 3.198; 'guileful'). Ogilby draws royalist parallels when Athena sanctions Orestes' murder of Aegisthus as revenge for Agamemnon's death, and hopes that he will act as an example to others: 'καὶ λίην κεῖνός γε ἐοικότι κεῖται ὀλέθρῳ· / ὡς ἀπόλοιτο καὶ ἄλλος, ὅτις τοιαῦτά γε ῥέζοι' (*Odyssey* 1.46–7; 'clearly that man lies low in a destruction that is his due; so, too, let any other also be destroyed who does such deeds'). Ogilby preserves Athena's approval, but places the sentiment in an explicitly royalist post-Restoration context. Ogilby's Athena says of Aegisthus 'Deservedly he fell, and may they all / Who murther Princes in like manner fall' (*Odysses*, p. 3). As with his use of 'Regicide', Ogilby portrays the murder of a monarch as the most transgressive act imaginable and worthy of the harshest punishment.

Despite its references to a regicide, the focus in *Odysses* is more on future possibilities than past outrages. Ogilby's translation makes the parts of Homer's text that are concerned with securing reconciliation between opposing factions speak to the moment of its publication in the 1660s. The text concludes with an entreaty from Athena (disguised as Mentor) to Odysseus:

"διογενὲς Λαερτιάδη, πολυμήχαν᾿ Ὀδυσσεῦ,
ἴσχεο, παῦε δὲ νεῖκος ὁμοιίου πολέμοιο,
μή πως τοι Κρονίδης κεχολώσεται εὐρύοπα Ζεύς."
ὣς φάτ᾿ Ἀθηναίη, ὁ δ᾿ ἐπείθετο, χαῖρε δὲ θυμῷ.
ὅρκια δ᾿ αὖ κατόπισθε μετ᾿ ἀμφοτέροισιν ἔθηκεν
Παλλὰς Ἀθηναίη, κούρη Διὸς αἰγιόχοιο,
Μέντορι εἰδομένη ἠμὲν δέμας ἠδὲ καὶ αὐδήν.

(*Odyssey* 24.542–8)

('"Son of Laertes, sprung from Zeus, many-skilled Odysseus, hold your hand, and stop the strife of war, common to all, for fear Zeus son of Cronus, whose voice is borne afar, may perhaps become angry with you." So spoke Athene, and he obeyed, and was glad at heart. Then for the future a solemn truce between the two sides was made by Pallas Athene, daughter of Zeus, who bears the aegis, in the likeness of Mentor both in form and in voice.')

Jove's Off-spring, stand, stand *Laertiades*,
No farther in this War thou must engage,
Lest thus displeasing, *Jove* thou should'st enrage.
<u>The King</u> at *Pallas* threatnings makes a stand,
And joyfully obeys the Maids command.
Pallas, like *Mentor*, as she had design'd,
Thus them again <u>in happy Peace conjoyn'd</u>.

(*Odysses*, p. 366)

Ogilby's interpolation of 'The King' here suggests another connection between Odysseus and Charles II. Ogilby also refers to a more permanent state of peace than is present in Homer by translating 'ὅρκια' ('solemn truce') as 'happy Peace', the same phrase that Ogilby adds to Zeus's speech in the council that opens *Iliad* 4. Ogilby also refers to Odysseus securing an 'everlasting Peace' (*Odysses*, p. 364) earlier in Book 24, with no prompting from Homer. In doing so, Ogilby presents an Odysseus who corresponds with the royalists' own idealised version of Charles II, or at least the providential divine will that acts through Charles II. He unites the nation, banishes discord and ushers in a secure peace.

The hopes that Ogilby expresses for the future in his *Odyssey* are akin to much early 1660s panegyric. Both Ogilby's Virgil and *Iliads*, however, indicate that he was capable of expressing such sentiments even when royalist fortunes were at their nadir. It does not necessarily follow that he could only articulate his hopes for Charles II in this manner after the Restoration. The 1656 Stationer's Register entry for Ogilby's *Iliad* refers to a translation of the *Odyssey* too, and in the appeal to subscribers for his Homer that Ogilby circulated in 1660 he claims that his *Odyssey* translation will appear 'by the end of the year following'.[51] Ogilby may simply have overstated the imminence of the volume's completion for the purposes of attracting more subscribers, but is also worth noting that the highly specific moments of royalist commentary in Ogilby's *Odyssey* look back to events of the 1640s and early 1650s, but the passages that outline a lasting peace are much more generic. It is thus possible that, at least for parts of the *Odyssey*, as with his Virgil, Ogilby translated the original not as a means of reflecting on his present circumstances but of anticipating the future that he hoped (or had convinced himself) would come to pass, both before and after the Restoration; his Virgil and Homer are written in a more confident and assertively optative mood than are the translations of his contemporaries.

Odysses is not the first time that Ogilby takes inspiration from passages from Virgil, or even directly quotes his own versions of Virgil, in another text: he first did so in his 1651 edition of Aesop. Notwithstanding the royalist nature of that volume, and the fact that he frequently quotes lines from his Virgil that functioned as royalist statements, the Virgilian quotations it contains do not provide overt political commentary.[52] Rather, their use appears to have been prompted simply by the subject matter of a particular fable or to give a mock epic grandeur to the individual tales. Ogilby uses Virgil in his Aesop less as an expression of royalism and more as a storehouse of poetical turns of phrase.

A closer precedent for Ogilby's use in *Odysses* of quotations from his Virgil as a means of incorporating ultra-loyalist beliefs lies in his contributions to Charles II's coronation procession. Ronald Knowles has established that the designs for the arches that formed part of the procession were largely inspired by those that Rubens had designed for the Habsburg Prince Ferdinand's 1635 triumphal entry into Antwerp but that the Virgil quotations on the arches were Ogilby's own additions.[53] Ogilby published an account of the procession in 1661 as *The Relation of His Majestie's Entertainment Passing through the City of London, To His Coronation*. Following the precedent of his Virgil, he later brought out an expanded version that contained an extensive scholarly commentary. My analysis in what follows, however, focuses on the material that Ogilby devised specifically for the day of Charles's procession, the description of this material in *Relation* and its connection to Ogilby's previous engagement with Virgil.

The Relation of His Majestie's Entertainment

Ogilby's past experience as a theatrical impresario in 1630s Ireland no doubt influenced his commission by the City of London to contribute to the act of spectacular public theatre that was the coronation procession, but there were other individuals with more extensive and more recent theatrical experience that the City could have appointed. That Ogilby was chosen over these other candidates was likely the result of his ultra-loyalism and the belief in a sacred monarchy he had expressed in his translations. Ian W. Archer has suggested that 'the rather messy facts of London's past and present circumstances' regarding its relationship to the Crown required, officially at least, some form of penance, and that 'the City had to perform some delicate manoeuvring to establish its loyalist credentials'.[54] It was not enough just to be a royalist; Ogilby was the right kind of royalist for the City's needs.

The inscriptions that Ogilby contributed for the '*Poetical Part*' of the procession are taken from a number of classical authors, but Virgil is the author he returns to most frequently for these purposes. It was common to herald the Restoration in Virgilian terms. Dryden's *Astræa Redux* and Rachel Jevon's *Exultationis Carmen* both use 'redeunt Saturnia regna' (*E* 4.6; 'the reign of Saturn returns') as an epigraph.[55] Cowley chooses a different Virgilian epigraph for his *Ode Upon his Majesties Restoration and Return*: 'quod optanti divum promittere nemo / auderet, volvenda dies en attulit ultro' (*A* 9.6–7; 'what no god dared to promise to your prayers, the circling hour brings of its own accord').[56] The presence of both these lines on the first of the arches, the latter 'Under the . . . Representation of the King pursuing *Usurpation*', may have been prompted by Ogilby's reading of these panegyrics.[57] The latter quotation would also correspond with Ogilby's earlier exhortations in his Virgil and Homer translations to await what he believed to be the inevitable Stuart restoration without actively pursuing it through armed uprisings. Like many other writers on the Restoration, Ogilby emphasises the fact that Charles's return to the throne occurred without further armed conflict and the shedding of blood.

Ogilby's use of Virgilian inscriptions in the ceremony does not simply pay lip service to the tradition of using Virgil for panegyrical purposes or to reproduce the quotations of his contemporaries. Deciding which lines and phrases should serve as inscriptions represents Ogilby's most personal response to the Restoration. Around a third of the Virgilian mottos on the arches quote lines whose translations Ogilby italicises in his 1649 Virgil. The majority of the lines focus on the dangers of rebellion and its terrible consequences: he quotes 'en quo discordia cives' (*E* 1.71; 'see where strife has brought our citizens') and 'discite iustitiam moniti' (*A* 6.620; 'be warned, learn to be just'); he also slightly adapts 'ausi omnes immane nefas ausoque potiti' (*A* 6.624; 'all dared shameful crimes, and attained what they dared').[58] A more positive resonance comes in Ogilby's use of a quotation from the *Georgics*, 'regi incolumi mens omnibus una' on the third arch.[59] As discussed above, Ogilby italicises his translation of this passage in his 1649 Virgil as a means of acknowledging what he considered to be the destructive social consequences of Charles I's death. In 1661, however, Ogilby is able to use the same passage not to mourn a king's death, but to hail a coronation.

An additional piece of direct self-quotation comes in the use of the phrase 'in solido rursus fortuna locavit'. In his commentary Ogilby notes that the phrase is a quotation from Virgil, then gives the sentence from which it is taken, and provides a translation:

> Alluding to that of *Virgil*,
> *Multa dies* variusque labor, mutabilis ævi
> Rettulit in melius, multos alterna revisens
> Lusit, & in solido rursus Fortuna locavit.
> Thus rendred,
> "The various Works of Time, and many Dayes,
> "Often Affairs from worse to better raise,
> "Fortune reviewing those she tumbled down,
> "Sporting restores again unto the Crown.[60]

I discussed Ogilby's translation of this passage earlier in the chapter as an example of the status certain italicised lines in the 1649 Virgil have as predictions of a Stuart restoration whilst presenting themselves as moral *sententiae*. Citing the same translation from his *Aeneid* practically verbatim in *Relation* vindicates the prophetic element that he had sought to grant their first appearance in print.

Aubrey said that it was 'as if by a prophetique spirit' that Ogilby dedicated a different publication, a deluxe edition of the Bible, to Charles II before the Stuart restoration seemed likely.[61] The Virgilian inscriptions that are associated with Charles II's coronation procession and Ogilby's account in *Relation* offer an even more extensive (if largely private) incidence of Ogilby granting a prophetic quality to his publications. The inscriptions not only herald the return of the monarchy, they also demonstrate that Ogilby's prophecies of a Stuart restoration had actually come to pass. Even though it was more a triumph of hope than experience, Ogilby did acquire the status of a Virgilian *vates*.

Virgilian Parliaments: John Ogilby and Robert Heath

Ogilby's ultra-loyalism meant that he believed responsibility for the outbreak of civil war in the Stuart kingdoms lay solely with Parliament. A similar mindset characterises a translation that was produced at the same time as the first version of Ogilby's Virgil: Robert Heath's *Virgil's Æneis Translated in English Heroick Verse*. Because of Heath's status as a minor literary figure and the inaccessibility of this text – it survives in a single manuscript, only one small section of which has ever been printed – the following paragraphs give a brief account of Heath himself before discussing the political beliefs that informed the composition of his translation.[62]

Heath was from a family with close connections to the Stuart court; his father, Sir Robert Heath, was Charles I's Chief Justice.[63] Along with his father, Heath was resident in Oxford, the royalist capital, in the mid-1640s, and it was in this period that he produced his *Aeneid* translation. The manuscript of *Virgil's Æneis* records the date that Heath completed work on each book of the translation; *Aeneid* 1–3 were the product of 1644 and 1645, and he translated the other books between May and September 1646. Sheldon Brammall, the author of the only critical discussion of the translation, has established that Heath made significant use of John Vicars's *Aeneid* when preparing his own translation, but when he did so he rewrote Vicars's expressions of Parliamentarian sympathy to make them function as more royalist statements.[64] One example of the difference in Vicars's and Heath's political loyalties can be seen in their respective versions of Virgil's reference to the 'sideream . . . sedem' (*A* 10.3; 'starry dwelling') in which the Olympian gods meet. Where Vicars translated the phrase literally (and somewhat infelicitously) as 'stelliferous seat', Heath's *Virgil's Æneis* refers to 'Heav'ns Star-chamber'.[65] As with Ogilby's use of the same term over a decade later in his *Iliads*, Heath can only have intended it to evoke the royal Court of Star Chamber in order to link divine and royal authority.

In this star-chamber, however, Heath's Jupiter 'calls a Parliament'.[66] Heath's use of 'star-chamber' thus differs from Ogilby's use of the term, since the Olympians are compared not to a royal council but to members of the House of Commons. There, after haranguing the gods for fomenting civil war in Italy, Jupiter instructs them to 'joyfull peace straight make' (p. 170, translating *A* 10.15; 'placitum laeti componite foedus'; 'accept the treaty that has been agreed, and be content'). Heath's loyalties thus combine elements of constitutional royalism, especially the conviction that the exertion of royal authority had to involve Parliament to acquire legal legitimacy, with the belief in sacred monarchy that is the hallmark of ultra-loyalism. Parliament may have played a vital role in Heath's preferred system of government, but this does not prevent him from using this passage from the *Aeneid* to intimate that the war which broke out was contrary to royal/divine will, and that the need to make peace lay with Parliament, not the monarch. A similar impulse to absolve a king of responsibility for ruling during a time of war comes in Heath's translation of Aeneas' reference to 'Priamique ... gentem / immeritam' (*A* 3.1–2; 'the innocent race of Priam') as 'Priams faultles Crowne' (p. 38). In Virgil the emphasis is on Priam's royal house and the people of Troy, not his personal status as a king. Heath completed work on *Aeneid* 3 on 13 August 1645, two months after the royalist defeat at Naseby. Although Heath's *Aeneid* lacks any explicit presentation of Priam as a proxy for Charles I, his reference to a 'faultles Crowne' at a time when the royalists' fortunes were at an especially low point does suggest that he encouraged some degree of connection between the two monarchs.

Although Heath's translation anticipates the exculpatory qualities of Ogilby's *Aeneid*, his broader poetic career reveals a much stronger connection to the work of another translator of Virgil, Sir Richard Fanshawe. The extent to which Fanshawe's influence on Heath was the result of a close association is not clear: although Fanshawe knew several members of the Heath family well and corresponded with them frequently, none of the surviving letters are addressed to Robert directly, and when they do refer to him it is only in passing.[67] Heath's self-fashioning as a poet was nonetheless highly indebted to Fanshawe. The engraving of Heath's interlinked initials surrounded by laurel leaves that appears on the title page of his 1659 publication *Paradoxical Assertions* is adapted from the engraving on the title pages of Fanshawe's publications from earlier in that decade.[68] One of the poems in Heath's only other published work, the verse collection *Clarastella* (1650), is entitled 'Dialogue between Sylvio and Mirtillo';[69] these names are taken from Fanshawe's *The Faithfull Shepherd*, his 1647 translation of Guarini's pastoral tragicomedy *Il Pastor Fido*. However much Heath took from Fanshawe poetically, the two men's political attitudes diverged sharply, especially with regard to Charles I. Fanshawe, unlike Heath, held Charles to be far from faultless. The following chapter considers why Fanshawe believed the king was both personally responsible for the outbreak of civil war and an obstacle to securing a royalist revival.

Notes

1. John Ogilby, *The Works of Publius Virgilius Maro* (London, 1649) (hereafter Ogilby, *Works* (1649)), sig. E2v.
2. There are parallels here with Cowley's presentation in *The Civil War* (1643) of leading Parliamentarians as agents for the forces of the Underworld: see pp. 60–1, above.
3. See Alan Ereira, *The Nine Lives of John Ogilby: Britain's Master Map Maker and His Secrets* (London, 2016), p. 88; for the Register entry, see G. E. B. Eyre (ed.), *A Transcript of the Registers of the Worshipful Company of Stationers, From 1640–1708 AD*, 3 vols (London, 1913–14), vol. 1, p. 303.
4. Tanya Caldwell, 'Translation', in *The Oxford Handbook of British Poetry, 1660–1800*, ed. Jack Lynch (Oxford, 2016), pp. 596–614 (601).
5. Ogilby, *Works* (1649), sig. ²D6v. As in my other chapters, underline indicates where the translations substantially depart from or add to the Virgilian original.
6. As discussed above on p. 29 with regard to Denham's translation of this passage in *The Destruction of Troy*.
7. Syrithe Pugh, *Herrick, Fanshawe and the Politics of Intertextuality: Classical Literature and Seventeenth-Century Royalism* (Farnham, 2010), p. 3.
8. Ogilby prints a passage from *Carolies* that refers to Charles as 'the royal martyr' in his *Africa* (London, 1670), sig. c2r, where he states the *Carolies* manuscript was destroyed in the Great Fire of London. He had previously published the lines as an inscription for a 1661 portrait of Charles II.
9. As discussed on pp. 66–7; 74, above.
10. John Ogilby, *The Relation of His Majestie's Entertainment Passing through the City of London, To His Coronation: with a Description of the Triumphal Arches, and Solemnity* (London, 1661) (hereafter Ogilby, *Relation*), sig. a1v.
11. Ogilby, *Works* (1649), sig. B1r.
12. Annabel Patterson, *Pastoral and Ideology: Virgil to Valéry* (Oxford, 1988), p. 171.
13. Ogilby, *Works* (1649), sig. C1r.
14. John Ogilby, *The Works of Publius Virgilius Maro* (London, 1650), p. 14.
15. See, for example, Paulus Manutius and Georgius Fabricius (eds), *Opera P. Virgilii Maronis* (Cambridge, 1632), pp. 11–12.
16. Ogilby, *Works* (1649), sig. H4v.
17. I discuss this text in the following chapter: see p. 123, below.
18. See Thomas Farnaby (ed.), *Publii Virgilii Maronis Opera* (London, 1634), pp. 36, 37, 42, 62, 68, 79, 133, 134, 149, 159, 169, 180, 210, 235, 320, 329, 330, 353, 390.
19. I discuss this technique in the context of the italicised lines in other royalist texts of the late 1640s in Ian Calvert, 'Slanted Histories, Hesperian Fables: Material Form and Royalist Prophecy in John Ogilby's *Works of Publius Virgilius Maro*', *The Seventeenth Century*, 33 (2018), 531–55 (pp. 536–7; 540–1).

20. Ogilby, *Works* (1649), sig. ²B5v, translating *A* 1.207; 'durate, et vosmet rebus servate secundis'; 'endure, and preserve yourselves for a happier day'; sig. Hhh5r, translating *A* 11.362; 'nulla salus bello'; 'there is no safety in war'.
21. The information here and in the following paragraph is indebted to Nicholas McDowell, 'Herrick and the Order of the Black Riband: Literary Community in Civil-War London and the Publication of *Hesperides* (1648)', in *'Lords of Wine and Oile': Community and Conviviality in the Poetry of Robert Herrick*, ed. Ruth Connolly and Tom Cain (Oxford, 2011), pp. 106–26.
22. Ogilby, *Works* (1649), sig. ²H2v.
23. Ogilby, *Works* (1649), sig. F4v, translating *G* 2.401–2; 'redit agricolis labor actus in orbem, / atque in se sua vestigia volvitur annus'; 'the farmer's toil returns, moving in a circle, as the year rolls back upon itself over its own footsteps'; Ogilby, *Works* (1649), sig. ²F1v, translating *A* 3.415; 'tantum aevi longinqua valet mutare vetustas'; 'such great change length of time can affect'.
24. Ogilby, *Works* (1649), sig. Hhh6v.
25. John Vicars, *The XII Aeneids of Virgil* (London, 1632), p. 353.
26. For the politics of Vicars's translation, see Sheldon Brammall, *The English Aeneid: Translations of Virgil, 1555–1646* (Edinburgh, 2015), pp. 150–65.
27. Ogilby, Works (1649), sig. E5v; Ogilby, Works (1654), p. 85.
28. Ogilby, *Works* (1654), p. 2.
29. Ogilby, *Works* (1649), sig. B2v.
30. See Ogilby, *Works* (1654), p. 426.
31. Ereira, *Nine Lives*, pp. 124–6.
32. John Ogilby, *The Fables of Æsop* (London, 1651), sig. Gggg2v. For other representations of St Edward's Crown at the time of the regicide, see *The Complete Poetry of Robert Herrick*, ed. Tom Cain and Ruth Connolly, 2 vols (Oxford, 2013), vol. 1, p. 406.
33. Matthew Jenkinson, *Culture and Politics at the Court of Charles II, 1660–1685* (Woodbridge, 2010), p. 51.
34. Arvid Løsnes, *'Arms, and the Man I sing . . .': A Preface to Dryden's Æneis* (Newark, DE, 2011), p. 328.
35. See Ogilby, *Works* (1654), p. 42.
36. Ogilby, *Works* (1649), sig. ²E1r; Ogilby, *Works* (1654), p. 227.
37. See Antonia Fraser, *King Charles II* (London, 1979), pp. 3–4.
38. John Ogilby, *Homer his Iliads Translated, adorn'd with Sculpture, and illustrated with Annotations* (London, 1660) (hereafter *Iliads*), sig. a1v; roman/italic fonts reversed.
39. Jack Lynch, 'Political Ideology in Translations of the *Iliad*, 1660–1715', *Translation and Literature*, 7 (1998), 23–41 (p. 26).
40. Ogilby, *Iliads*, sig. A2r; roman/italic fonts reversed.
41. See Eyre (ed.), *Transcript*, vol. 2, p. 51.
42. For which see Niall Allsopp, *Poetry and Sovereignty in the English Revolution* (Oxford, 2020).
43. See Ereira, *Nine Lives*, p. 132.
44. See Katherine S. Van Eerde, *John Ogilby and the Taste of His Times* (Folkestone, 1976), p. 22.

45. Sir John Denham, *Coopers Hill. A Poëme* (London, 1642), p. 19.
46. See pp. 64–5, above.
47. Examples include John Ogilby, *Homer his Odysses Translated, adorn'd with Sculpture, and illustrated with Annotations* (London, 1665) (hereafter *Odysses*), pp. 40, 120, 273.
48. See 'On *The New Inn* Ode. To Himself', lines 51–60, in Ben Jonson, *The Complete Poems*, ed. George Parfitt (London, 1988); 'Charles His Waine', in *The Poems of Sir John Davies*, ed. Robert Krueger and Ruby Nemser (Oxford, 1975).
49. See Edward Matthew, *The Most Glorious Star, or, Celestial Constellation of the Pleiades, or Charles Waine* (London, 1660).
50. Translating *A* 2.11–13. The equivalent lines in the 1649 translation read 'Though at the thought such horror I within / My wounded soul conceive, yet Ile begin' (Ogilby, *Works* (1649), sig. ²C6v). 'Sad remembrance' may have been prompted by, or helped to prompt, Denham's use of the phrase when translating the same line in *The Destruction of Troy*. As both poets borrow from the work of others for their respective translations, the original authorship of the phrase cannot be ascertained, but it is more plausible that it is Ogilby who borrows from Denham. It is possible, then, that Ogilby had access to Denham's translation before its publication, like (as discussed in Chapter 1) he also had for Godolphin/Waller's *The Passion of Dido for Æneas*.
51. John Ogilby, *The Translation of Homers Works into English Verse being Undertaken by John Ogilby* (London, 1660).
52. I discuss examples of Ogilby's self-quotations from the 1649 Virgil in his 1651 Aesop in Calvert, 'Slanted Histories', p. 544.
53. See 'Introduction', in John Ogilby, *The Entertainment of His Most Excellent Majesty Charles II: A Facsimile*, ed. Ronald Knowles (Binghamton, NY, 1988), pp. 9–49 (12).
54. Ian W. Archer, 'Royal Entries, the City of London, and the Politics of Stuart Successions', in *Stuart Succession Literature: Moments and Transformations*, ed. Paulina Kewes and Andrew McRae (Oxford, 2019), pp. 257–81 (258; 266).
55. John Dryden, *Astræa Redux* (London, 1660); Rachel Jevon, *Exultationis Carmen* (London, 1660).
56. Abraham Cowley, *Ode, Upon The Blessed Restoration and Returne of His Sacred Majestie, Charls the Second* (London, 1660).
57. Ogilby, *Relation*, p. 4.
58. See Ogilby, *Relation*, pp. 6, 7, 4; cf. Ogilby, *Works* (1649), sigs B3v; L1v.
59. Ogilby, *Relation*, p. 23.
60. Ogilby, *Relation*, p. 3.
61. *Aubrey's Brief Lives*, ed. Oliver Lawson Dick (London, 1949), p. 220.
62. Citations from Heath's *Aeneid* are by page number, and are taken from a transcript of the manuscript (Los Angeles, William Andrews Clark Memorial Library, MS.1946.007) which Stuart Gillespie has very generously made available to me. For the published extract from the translation, see *Newly Recovered English Classical Translations 1600–1800*, ed. Stuart Gillespie (Oxford, 2018), pp. 480–1.

63. Biographical information on Heath and his family is taken from the *Oxford Dictionary of National Biography* (*ODNB*), www.oxforddnb.com.
64. See Brammall, *English Aeneid*, pp. 171–81 (174–6).
65. Vicars, *Aeneids of Virgil*, p. 292; Heath, *Virgil's Æneis*, p. 170.
66. Heath, *Virgil's Æneis*, p. 170; cf. the opening line of Vicars's argument to *Aeneid* 11: 'The Gods convoke a parliament' (Vicars, *Aeneids of Virgil*, p. 292; roman/italics font reversed).
67. I draw here on Heath's entry in *ODNB*.
68. Cf. the title pages of Robert Heath, *Paradoxical Assertions and Philosophical Problems* (London, 1659) and Sir Richard Fanshawe, *Selected Parts of Horace, Prince of Lyricks; and of all the Latin Poets the fullest fraught with Excellent Morality* (London, 1652).
69. Robert Heath, *Clarastella* (London, 1650), pp. 28–9.

Chapter 5

Hopeful Prince: Sir Richard Fanshawe

Introduction

Like the other translators considered in this study, Fanshawe engaged with the early modern traditions of the Virgilian poet–counsellor and the poet as *vates*. He tended, however, to privilege the first of these traditions over the second. When Fanshawe did present an imagined future it was to outline the benefits that he believed following his advice would bring. Such an attitude was consonant with his membership of several royal councils from the 1630s until his death in 1666. His long-standing service to the Stuart monarchy should not, though, be misconstrued as unswerving, uncritical loyalty. Fanshawe's poetry regularly opposes Charles I, his policies and his myth-making in a manner that is consonant with the principles of constitutional royalism.[1] This chapter first discusses the factors that inform Fanshawe's criticism of Charles I and his conviction even several years prior to the regicide that the best hopes for the royalists lay with the Prince of Wales, hence my contention that, despite his affinities with constitutional royalism, 'Prince's Party royalism' is a more useful term to describe his loyalties in the 1640s. It then considers Fanshawe's translation of Battista Guarini's pastoral tragicomedy *Il Pastor Fido* as *The Faithfull Shepherd* (1647), his translations from the *Aeneid* (1648), the collection *Selected Parts of Horace* (1652), and *The Lusiad* (1655), a translation of Luís Vaz de Camões' epic *Os Lusíadas*. In these texts Fanshawe presents himself as a Virgil to the Prince's Augustus. Through his translations he provides the Prince with counsel on how to secure a royalist revival and rule with both clemency and in the public interest once he has been enthroned as Charles II.

Fanshawe, Charles I and the Prince of Wales

Fanshawe's presentation of Charles I in the occasional poem *On His Majesties Great Shippe lying almost finisht in Woolwich Docke Anno Dom. 1637. and afterwards called The Soveraigne of the Seas* initially appears to be very fulsome. Its claim that '*Charles* his Shipp shall quite Ecclipse his *Wayne*' (line 110) capitalises on the connection between the Stuart monarchy and the constellation then known as 'Charles's Wain' that, as we saw in the previous chapter, several mid-seventeenth-century royalist panegyrics used to connect royal and divine authority.[2] *On His Majesties Great Shippe* was first published in the supplementary material that was appended to the 1648 edition of *The Faithfull Shepherd*; Syrithe Pugh has suggested that the decade which elapsed between the construction of the royal flagship and the publication of *On His Majesties Great Shippe* likely affected any potentially laudatory associations in the poem's reference to Charles's Wain. According to Pugh, on reading the line 'in 1648 it must have been tempting to hear … a reference to Charles's *wane*, his fall from power'.[3] Whether or not readers interpreted the line in this way, the temporal gap between composition and publication did affect the reception of another poem in the edition, *An Ode Upon occasion of His Majesties Proclamation in the yeare 1630*. Fanshawe's reference in this poem to the England of 1630 as '(A world without the world)' (line 34) is indebted to 'et penitus toto divosos orbe Britannos' (*E* 1.66), the same line from Virgil's *Eclogues* that Abraham Cowley evokes in the opening lines of *The Civil War* (1643).[4] At the time of its composition Fanshawe's imitation of *Eclogue* 1 celebrated an England at peace whilst Europe was at war; by the time of its publication in 1648 this situation had been reversed.

The context of 1648 also brings the imitation closer to the tone of the Virgilian original. The reference by the displaced shepherd Meliboeus to Britain as 'penitus toto divisos orbe' is meant as lament, not praise. The connection between Fanshawe and Meliboeus is all the more striking because elsewhere in the poem Fanshawe expresses his desire to imitate the other speaker of *Eclogue* 1, Tityrus, whose experiences run counter to Meliboeus'. Fanshawe exploits the traditional interpretation of Tityrus as a proxy for Virgil himself in order to present an imagined English Augustan future that remained plausible in 1630:

> And if the Fields as thankfull prove
> For benefits receiv'd, as seed,
> They will, to quite so great a love,
>   A *Virgill* breed;

> A *Tytirus*, that shall not cease
> Th' *Augustus* of our world to praise
> In equall verse, author of peace
>   And *Halcyon* dayes.
>
> (lines 73–80)

Fanshawe suggests here that he could be a second Tityrus/Virgil, praising a second Augustus; unlike in other seventeenth-century texts, Augustus invariably serves as a positive model in Fanshawe's writing. On its publication the passage carried an implicit reminder that the shift in the political situation which occurred between 1630 and 1648 had prevented Fanshawe from achieving this potential.

The first draft of the 'Proclamation' ode was written more or less contemporaneously with the events that it describes, but there are differences between its manuscript and print versions.[5] Fanshawe's practice is thus superficially reminiscent of those of his contemporaries who revised certain texts to grant them the status of vatic utterances. However, Pugh has shown that the more apprehensive elements of the poem are present from its first version and that Fanshawe's revisions were concerned with making aesthetic improvements, not adding or reshaping his political commentary with the benefit of hindsight.[6] The use of 'et penitus toto divisos orbe Britannos' in the 'Proclamation' ode is adjacent to, but differs from, Cowley's imitation of that line in the opening of his *Civil War*. In Cowley the line bewails how circumstances have caused the panegyric of the 1630s to mutate into a 1640s lament; Fanshawe's use of it was always contingent.

In his political and literary career Fanshawe consistently expresses concerns regarding the prospect of autocratic monarchical rule that excluded Parliament from governance.[7] It is worth noting in this context that the events commemorated in both *On His Majesties Great Shippe* and the 'Proclamation' ode are connected to signature policies from the period of Charles's reign when he ruled without Parliament. The 'great shippe' in question was funded through the raising of the Ship Money levy; the 'Proclamation' ode was a response to the royal command that members of the gentry resident in London (a group which included many former Members of Parliament) leave the city and return to their country estates. Fanshawe engages with the Virgilian tradition of the poet as *vates* to indicate he anticipated a crisis in royal authority before the outbreak of civil conflict, and to present certain royal policies as responsible for precipitating this crisis. Fanshawe shows genuine foresight with regard to the potential for loyalist discourse to anticipate future travails.

Fanshawe provides more specific and explicit guidance than many of his Virgilian contemporaries do on how the monarchy could overcome these travails and create the conditions in which an English Tityrus could praise an English Augustus. He incorporates into his texts a series of types and antitypes drawn from history, literature and myth for the sovereign to follow and avoid. As in *On His Majesties Great Shippe* and the 'Proclamation' ode, they frequently appear alongside, and subvert, ultra-loyalist tropes. In *Presented to His Highnesse, In the West, Ann. Dom. 1646* Fanshawe compares an imminent return of Stuart power to the return of the phoenix: like the phoenix the monarch comes from 'his Sires Urn' and 'brings / His Fathers honour'd ashes on his wings, / And funerall odours' (lines 32, 37–9). *Ann. Dom. 1646* translates a Latin poem by George Buchanan on the birth of Charles's own father, James VI and I, so addressing the poem to Charles I would strengthen the emphasis the phoenix myth places on patrilineal succession and the continuity between father and son. Yet the 'Highnesse' of the poem's title is not Charles I, but his son. Fanshawe's presentation of the Prince's potential was no doubt partly influenced by his appointment in the mid-1640s to the Council in the West, which was specifically tasked with advising the Prince. His conviction that the Prince represented the best chance of a royalist revival was not, however, simple careerism. Fanshawe's phoenix preserves the traditional emphasis on rebirth, but it underlines the poem's distinctive treatment of Charles I as someone already deceased, and provides little sense of the son as a phoenix-like reincarnation of his father. The poem challenges Charles's authority by suggesting that the transfer of power from father to son has already occurred and that a royalist revival is predicated on the Prince's assumption of his father's role. As early as 1646, then, Fanshawe was starting to think of the Prince as king in all but name, and was concentrating on advising the Prince rather than his father. Fanshawe implies that, although Charles I had not fulfilled his potential to be the English Augustus, the Prince still could.

Despite these established associations with Augustus, Fanshawe offers Julius Caesar as a model for the Prince to follow in *Ann. Dom. 1646*'s companion poem, *Presented to His Highnesse the Prince of Wales, At his going into the West, Anno M.DC.XLV. Together with Cesar's Commentaries*. Yet Fanshawe's Caesar is not necessarily consonant with his general reputation:

> Before hee fought,
> Observe how *Peace* by him was ever sought:
> How bloodlesse Victories best pleas'd him still,

Grieving as oft as he was forc'd to kill,
How most religiously he kept his word,
And conquer'd more that way then by the sword.

(lines 9–14)

In both the 'Presented to His Highnesse' poems Fanshawe intimates that the Prince could fulfil the potential that his father never realised by achieving bloodless victories. He strengthens this connection by portraying the historical Augustus as someone who followed the admirable qualities of Julius Caesar and learned from his errors to achieve a lasting peace. *Ann. Dom. 1646* addresses the Prince as the '*Father of his People*' (line 58). The term is more usually assigned to the monarch, not the heir apparent, so its use here acts as a subtle rebuke to Charles I. It also seems inspired by the Latin title of 'Pater patriae', 'Father of the Country', which was awarded to those who brought civil war to an end.

Fanshawe also identifies the Prince's potential as an author of peace in 'this *Prince's* Starrs / Promise an end to all our *Civill Wars*' (lines 13–14); the stars in question are presumably those of the 'Charles's Wain' constellation. These lines contain less potential criticism than the equivalent reference in *On His Majesties Great Shippe*, because the association has passed from father to son. This end to civil wars, and the implied royalist revival, is also not something that the poem claims is destined to happen, as Ogilby's uses of ultra-loyalist tropes assert.[8] When Fanshawe incorporates panegyrical terms into his poetry, he does so optatively as well as proleptically, in recognition of their contingency and as a reminder that their positive associations have to be earned, rather than assumed.

Unlike *On His Majesties Great Shippe* and the 'Proclamation' ode, the 'Presented to his Majesty' poems were published soon after their composition; they were the final poems in the original (1647) edition of *The Faithfull Shepherd*. Both this edition and the expanded version of 1648 continue Fanshawe's duties as a royal counsellor, since they take the Prince as its imagined reader. The 1647 edition opens with a dedication to 'the most Illustrious and most hopefull Prince Charles, Prince of Wales';[9] the 1648 edition reprints this dedication and adds a second address that is headed by a sizeable ornament of the traditional heraldic badge and motto of the Prince of Wales and hails its dedicatee as the 'Hope and Lustre of Three Kingdomes'.[10] Both volumes intimate that the Prince will be able to fulfil the hopes that he represents by heeding Fanshawe's counsel.

Fanshawe believed that a monarch could avoid becoming a tyrant by acquiring self-mastery.[11] His poems consistently articulate the setbacks and disasters that arise when rulers lack this quality. On occasion Fanshawe either replaces or combines this moral instruction with material that expresses the belief that the most effective way the Prince could be the author of peace in the Stuart kingdoms and inaugurate a period of national revival was through marriage to an Iberian princess. Fanshawe was considering potential marriage partners for the Prince from the 1630s: *On His Majesties Great Shippe* anticipates the ship fetching 'for our young Prince a Princely Bride' (line 94). The possibility that Fanshawe was thinking specifically of an Iberian bride increases when the poem is taken alongside a reference to Philip II of Spain's marriage to Mary I as 'Our *English* joyn'd with *Spaine* by Mariage late' in his *The Escuriall* (line 40). This text immediately follows *On His Majesties Great Shippe* in the 1648 edition of *The Faithfull Shepherd*; *On His Majesties Great Shippe* also opens with an address to the ship as the '*Escuriall of the Sea*' (line 1). The Spanish Infanta at the time of these poems' publication, Maria Theresa, was only nine years old, and the question of her marriage had yet to be settled. A match between her and the Prince was therefore possible, albeit (given the Prince's reduced circumstances) extremely unlikely. The following section considers the more extensive account of Fanshawe's belief in the value of a marriage between the Prince and the Spanish Infanta that is present in the preface to *The Faithfull Shepherd*.

The Faithfull Shepherd

The play is set in a cursed Arcadia, where a prophecy states that the curse can only be lifted '*when two of Race Divine / Love shall combine*' (*Pastor Fido* (1647), p. 23). Fanshawe recodes this prophecy as it appears in Guarini's original to better suit his purposes, by conflating divine with royal ancestry. In the volume's dedicatory epistle to the Prince, Fanshawe links the plot of *Il Pastor Fido* to the circumstances of its first performance, and of his own translation, to underline the benefits he believed a royal match could bring. Fanshawe notes that *Il Pastor Fido* was performed in 1585 for the marriage celebrations of Catalina Micaela, daughter of Philip II of Spain, and Charles Emmanuel I, Duke of Savoy, 'the same *Charles Emanuel* who proved afterwards in his riper yeers, by his Councels and by his Prowesse, *the Bulwark* indeed *of Italie*' (*Pastor Fido* (1647), sig. A4v). Print editions of Guarini's original play were dedicated to Charles Emmanuel, and Fanshawe's epistle indicates that he hoped the dedicatee of *The Faithfull Shepherd* would recognise the parallel and imitate the actions of his Savoyard namesake. Guarini, in Fanshawe's account, gives

> another and more suitable object to his *Royall Spectators*. He shews to *them* the image of *a gasping State* (once the most flourishing in the world): *A wild Boar (the sword)* depopulating the *Country*: *the Pestilence* unpeopling the *Towns*: their gods themselves in the mercilesse *humane Sacrifices* exacting bloody contribution from *both*: and the *Priests (a third Estate of misery)* bearing the burthen of *all* in the *Chorus*, where they deplore their *owne* and the *common* Calamitie. Yet in the *Catastrophe, the Boar slain; the Pestilence* (but this was before upon that miserable composition with their Gods) *ceased*; *the Priests* above all others *exulting* with pious joy: and all this miraculous change occasioned by the presaged Nuptials of two of Divine (that is, Royall) extraction; meaning those at that time of the *Duke of Savoy* with the *Infanta of Spain*, from which fortunate Conjunction hee prophesies a finall period to the troubles that had formerly distracted that State: *So much depends upon the Marriages of Princes.*
>
> (*Pastor Fido* (1647), sig. A4r)

As Fanshawe places parts of his text with a royalist application in italics to make its contemporary resonances all the more apparent, the Prince could hardly have missed the point.

Leaving nothing to chance, though, Fanshawe goes on to exhort his dedicatee

> to reflect upon the sad *Originall*, not without hope to see it yet speedily made a perfect *parallel* throughout; and also your self a great Instrument of it. Whether by some happy Royall Marriage (as in this *Pastorall*, and the case of *Savoy*, to which it alludes) thereby uniting a miserably divided people in a publick joy; or by such other wayes and means as it may have pleased *the Divine Providence* to ordain for an *end of our woe*; I leave to that Providence to determine.
>
> (*Pastor Fido* (1647), sig. (a)1v)

Graham Parry claims that Fanshawe's references to marriage look 'with a wild optimism beyond the present catastrophe of royalist fortunes to a time when Charles will be an instrument of recovery',[12] but it is more accurate to state that Fanshawe's concerns are grounded firmly in the present. It is through his marriage, specifically to the Spanish Infanta, that Fanshawe sees the Prince becoming an instrument of recovery. Such a marriage could secure an alliance with a foreign power that would give the royalists the necessary resources to ensure their victory in the civil wars.

Fanshawe both retains and refocuses the emphasis on marriage that dominates the preface to his Guarini translation in his rendering of *Aeneid* 4 as *On the Loves of Dido and Æneas*. This translation first appeared as part of the additional material in the 1648 edition of *The Faithfull Shepherd*. Where the preface to *The Faithfull Shepherd* stresses the benefits of the Prince's marriage to a Spanish princess, the references to marriage in *On the Loves of Dido and Æneas* form part of Fanshawe's broader strategy of using the translation as a vehicle of providing the Prince with ethical instruction. My analysis initially focuses on the relationship between Fanshawe's desire to moralise the *Aeneid* and the translation's formal properties. It then considers the references to marriage in the text, and their status as part of Fanshawe's strategy of foregrounding the need to possess emotional self-mastery and privilege public over private duty.

The Fourth Booke of Virgills Æneis On the Loves of Dido and Æneas

The most striking aspect of *On the Loves of Dido and Æneas*' form is its use of the Spenserian stanza, since by the 1640s heroic couplets had become the standard metre for translating Virgil and other classical epic poets. Pugh has drawn attention to Spenser's association with didactic poetry in the early modern period, and to the fact that Fanshawe's other work in Spenserian stanzas, *A Canto of the Progresse of Learning*, is explicitly framed as an instructional work.[13] In that poem, as elsewhere in his *oeuvre*, Fanshawe articulates the importance of self-control. *On the Loves of Dido and Æneas* devotes considerable attention to the dangerous consequences that arise when rulers do not possess this quality: Aeneas' arrival in Carthage causes both him and Dido to display a distinct lack of self-mastery. The monstrous goddess Fama reports 'hiemem inter se luxu, quam longa, fovere / regnorum immemores turpique cupidine captos' (*A* 4.193–4; 'they while away the winter, all its length, in wanton ease together, unmindful of their realms and enthralled by shameless passion'). Fanshawe translates this as 'now they spent / In Revells the long winter, wholly bent / On brutish Love, drowning affaires of State' (lines 225–7).[14] When Aeneas is with Dido, the construction of Carthage and the founding of the Roman nation are deferred, potentially indefinitely, in the interests of indulging 'brutish Love'.

Peter Davidson has argued that the Spenserian stanzas lead to a lack of narrative momentum and reduce the overall effectiveness of the translation.[15] Yet the longueurs of the Spenserian stanza make it a particularly appropriate choice for a stand-alone version of *Aeneid* 4 that has instructional designs on its intended reader. The reference to Dido and Aeneas' behaviour suggests that stasis is precisely what defines Aeneas' time in Carthage and what Fanshawe wishes to highlight in his translation. Fanshawe's especial keenness to embed the idea of delay informs not only his choice of verse form, but also the duplication of terms in certain lines. Although Dido has forsworn a second marriage on account of the vows she made to Sychaeus, her passion for Aeneas causes her to admit 'Did I not loath the Nuptiall Torch and Bed, / To this one fault perchance, <u>perchance</u> I might be led' (lines 17–18); 'perchance' translates Virgil's 'forsan' (*A* 4.19; 'perhaps'), but the term only appears once in the Latin.[16]

The associations of the Spenserian stanza with didacticism and deferred resolution complement Fanshawe's desire for his translation of *Aeneid* 4 to function as princely counsel. The Trojans wintering in Carthage during their voyage from Troy parallel the royalists in their peripatetic European exile. For both groups, the locale in which they find themselves – Carthage for the Trojans, France (in this period) for the royalists – should function as a place of temporary respite, not as an alternative destination. Remaining there delays their true purpose and destined mission. Once Aeneas finally prepares to leave Carthage he tells Dido he has been visited by the spirit of his father Anchises, who laments that Aeneas' actions are keeping Ascanius from 'regno Hesperiae ... et fatalibus arvis' (*A* 4.355; 'a Hesperian kingdom ... and predestined lands'). Fanshawe translates this phrase as 'his destin'd Crowne' (line 410), which adds a royalist resonance to his presentation of Carthage as a place of delay.

This sense of stasis and the use of Spenserian stanzas, in conjunction with an added reference to Carthage as a '<u>Land / Of sweet inchantments</u>' (lines 321–2), makes Carthage akin to a Bower of Bliss from which Aeneas must escape. That episode from *The Faerie Queene* occurs in the book that is dedicated to Guyon, the knight of Temperance, which corresponds to Fanshawe's interest in advocating self-control and the avoidance of indulgence. The reference to '<u>Don</u> *Æneas*' (line 248) and the translation of Dido's 'quem sese ore ferens, quam forti pectore et armis' (*A* 4.11; 'What a countenance he bears, how brave in heart and feats of arms') as 'How wise! How valiant! What a Face he has!' (line 11), also make Aeneas a knightly figure. Davidson suggests that the connections between *On the Loves of Dido and Æneas* and *The Faerie Queene* extend to Dido: she is an enchantress to his knight.[17] Yet, in Fanshawe's translation, the individual whom Juno perceives to be 'drown'd / <u>In witchcrafts</u>' (lines 101–2) is Dido, not Aeneas. In Virgil Dido is simply 'tali ... peste teneri' (*A* 4.90; 'held in so fatal a disease'). Fanshawe translates a reference to how Dido 'pendetque ... ab ore' (*A* 4.79, 'hangs on [Aeneas'] lips'), as 'at his <u>charming</u> Lips againe shee fondly hung' (line 86). Again it is Dido who is under a form of enchantment.

Significantly, the reference to Aeneas' 'charming Lips' comes from the narrator rather than Dido herself. By collapsing the boundaries between Dido and narrator, Fanshawe has the reader experience the narrative more via Dido's point of view than is the case in other early modern translations of *Aeneid* 4. This decision influences Fanshawe's distinctive presentation of Dido and Aeneas' relationship. In Virgil, the events following Dido and Aeneas taking shelter from a thunderstorm in the same cave accommodate different interpretations:

> speluncam Dido dux et Troianus eandem
> deveniunt. prima et Tellus et pronuba Iuno
> dant signum; fulsere ignes et conscius Aether
> conubiis, summoque ululaunt vertice Nymphae.
> ille dies primus leti primusque malorum
> causa fuit. neque enim specie famave movetur
> nec iam furtivum Dido meditatur amorem;
> coniugium vocat; hoc praetexit nomine culpam.
>
> (*A* 4.165–72)

('To the same cave come Dido and the Trojan chief. Primal Earth and nuptial Juno give the sign; fires flashed in Heaven, the witness to their bridal, and on the mountaintop screamed the Nymphs. That day was the first cause of death, the first of calamity. For Dido is no more swayed by fair show or fair fame, no more does she dream of a secret love: she calls it marriage; with that name she hides her *culpa*.')

Virgil structures this passage so it moves between Dido's and the narrator's viewpoints, but ultimately suggests that, whilst the encounter between Dido and Aeneas has the trappings of a marriage, they do not leave the cave as husband and wife. Fanshawe, by contrast, translates the key lines as 'Earth gives the signall word, / And *Juno*, Queene of Marriage, doth their hands accord' (lines 193–4); these additional details suggest that a formal marriage ceremony has been performed and witnessed.[18]

Fanshawe's version is unique in having Juno not just present at Dido and Aeneas' encounter, but actively officiating in her capacity as the goddess of marriage to make them husband and wife. It follows that his rendering of 'coniugium vocat; hoc praetexit nomine culpam' as 'She calls it Wedlock, gives her fault an honest name' (line 203) is relatively non-judgemental. *Culpa* has a wide range of possible meanings, from the sympathetic to the highly condemnatory. Fanshawe's contemporaries veer more to the latter, by making Dido know her union with Aeneas is invalid: '[she] names / It, marriage: this pretence t' her fault she frames'; 'She stiles it wedlock, gives her crime that name'; 'Her Crime she justifies by Wedlocks name'.[19] Fanshawe's Dido, by contrast, is not conniving; instead she suffers from errors and faults that are not of her own making. His translation of 'fulsere ignes et conscius Aether / conubiis', as 'The guilty Heav'ns, as blushing to have been / An instrument this meeting to fulfill, / With flashing lightning shone' (lines 195–7) transfers much of the shame the text implies the lovers should feel on to the (super)natural world. It is the gods who are at fault, not Dido. A consequence of this characterisation is that Fanshawe's Aeneas is more fickle than his Virgilian counterpart. It makes his claim 'much lesse did I Wedlock-bands pretend, / Neither to such a treaty ever condescend' (lines 391–2) more disingenuous than the original 'nec coniugis umquam / praetendi taedas aut haec in foedera veni' (*A* 4.338–9; 'I never held out a bridegroom's torch or entered such a compact'). Fanshawe's Aeneas initiates, or at least acquiesces to, the union where the Virgilian original leaves the nature of the pledge more uncertain and not necessarily mutually decided.

The Aeneas of Fanshawe's *On the Loves of Dido and Æneas* consequently seems more of an antitype whose behaviour is to be avoided than a model for the Prince to imitate. Pugh argues that Fanshawe bifurcates the contemporary application of Aeneas in his translation to provide counsel that is consistent with his other advice, as he bifurcates the application of Julius Caesar in the 'Presented to his Majesty' poems.[20] The Aeneas who is 'uxurious' (line 308, which directly replicates 'uxorius' at *A* 4.266), in Pugh's reading, represents Charles I. In a clear point of contact with anti-Caroline propaganda, Fanshawe finds that a leader who is overly dominated by his wife fosters conditions which make warfare inevitable; this Aeneas provides a model of what the Prince's rule would be like were he to imitate his father. The more admirable elements of Aeneas' behaviour, principally his willingness to obey the orders of the gods and leave Carthage for Italy, represent the Prince, or at least the type of idealised Prince who is not in thrall to the passions. Pugh's reading is persuasive, and corresponds to the humanist reading of *Aeneid* 4 as a work which emphasises the importance of duty over pleasure, and of *pietas* over *luxus*. Having Aeneas marry, and then abandon, Dido heightens the necessary process of Aeneas' maturation and the reacquisition of his defining status as 'pius Aeneas' (*A* 4.393). Tellingly, Virgil uses this term for the first time in *Aeneid* 4 when Aeneas follows the gods' orders and sails for Italy. The departure from Carthage shows Aeneas resuming his destined fate, as foretold to him by the ghost of his Trojan wife Creusa, that a new nation and wife await him in Latium (*A* 2.781–4). Aeneas had forgotten, repressed or ignored this information when in Carthage. For Fanshawe, the Prince too must learn to subordinate his own interests and desires to the needs of his people.

A Summary Discourse of the Civil Warres of Rome

The counsel Fanshawe provides in *On the Loves of Dido and Æneas* regarding the necessity of not letting passion dictate royal conduct or policy is also present in the other Virgil translations that appear in the 1648 edition of *The Faithfull Shepherd*: Anchises' encomium of Augustus (*A* 6.791–805) and his delineation to Aeneas of the Roman imperial mission (*A* 6.847–53). Both of these translations appear in the volume's closing text, *A Summary Discourse of the Civil Warres of Rome*. They draw not only on the parallels Fanshawe finds between the Prince and Aeneas in *On the Loves of Dido and Æneas*, but also on the associations between the Prince and Augustus that are made in the 'Presented to his Highness' poems. The first translation begins at the moment that Anchises points out Augustus to Aeneas in the parade of Roman heroes:

> hic vir, hic est, tibi quem promitti saepius audis,
> Augustus Caesar, divi genus, aurea condet
> saecula qui rursus Latio regnata per arva
> Saturno quondam.
>
> (*A* 6.791–4)

('here is the man, here he is, whom you so often hear promised to you, Augustus Caesar, son of a god, who will found a golden age again in Latium amongst fields once ruled by Saturn'.)

Fanshawe translates this passage:

> This is that man of men Augustus, hee
> Whom (sprung from Heaven) Heaven oft hath promised thee,
> That man that shall to *Italy* restore
> *The Golden Age* which *Saturne* gave before.[21]

Henry Power has noted that Fanshawe's use of 'restore' departs from the original, since Virgil's *condet* 'indicates a new foundation rather than a restoration'.[22] As the *Summary Discourse* prints the Latin text immediately before the translation Fanshawe would have expected at least some of his readers to recognise the difference between 'condet' and 'restore'. According to John Aubrey the Prince 'understood not Latin well', so even if he did read this translation the difference, and its concomitant royalist resonance, may have passed him by.[23]

Charles's lack of facility with Latin potentially informs Fanshawe's more overt adaptation of Virgil in the *Summary Discourse*'s second translation from *Aeneid* 6:

excudent alii spirantia mollius aera
(credo equidem), vivos ducent de marmore vultus,
orabunt causas melius, caelique meatus
describent radio et surgentia sidera dicent:
tu regere imperio populos, Romane, memento
(haec tibi erunt artes) pacique imponere morem,
parcere subiectis et debellare superbos.

(A 6.847–53)

('Others, I doubt not, shall with softer mould beat out the breathing bronze, coax from the marble features to the life, plead cases with greater eloquence and with a pointer trace heaven's motions and predict the risings of the stars; you, Roman, be sure to rule the world (these will be your arts), to crown peace with justice, to spare the vanquished and to crush the proud.')

Others may breathing Mettals softer grave,
Plead Causes better, <u>and poore Clients save
From their oppressours</u>: with an Instrument
They may mete out the spacious Firmament,
And count the rising starres with greater skill,
<u>Reyne the proud Steed, and breake him of his will.
Better their Sword, and better use their Pen.</u>
Breton remember thou to governe men,
(Be this thy trade) And to establish Peace,
To spare the humble, and the proud depresse.[24]

Fanshawe's substitution of 'Breton' for 'Romane' to elide Aeneas, Augustus and the Prince has been much discussed.[25] Less attention has been paid, however, to the emphasis that establishing peace plays in the translation relative to the original. The instruction that the Prince should '*depresse*' the proud could engage with the definition of the term as 'to subjugate, vanquish',[26] but this meaning was starting to become obsolete by the mid-seventeenth century. If Fanshawe did use 'depresse' in this way its martial implications remain more obscure than in the original term 'debellare', which derives from 'bellare', 'to wage war', and means 'to conquer completely'.[27] As in other texts in the 1648 volume, the translation stresses the importance of curbing strong emotions. Fanshawe's pacification of *Aeneid* 6 also corresponds to the value the *Summary Discourse* places on leaders pursuing 'clemencie and moderation' and the dangers of embarking on 'a *new civil Warre*'.[28]

The desire to provide the Prince with further counsel and register anxieties regarding the prospect of a new civil war also shapes Fanshawe's *Selected Parts of Horace* (1652). In addition to the translations of Horace which comprise the bulk of the volume, *Selected Parts* translates an extract from the *Georgics* (G 3.219–41) under the title *Virgil's Bull*. The episode's interest in exploring the effectiveness of violence in securing the intended outcome for its instigators would have given it a particular resonance following its publication after successive armed risings by the royalists; these attempts to restore royal authority had led to catastrophic defeats at the Battle of Preston (1648) and the Battle of Worcester (1651). In order to identify what prompted Fanshawe to translate and publish *Virgil's Bull* it is first necessary to consider the status of *Selected Parts* as a volume that addresses the Prince, and the didactic elements in the stand-alone translations from the *Georgics* that were published prior to *Virgil's Bull*.

Selected Parts of Horace and Virgil's Bull

Fanshawe spent part of the early 1650s in prison; he had followed the Prince to Worcester and he was captured as he tried to escape the area in the aftermath of the royalists' defeat. One of the conditions of his release was that he write no more works in support of the royalist cause.[29] The publication of *Selected Parts*, however, represents a clear attempt to overcome this restriction. It is likely that had he been able to Fanshawe would have formally dedicated *Selected Parts* to the Prince, as he had the 1647 and 1648 editions of *The Faithfull Shepherd*. The reference on the volume's title page to Horace as the 'Prince of Lyricks' functions as a substitute for a formal dedication to the Prince. The likelihood that Fanshawe's use of 'Prince' gestures towards the volume's intended reader is strengthened when it is compared to the reference to Horace as 'the best of Lyrick Poets' on the title page of Barten Holyday's collection of Horace which was also published in 1652.[30] Fanshawe, unlike Holyday, grants Horace the trappings of royalty to praise his poetic abilities.

Many of Fanshawe's Horace translations had been circulating in manuscript for almost two decades before their publication. Comparisons between the manuscript and print versions suggest that, in contrast to *On His Majesties Great Shippe* and the 'Proclamation' ode, Fanshawe revised some of them for publication for political rather than aesthetic reasons. Cognates of 'prince' occur with greater frequency in the published translations than in the earlier manuscript versions. One poem, a version of *Odes* 2.15, begins 'Our Princely Piles will shortly leave / But little Land for Ploughs to cleave', whereas an earlier manuscript version begins 'Our sumptuous Piles will leave small space, / To plough ere long'.[31] All the Horatian odes in *Selected Parts* are, like several poems in the 1648 *Faithfull Shepherd*, published alongside their equivalent Latin texts. Horace's original reads 'iam pauca aratro iugera regiae / moles relinquent' (*Odes* 2.15.1–2; 'soon our princely piles will leave only a few acres for the plough'). The replacement of 'Princely' for 'sumptuous' could, though, simply represent a more accurate rendering of Horace's original. As in the appearance of 'Prince' on the volume's title page, the presence of 'Princely' in the poem reveals the volume's intended reader without necessarily incorporating any noticeably royalist sentiment or counsel. *Selected Parts* does contain a noticeably didactic element, as a number of poems advocate temperance, self-mastery and clemency: the titles that Fanshawe gives to *Odes* 1.18 and 1.27, for example, emphasise the significance of drinking in moderation.[32] Such advice is consonant with the counsel that Fanshawe provides in earlier poems that are explicitly addressed to the Prince. This instruction, however, is of a noticeably general kind that could easily be held to impart ethical advice that is applicable to any reader, not just its implied one.

Other lyrics are both more specifically targeted at the Prince and politically engaged. These moments are generally concerned with the poems that are addressed to Augustus: the subtitle of *Odes* 1.2, for example is 'That all the Gods are angry with the *Romans* for the killing of *Julius Caesar:* That the only hope of the Empire is placed in *Augustus*'. Such a title indicates that Fanshawe uses the poem to reaffirm the presentation of the Prince as a potential second Augustus who could be the author of peace, as outlined in the 'Presented to his Majesty' poems and his *Summary Discourse*. *Odes* 4.5, which is also addressed to Augustus, opens with the exhortation

> Heav'ns choicest gift, *Rome*'s greatest stay,
> Now thou art too too long away:
> The holy Senate urge thy word
> For soon Return, Return.
>
> (lines 1–4)

The contemporary application of this wish is hardly Fanshawe's most subtle royalist statement.

In several of the poems that precede *Virgil's Bull* in *Selected Parts*, then, Fanshawe reasserts his status as a counsellor who provides moral and political instruction. But the precedents for politicised translation in the volume do not necessarily indicate that Fanshawe wanted his *Georgics* translation to be read in this manner. The only non-Horatian poem other than *Virgil's Bull* in *Selected Parts* is a translation of Ausonius' *De Rosis Nascentibus*, which does not carry any political overtones. In addition, whilst there was an extensive tradition of publishing partial, as well as complete, English versions of other poems by Virgil (and indeed Horace), there are only two occasions before *Virgil's*

Bull when an extract from the *Georgics* functions as a stand-alone poem (the politically charged translation from the *Georgics* by Cowley that was discussed in Chapter 3 was not published until over a decade after *Selected Parts*). Richard Crashaw and Henry Vaughan, the poets in question, do have royalist credentials. Their poetry is frequently informed by their royalism, and Vaughan sometimes engages with Virgil as a means of reflecting on his experiences of the civil wars.[33] But in both cases their translations from the *Georgics* serve purely devotional purposes. Crashaw's 1646 collection *The Delights of the Muses* is divided into religious and secular poetry. His 'Out of Virgil, In the praise of the Spring' (a translation of *G* 2.323–45) appears among the secular poems in this collection.[34] The translation, however, Christianises Virgil's account of the spring to make it a meditation on the lost prelapsarian world; Crashaw does not make any connection between this lost world and the 'halcyon days' of the Caroline period. Vaughan's 'Man in Darkness, or, A Discourse of Death' includes a translation from the celebrated passage from *Georgics* 4 on the Corycian farmer (*G* 4.125–38).[35] The translation heightens the poverty of Virgil's farmer to stress his ability to find contentment in his present surroundings and the virtues of labour. Crashaw and Vaughan moralise the *Georgics*' own didactic elements to accommodate Christian ethics, but they neither retain Virgil's own political commentary in these passages nor update it to their own times.

Nonetheless, given Fanshawe's habitual desire that his poetry serve an instructive purpose it is likely that Fanshawe intends *Virgil's Bull* to provide the Prince with counsel. The passage Fanshawe selected for translation concerns a bull who fails to see off a rival's challenge for his possession of his mate and the preparations he undergoes to avenge his defeat. Fanshawe's translation increases the sympathy that Virgil's original invites for the defeated bull, rather than his successful challenger:

> nec mos bellantis una stabulare, sed alter
> victus abit longeque ignotis exulat oris,
> multa gemens ignominiam plagasque superbi
> victoris, tum quos amisit inultus amores,
> et stabula aspectans regnis excessit avitis.
>
> (*G* 3.224–8)

('nor is it the rivals' custom to herd together, but the vanquished one departs, and dwells an exile in unknown scenes far away. Much does he bewail his shame, and the blows of his haughty conqueror, and much the love he has lost unavenged – then, with a wistful glance at his stall, he has quitted his ancestral realm.')

> Nor is't the fashion when the War is done,
> For these stout Combatants to live in one
> And the same Field. The vanquish't quits the place,
> Exil'd in parts far off: his own disgrace
> Lamenting deep, and the proud Victors blowes,
> Also the *Love* he (unreveng'd) did lose:
> And, casting back a <u>ruefull</u> look, is fain
> To leave the Pastures where <u>his Sire</u> did raign.
>
> (lines 7–14)

The 'ruefull' look the defeated bull gives to his lost lands gives the bull human qualities and emotions. As the translation of 'regnis . . . avitis' as 'the Pastures where his Sire did raign' helps to prompt memories of Charles I, the bull who is bent on revenge could also act as a proxy for the Prince, especially with the references to his being 'vanquish't' and 'Exil'd'.

The passage's emphasis on conflict initially seems to be at odds with the counsel that Fanshawe gives the Prince in his other translations, but overall it suggests the risks of attempting violent reprisals are too great to be worthwhile. *Virgil's Bull* describes the defeated bull's preparation for a second combat at length, but the episode ends abruptly after using an extended simile to dramatise his second charge:

> post ubi collectum robur viresque refectae,
> signa movet praecepsque oblitum fertur in hostem:
> fluctus uti medio coepit cum albescere ponto,
> longius ex altoque sinum trahit, utque volutus
> ad terras immane sonat per saxa, neque ipso
> monte minor procumbit; at ima exaestuat unda
> verticibus nigramque alte subiectat harenam.[36]
>
> (G 3.235–41)

('soon, when his power is mustered and his strength renewed, he advances the colours, and dashes headlong on his unheeding foe: as, when a wave begins to whiten in mid-sea, from the farther deep it arches its curve, and, rolling shore-ward, roars thundering along the reefs, and, huge as a very mountain, falls prone, while from below the water boils up in eddies, and tosses black sand aloft'.)

> Before the fight doth flourish, having knit
> His slackend Nervs, he doth his Trumpet blow,
> And rushes headlong on his <u>secure</u> Foe:
> As when a Billow in the midst o'th' *Maine*
> Began to Foam, and gathers a long Train
> Advancing through the *Deep*: and rowled to Land
> Roares in the Rocks, nor overlays the Strand
> Less heavie then a Mountain: but boils up

> With curling Whirlpools to the *Ocean*'s top,
> And throws high Works up of black Sand.
>
> (lines 22–31)

The next line in Virgil's *Georgics* starts a new verse paragraph that returns to the poem's more general concerns about the power of desire. As the narrative regarding the contest of the bulls is not resolved, the passage suggests that it is possible the exiled bull will be victorious and regain his former position; his strength has been renewed and he is able to operate at the height of his powers. This outcome, however, is not presented as inevitable. The translation of the reference to the bull's enemy being 'oblitum' ('unheedful') as 'secure' adds to the poem's indeterminacy. The term may simply indicate that the bull's enemy is wrong to think that he is secure in his status as a victor. Yet both 'oblitum' and 'secure' can also carry associations of unassailability, and hint that the challenge will not be successful. In isolation, *Virgil's Bull* reads as if it supports military action. Yet, when placed at the end of a collection in which so many poems warn against renewing civil conflict, and when considered alongside the original passage, it reveals greater qualms about the risks such a policy entailed. Its account of the potentially self-destructive behaviour to which creatures who are under the sway of passionate emotion are driven also reiterates the advice regarding the necessity of acquiring self-mastery that informs Fanshawe's other translations from Virgil.

As there is no manuscript provenance for *Virgil's Bull* its composition date cannot be established with certainty, but its publication in *Selected Parts* rather than in the 1647 or 1648 *Faithfull Shepherd* volumes suggests it is a product either of the late 1640s or early 1650s. The events of the episode where the bull seeks reprisals for an earlier defeat speak most immediately to the period that came between Charles I's surrender after the royalist defeat at Newbury in 1645 and the later defeat at Preston in the summer of 1648. *Virgil's Bull* may be a retrospective response to the state of the royalists' fortunes after Preston. It may also represent something written before Preston that provides a sufficiently open-ended appraisal of the policy that instigated a second phase of armed conflict that it would acquire prophetic status irrespective of the events that followed. The general absence of specific *post eventum* prophecies in Fanshawe's oeuvre suggests that the latter is more likely. However finely balanced the *Georgics* passage is when it comes to documenting the potential ramifications of seeking further violent conflict after a defeat, *Virgil's Bull* concentrates more on the risks of defeat than the rewards of victory. The defeat at Worcester in 1651 would have provided additional vindication for such emphasis when *Virgil's Bull* appeared in print the following year.

It was during his aforementioned period of enforced retirement from direct royal service that followed the Battle of Worcester that Fanshawe began work on his most substantial literary project: a complete English translation of Camões' *Os Lusíadas* (1572) as *The Lusiad, or Portugals Historicall Poem* (1655). Despite its composition during the Interregnum, in *The Lusiad* – and *Specimen Rerum a Lusitanis*, a partial translation of *Os Lusíadas* into Latin – Fanshawe offers a more confident, hopeful future for the Prince and his dynasty than is present in *Virgil's Bull*. The Camões translations combine Fanshawe's earlier practice of providing the Prince with models of good governance and of advocating a political alliance that would be secured through marriage to an Iberian princess. His choice of *Os Lusíadas* to provide this counsel indicates that by the mid-1650s Fanshawe no longer felt, as he had at the time of his *Il Pastor Fido* translation, that the Prince should marry the Spanish Infanta, and instead he was advocating that the Prince marry into the Portuguese royal family. The failure of the 1649–51 diplomatic mission to Spain (in which Fanshawe participated) to secure meaningful support for the royalists, and the support Portugal gave to prominent royalists in the aftermath of Charles's execution, was likely a primary influence behind this shift. At the time of Fanshawe's *Os Lusíadas* translation the Portuguese Infanta was Catherine of Braganza. Catherine had been suggested as a possible bride for Charles in the early 1640s, but discussions had stalled following the outbreak of civil war.[37] Yet circumstances changed sufficiently in the aftermath of the Restoration that this alliance did indeed come to pass in 1662. Unlike other poems by Fanshawe that engage with the tradition of the poet as *vates*, such as the 'Proclamation' ode (and potentially *Virgil's Bull*), his *Os Lusíadas* translations ultimately justified hopes rather than fears. Nonetheless, as the final section of this chapter considers, the future that these translations anticipate was only partially fulfilled.

The Lusiad, or Portugals Historicall Poem

The conditions of Fanshawe's release from prison meant that, as with *Selected Parts*, he was unable to include a formal dedication to the Prince in his *Lusiad*. Instead he dedicated it to William Wentworth, 2nd Earl of Strafford, at whose estate (Tankersley Park) Fanshawe completed the translation.[38] This Strafford was the son of the first Earl, for whom Fanshawe had worked in Ireland during the 1630s (the same period in which Ogilby was Strafford's Master of the Revels).[39] Despite the dedicatee, the Prince remains Fanshawe's imagined reader. In his *Lusiad*, as in his other translations, Fanshawe finds parallels between his motives and those of the original author. Camões' approach to the *Aeneid* was informed by its reception as a work in which Virgil provided Augustus with counsel.[40] Camões fashioned himself as a Virgil addressing an Augustus by framing *Os Lusíadas* with direct addresses to Portugal's young King Sebastião I (*reg.* 1557–78) which advise him on how to fulfil his promise to become a model ruler (*Os Lusíadas* 1.6–18; 10.146–56).[41]

The Lusiad, like Fanshawe's other translations, presents the Prince with idealised types whose example he should follow. The most significant of these is not the original poem's dedicatee Sebastião, but Infante Dom Henrique (1394–1460). Henrique was a member of the 'Ínclita geração' (*Os Lusíadas* 4.50.8; 'the illustrious generation'), the sons of King João I (*reg.* 1385–1433) who were hailed as ideal early modern princes who spearheaded a revival of Portugal's power and influence. He was celebrated as a pioneer of Portuguese navigation who sponsored expeditions to Africa and India; these expeditions made possible the voyages of da Gama that comprise the main narrative of *Os Lusíadas*. Fanshawe's *Lusiad* has to grant Henrique a prominence that he does not possess in Camões' original to have him serve as a model for the Prince, since his appearance in the original text is confined to the parade of Portuguese heroes who are depicted on the sails of da Gama's ship (*Os Lusíadas* 8.37). The *Lusiad* draws attention to Henrique through the full-page engraving of 'Prince Henry of Portugal' that forms part of the volume's front matter.[42] The only other two portraits in Fanshawe's volume are based on woodcuts of da Gama and Camões that appear in *Lusíadas Comentadas*, a 1639 edition of the poem by the critic and poet Manuel de Faria y Sousa which Fanshawe consulted when working on his translation of the poem.[43] Neither this nor any other edition of Camões' poem prior to the *Lusiad* contains an illustration of Henrique, so Fanshawe must have commissioned it specially to serve this instructional purpose.

The illustration of Henrique in Fanshawe's *Lusiad* provides a reminder of his connections to the English court. Henrique's mother was Philippa of Lancaster (a daughter of John of Gaunt), and the portrait incorporates the Portuguese royal crest encircled by the Order of the Garter; Henrique was, in fact, one of several Portuguese princes who were made Garter Knights in the early modern period. That the history and role of the Order was clearly on Fanshawe's mind during this time explains a reference in his *Querer por solo Querer* – a translation of a play by the

Spanish dramatist Mendoza which he worked on at the same time as his *Lusiad* – to 'the *Garter'd English* MARS' (3.8.43); the equivalent character in the original adapts a traditional Spanish battle cry that refers to Spain's patron saint, 'Santiago, y cierra España' ('For Saint James, and march on, Spain').[44] Fanshawe was made pro tem Chancellor of the Order of the Garter soon after the Restoration, and the prominence that the *Lusiad*'s paratexts grant to the Order may explain why Fanshawe was felt to be an appropriate candidate for that office.

Brian Lockey has suggested that Fanshawe's interest in the Garter shows a 'faith in a voluntary international order involving a network of like-minded sovereigns, linked to the English crown by virtue of their personal and political values'.[45] Such a faith may well have been on Fanshawe's mind when producing the *Lusiad*, but it is also likely that his references to the combined arms of Portugal and England were primarily prompted by a desire to advocate a further alliance of those two kingdoms by a marriage between the Prince and the Portuguese Infanta. Fanshawe's reference to Portuguese as 'so *uncourted a language*' (*Lusiad*, sig. A2r) in his dedication may serve as an oblique hint of the translation's design. It courts the Portuguese Infanta on the Prince's behalf. Advising the poem's addressee about a suitable marriage partner also formed part of Camões' original design: in its opening address to Sebastião the poem's reference to the sea goddess Tethys preparing the oceans as a dowry (*Os Lusíadas* 1.16.5–8) serves as a reminder of the king's duty to marry.[46] Fanshawe applies this aspect of Camões' counsel in *Os Lusíadas* to the Prince's own situation.

Although the intended bride was the Portuguese rather than the Spanish Infanta, Fanshawe's strategy in his *Lusiad* is indebted to the equation of a royal marriage and the revival of a country's fortunes that frames his translation of *Il Pastor Fido* (1647). At the time of the marriage of Henrique's parents in 1387 Portugal was emerging from a period of instability and civil conflict. Fanshawe uses this reference to a former marriage alliance between the royal houses of England and Portugal as a harbinger of imperial expansion and revival in influence. Fanshawe seeks to evoke the historical precedent for the advantages that a marriage between the English and Portuguese royal families could bring. He also wants to co-opt the cultural authority that was attached to Camões, Portugal's Virgil, to suggest that the nation's own foundational text, *Os Lusíadas*, advocates such a match.

The attention that Fanshawe grants the Anglo-Portuguese princes in the *Lusiad* suggests that Fanshawe was as (if not more) concerned with the imagined offspring of the marriage between Charles and the Portuguese Infanta, and their potential to become a second 'Illustrious

Generation', as he was with the more immediate benefits that the marriage could bring in the 1650s to advance the royalist cause. This focus on the 'Illustrious Generation' would have received more attention from the Portuguese who needed to be courted to secure an alliance between the Prince and the Infanta than Fanshawe's English counterparts. A desire to emphasise the value for Portugal of an earlier Anglo-Portuguese marriage alliance motivates *Specimen Rerum a Lusitanis*, a Latin translation of *Os Lusíadas* 1.1–43 and 4.1–47. *Specimen* survives in a manuscript which also contains a Latin commentary by Fanshawe on the origins and history of the royal arms of Portugal. The commentary pays special attention to the inclusion of the Garter in the arms of King João II (*reg.* 1481–95). Fanshawe's decision to write this commentary and to translate sections of the *Lusiad* into Latin as well as English is prompted by a recognition that using the international language of diplomacy would increase the chances of its intended Portuguese audience reading it; the same could not be assumed of the English *Lusiad*. *Specimen* certainly seems more directly oriented to flatter Portuguese egos. The commentary on Portugal's arms, for example, focuses on the status of the Portuguese as a divinely favoured people, how Portugal's coat of arms had its origins in heroic acts of the founder of the country's ruling dynasty, the matching of these heroics by João I overcoming his enemies in the Portuguese war of succession, and his marriage to Philippa that followed soon after. The reference to the marriage in *Specimen* thus acts as a culmination of a panegyric in a way that it does not in Camões' original, and becomes more like the end that is promised by the *Aeneid* through the marriage of Aeneas and Lavinia. By translating into Latin the passages from *Os Lusíadas* which record previous Anglo-Portuguese marriage alliances Fanshawe also intimates that they foretell another union of this kind between the Prince and Catherine of Braganza.

As with his translations from Guarini and the *Aeneid*, Fanshawe's *Lusiad* and *Specimen* delineate the political future that he hoped would come to pass. Whilst this alliance was eventually realised, it was *realpolitik* rather than the combined literary authority of Virgil, Camões and Fanshawe that caused the Portuguese to open marriage negotiations with England after the Restoration: Portugal was in need of an ally against Spain, and promised a sizeable dowry to England if Catherine were to marry Charles II. Fanshawe himself was involved in these negotiations only at a relatively late stage, but his translations of *Os Lusíadas* (as well as his prior diplomatic experience) may well have helped him secure this role. Even without this involvement, Fanshawe's focus on marriage and national revival means that the parts of the English *Lusiad* which focus on an Anglo-Portuguese marriage alliance would have given it a prophetic status for any royalists who read it after the Restoration. *Specimen*, however, may only have been composed after the Restoration, when the future that it imagines was more plausible.

The concluding stanza of *Specimen*, which has no equivalent in *Os Lusíadas*, capitalises on Fanshawe's vindicated prophecy of Charles II's marriage to Catherine in 1662 to predict further achievements:

> Quondam Hymen erit alter, et altera Regia Virgo
> Quae, vice tunc versa, Diademate laeta Britanno
> Lusa nurus fulgebit; erint etiam altera Bella
> Hesperidum: Haec eadem semper Fortuna Sequetur;
> Haec itidem Regi Rex Anglus amicus utrique
> Inter Ulysseum componet et inter Iberum.

> ('One day there will be another marriage, another Royal virgin; who, with roles reversed, a happy daughter of Lusus, will shine in the British diadem; and there [will] also be another war of the Hesperians; this same Fortune will always follow in the same way. The English king will be friend to this same king, and will compact peace between Spain and Portugal.')[47]

The last lines of the stanza refer to Fanshawe's involvement in diplomatic attempts in the last year of his life to broker a peace between Spain and Portugal. The account of Charles's marriage to Catherine is presented as something that will happen, not as an event that has already occurred; Fanshawe's past diplomatic successes anticipate even greater triumphs. The stanza provides the only confirmed example of a *post eventum* prophecy of Fanshawe's poetic career; the shift in technique is possibly (as Davidson records) the result of the stanza not being the work of Fanshawe himself, but of his brother Lyonel.[48] In any case, the peace accord between Spain and Portugal, predicted so confidently here, collapsed soon after Fanshawe's death.

The imagined future of a new 'Illustrious Generation' of Anglo-Portuguese princes was also not fulfilled. Although Catherine was pregnant several times in the early 1660s, none of these pregnancies came to term. Charles and Catherine abandoned their attempt to conceive an heir following a traumatic miscarriage in 1669.[49] Fanshawe had died in 1666, but he lived long enough into the Restoration to be aware that the prospect of a new 'Illustrious Generation' was becoming increasingly unlikely. This absent generation represents the first of many lost heirs that would affect the dynastic hopes of the Stuarts for the remainder of the century.

Although the manuscript which contains the *Specimen* translation was intended for a Portuguese audience, it remained in Fanshawe's possession.[50] That Fanshawe kept hold of it explains the presence of three further Latin compositions by him in the manuscript, which record losses that are more immediately personal than the absence of a son to Charles II and Catherine of Braganza. One poem marks the death of a daughter, Elizabeth, another, the death of a son, Richard. The third is a translation of Sidney Godolphin's elegy for Lady Rich.[51] The translation adds a passage to the poem to mourn Godolphin's own death, which concludes with 'Manibus date lilia plenis'. The line quotes Anchises' speech on the death of Marcellus (*A* 6.883; 'grant me to scatter lilies from my hands').[52] For all the royal counsel that Fanshawe lived to see eventually come to pass, his final engagement with Virgil was closer to the melancholy Virgil of Cowley than the confident, even triumphalist, Virgil of Ogilby.

This chapter has argued that Fanshawe considered himself to be a latter-day Virgil whose works contained advice on good governance, which he addressed to a head of state whose achievements are repeatedly compared with those of Augustus. The same Virgilian self-fashioning is also true for the subject of the next chapter, James Harrington. The chapter delineates why Harrington found Augustus to be a more problematic figure and touchstone for a sovereign than Fanshawe did, and, despite his personal experience of royal service, Harrington's advice was directed neither to Charles I nor the Prince, but to Cromwell.

Notes

1. For which see p. 26, above.
2. Unless otherwise stated, Fanshawe's poetry is cited from *The Poems and Translations of Sir Richard Fanshawe*, ed. Peter Davidson, 2 vols (Oxford, 1997) (hereafter Fanshawe, *Poems and Translations*). For panegyrical uses of the 'Charles's Wain' constellation, see pp. 98–9, above.
3. Syrithe Pugh, *Herrick, Fanshawe and the Politics of Intertextuality: Classical Literature and Seventeenth-Century Royalism* (Farnham, 2010), p. 129.
4. As discussed on p. 60, above.
5. Recorded in Fanshawe, *Poems and Translations*, vol. 1, pp. 55–9.
6. In Pugh, *Politics of Intertextuality*, p. 108.
7. As outlined in Pugh, *Politics of Intertextuality*, pp. 87–173 *passim*.
8. For which see pp. 92–4, 98–9, above.
9. Sir Richard Fanshawe, *Il Pastor Fido, The Faithfull Shepherd* (London, 1647) (hereafter *Pastor Fido* (1647)), sig. A3r.
10. Sir Richard Fanshawe, *Il Pastor Fido The Faithfull Shepheard with an Addition of divers other Poems Concluding with a short Discourse of the Long Civill Warres of Rome. To His Highnesse the Prince of Wales* (London, 1648) (hereafter *Pastor Fido* (1648)), sig. A2r.

11. See Pugh, *Politics of Intertextuality*, pp. 119, 173.
12. Graham Parry, 'A Troubled Arcadia', in *Literature and the English Civil War*, ed. Thomas Healy and Jonathan Sawday (Cambridge, 1990), pp. 38–55 (42).
13. See Pugh, *Politics of Intertextuality*, pp. 165–6.
14. As in my other chapters, underline indicates where the translations substantially depart from or add to the Virgilian original.
15. In Fanshawe, *Poems and Translations*, vol. 1, pp. 366–7.
16. Similar unprompted duplications occur elsewhere in the text: cf. *On the Loves of Dido and Æneas*, line 252 and *A* 4.217–18; line 446 and *A* 4.383; line 766 and *A* 4.674.
17. See Fanshawe, *Poems and Translations*, vol. 1, p. 366.
18. I draw here on Pugh, *Politics of Intertextuality*, p. 165.
19. Los Angeles, William Andrews Clark Memorial Library MS.1946.007, p. 60 (Robert Heath, *Aeneid*); John Ogilby, *The Works of Publius Virgilius Maro* (London, 1649), sig. ²G1v; John Ogilby, *The Works of Publius Virgilius Maro Translated, adorn'd with Sculpture, and illustrated with Annotations* (London, 1654), p. 269. These, and other early modern renderings of the line, are discussed in Gordon Braden, 'The Passion of Dido: *Aeneid* 4 in English Translation to 1700', in *Virgil and His Translators*, ed. Susanna Braund and Zara Martirosova Torlone (Oxford, 2018), pp. 80–96 (85–6).
20. See Pugh, *Politics of Intertextuality*, pp. 165–7.
21. Fanshawe, *Poems and Translations*, vol. 1, p. 140; roman/italic fonts reversed.
22. Henry Power, 'The *Aeneid* in the Age of Milton', in *A Companion to Vergil's Aeneid and Its Tradition*, ed. by Joseph Farrell and Michael C. J. Putnam (Chichester, 2010), pp. 186–202 (189).
23. *Aubrey's Brief Lives*, ed. Oliver Lawson Dick (London, 1949), p. 75.
24. Fanshawe, *Poems and Translations*, vol. 1, p. 142; roman/italic fonts reversed.
25. See Colin Burrow, 'Virgil in English Translation', in *The Cambridge Companion to Virgil*, ed. Fiachra Mac Góráin and Charles Martindale, 2nd edn (Cambridge, 2019), pp. 109–27 (114); Pugh, *Politics of Intertextuality*, p. 172.
26. 'Depress, v. (1a)', *OED Online*, oed.com/view/Entry/50442.
27. Charlton T. Lewis and Charles Short, *A Latin Dictionary* (Oxford, 1879), s.v. 'bellare' 1a; 2a.
28. Fanshawe, *Poems and Translations*, vol. 1, p. 138.
29. See John Loftis (ed.), *The Memoirs of Anne, Lady Halkett and Ann, Lady Fanshawe* (Oxford, 1979), pp. 134–5.
30. Barten Holyday, *Horace. The best of Lyrick Poets. Containing much morality, and Sweetnesse* (London, 1652).
31. Cited in Fanshawe, *Poems and Translations*, vol. 1, p. 172.
32. 1.18: 'That with moderate drinking of Wine, the Minde is exhilarated: with immoderate, Quarrels begotten'; 1.27: 'To his Companions feasting together, that they should not quarrel in their drink, and fight with the Cups themselves, after the manner of the Barbarians'.
33. For a general overview of the Virgilian presence in Vaughan's civil-war

poetry, see Henry Power, 'Virgil's *Georgics* and the Poetic Landscape of the English Civil War', in *Interlacing Words and Things: Bridging the Nature–Culture Opposition in Gardens and Landscapes*, ed. Stephen Bann (Washington, DC, 2012), pp. 51–63 (53–5).
34. Richard Crashaw, *Steps to the Temple* (London, 1646), pp. 110–11.
35. Henry Vaughan, *The Mount of Olives* (London, 1652), pp. 71–131 (114–15).
36. Early modern editions of Virgil have 'receptae' ('recovered') for 'refectae' ('renewed') at *G* 3.235.
37. See Antonia Fraser, *King Charles II* (London, 1979), pp. 202–3.
38. I draw here on Loftis (ed.), *Memoirs of Ann, Lady Fanshawe*, p. 136.
39. For which see pp. 88, 96, 103, above.
40. Its status as a mirror for princes is by no means the only Virgilian aspect of *Os Lusíadas*. Camões wanted the poem to be Portugal's *Aeneid* and structured the poem accordingly. Both texts begin with the arrival of a fleet on the coast of Africa, where the protagonists (the Trojans; the Portuguese) are received by the local monarch (Dido; the Sultan of Malindi) and asked to speak of their travels, which their leader (Aeneas; Vasco de Gama) provides in a lengthy flashback. The poem also contains innumerable local borrowings and quotations from the *Aeneid*.
41. Citations from *Os Lusíadas* are taken from Luís Vaz de Camões, *Os Lusíadas*, ed. Álvaro Júlio da Costa Pimpão, 4th edn (Lisbon, 2000).
42. Sir Richard Fanshawe, *The Lusiad, or Portugals Historicall Poem* (London, 1655) (hereafter *Lusiad*), sig. b4v.
43. See Tiago Sousa Garcia, 'How *The Lusiad* Got English'd: Manuel Faria y Sousa, Richard Fanshawe and the First English Translation of *Os Lusíadas*', *Literature Compass*, 14 (2017), 1–18 (pp. 12–13).
44. Antonio Hurtado de Mendoza, *Querer por Solo Querer* (Lisbon, 1639), p. 39.
45. Brian C. Lockey, *Early Modern Catholics, Royalists, and Cosmopolitans: English Transnationalism and the Christian Commonwealth* (Abingdon, 2015), p. 256.
46. See Luís Vaz de Camões, *The Lusíads*, trans. Landeg White (Oxford, 2008), p. 229.
47. Fanshawe, *Poems and Translations*, vol. 2, pp. 362; 660 (Davidson's translation).
48. See Fanshawe, *Poems and Translations*, vol. 2, p. 660.
49. I draw here on Catherine's biography in the *Oxford Dictionary of National Biography* (*ODNB*), www.oxforddnb.com.
50. For speculation on why the manuscript remained with Fanshawe, see Roger Walker with W. H. Liddell, 'A Commentary by Sir Richard Fanshawe on the Royal Arms of Portugal', in *Studies in Portuguese Literature and History in Honour of Luís de Sousa Rebelo*, ed. Helder Macedo (London, 1992) pp. 155–70 (170).
51. As mentioned on p. 11, above.
52. Fanshawe, *Poems and Translations*, vol. 2, p. 663.

Chapter 6

Private Interest: James Harrington

Introduction

Harrington's first translation of Virgil was published in 1658 and contained his *Eclogues* 1 and 9 and *Aeneid* 1–2; a second volume, a translation of *Aeneid* 3–6, appeared the following year. Like other *Aeneids* that were written after 1649 which I have considered in this study, Harrington's uses Virgil's account of Priam's death to commemorate Charles I's execution and alters the text in order make the parallel between the two deaths explicit. Harrington's changes, however, are more extensive than those of his contemporaries. In the *Aeneid* Priam's decapitation is reported, not staged: it occurs *post mortem* after Pyrrhus has killed Priam with a sword thrust 'lateri capulo tenus' (*A* 2.553; 'into his side up to the hilt'). Other translators preserve this detail. In both the original (1649) and revised (1654) versions of Ogilby's *Aeneid* Pyrrhus 'buries' his sword in Priam's 'side', and in Denham's *The Destruction of Troy* (1656) Pyrrhus 'sheathes' his sword in Priam's 'Bosom'.[1] Harrington's Pyrrhus, by contrast, 'strikes off old *Priam*'s head'.[2] It is tempting to connect this highly explicit reference to Charles I's execution to Harrington's status as one of the king's personal attendants in the late 1640s. According to John Aubrey, Harrington was 'on the Scaffold with the King when he was beheaded; and I have oftentimes heard him speake of King Charles I with the greatest zeale and passion imaginable, and that his death gave him so great a griefe that he contracted a Disease by it'.[3] Aubrey is the only source for this claim, but whether or not Harrington had actually been present on the scaffold the fortitude that the king was said to have displayed there likely informs Harrington's interpolated reference to Priam as 'full of courage and resolv'd' (*Essay*, p. 37) as he approaches Pyrrhus and harangues him for his dishonourable conduct.

Despite Harrington's personal history of royal service and the vivid commemoration of Charles I's execution in his *Aeneid* translation it would not be accurate to label Harrington a royalist. His time in the king's service in fact emerged from an association not with royalism, but republicanism. Harrington was only appointed a Gentleman of the Bedchamber after the king had been taken into Parliamentary captivity. Harrington's cousin, the republican Member of Parliament Sir James Harrington, was a member of the committee that oversaw the conditions of Charles's captivity; he wanted someone who shared his principles and would not get involved in organising any escape attempts to monitor the king's activities. Harrington's experience of royal service did not cause him to alter his political outlook. All surviving accounts attest to the warm relationship that Harrington had with Charles, but Aubrey records that the king had to ask Harrington not to speak of republics in his presence.[4]

Harrington's legacy as a republican primarily stems from the theories he articulates in his 1656 political tract *The Commonwealth of Oceana*. Harrington's attitudes in *Oceana*, and in his other political tracts, have historically been associated with the intellectual tradition that modern historians term classical republicanism. The influence of this tradition can certainly be found in Harrington's belief that only a republic makes it possible to have a society function according to the '*ancient Prudence*' of government *de jure*, where 'a Civil Society of men is instituted and preserved upon the foundation of common right or interest', in contrast to the '*modern Prudence*' of government *de facto*, where 'some man, or some few men, subject a City or a Nation, and rule it according unto his or their private interest'.[5] Yet Harrington's classical republicanism was not necessarily hostile to periods of oligarchic or autocratic rule, despite the value it placed on common interest: as Rachel Hammersley has discussed, Harrington's conviction that 'certain political functions are best performed by a single individual' when new systems of government were being established and a significant amount of change was required in a short period of time owed much to Machiavelli, one of the most significant classical republican thinkers.[6]

Comments that Harrington made about Virgil illuminate his thinking about the value of single-person, even monarchical, rule. In a prefatory poem to his translation of *Aeneid* 3–6 he refers to Virgil as his '*Leige Lord*' and '*Soveraign in Poetry*', and he clearly means these terms positively.[7] Elsewhere Harrington claims that 'a Parliament of Poets' could never 'have written VIRGIL'S *Æneis*'.[8] To set Virgil against a 'Parliament of Poets' intimates that his poetry was inimical to that mode of government and instead advocates a more absolutist mode of rule.

Harrington does not imply that the *Aeneid* would have been better had it been written by a collective. In poetry, as in politics, monarchism, even absolute monarchism, has its place for Harrington. Hammersley has also stressed that, unlike other classical republicans, Harrington held that power concentrated in one individual had the potential to be a permanent feature of a republic provided that this represented the will of the populace.[9] As Harrington both expresses sympathy towards Charles I and advocates a form of single-person rule within the broader concept of government by popular consent, his convictions are best described as 'autocratic republicanism'.

This chapter relates Harrington's reception of Virgil to his autocratic republicanism. It extends and revises David Norbrook's contention that Harrington 'Virgilianized republicanism' and 'republicanize[d] Virgil'.[10] The paratextual and interpolated material in Harrington's translations from Virgil establishes that he was especially interested in Virgil's references to Augustus' land redistribution programme at the end of the Roman civil war, and that Harrington believed this policy informed the conditions of his own society that led him to advocate republican rule. Where this conviction shapes Harrington's translations from the *Eclogues*, it is, however, largely absent from his *Aeneid* translations. Harrington's *Aeneid* serves only rarely as a vehicle for direct or sustained commentary on contemporary politics; the connection between Charles I and Priam is the exception, not the rule.

I first outline the Virgilian presence in Harrington's political writings, before considering his translations from the *Eclogues* and *Aeneid*. Harrington used Virgil in *Oceana* to indicate his belief that in the 1650s there was the potential to secure a permanent republican, even proto-democratic, settlement in the former Stuart kingdoms. He incorporated didactic elements into *Oceana* not only through adaptive quotation from Virgil, particularly passages from the *Aeneid* that contain descriptions of trees, but also by engaging with the tradition that thought of Virgil as a counsellor to a sovereign discussed in previous chapters. *Oceana* documents the establishment of an 'equal *Common-wealth*' (*Oceana*, p. 22) through the actions of Oceana's 'Lord Archon' or chief magistrate, Olphaeus Megaletor. Harrington clearly intended Megaletor to function as a stand-in for Cromwell, and he strengthened the connection by dedicating *Oceana* to Cromwell. The presence of a Cromwell figure and Harrington's presentation of a society governed by the principles of autocratic republicanism in *Oceana* parallel the prophetic as well as the didactic elements in other Virgilian writings from the period. Hammersley has argued that the references to the three former Stuart kingdoms in *Oceana* under pseudonyms 'underscore the fact that what is being presented is not England, Scotland, and Ireland as they actually were in 1656, but rather those places as they could have been if different political decisions had been taken in 1653', the year Cromwell became Protector.[11] Nonetheless, *Oceana* still contains an optative element, since it intimates that this alternative society could yet become reality in Cromwellian England. The following section considers the didactic function that the references to Virgil in *Oceana* serve in articulating Harrington's belief that Cromwell was uniquely placed to secure a commonwealth 'upon the mightiest foundation that any hath been laid from the beginning of the World unto this day' (*Oceana*, sig. C1v). It then addresses the Virgilian presence in *Oceana*'s comments on what the best means were of ensuring a smooth transfer of power in this commonwealth and what the ideal relationship between the state's army and its governing bodies should be. It also relates his comparisons of Cromwell's achievements to those of the individual to whom Harrington felt that Virgil himself directed his counsel, Augustus.

The Commonwealth of Oceana

In *Oceana* Harrington presents certain events from the 1640s and 1650s as entirely foreseeable, even inevitable, consequences of fault lines within the English political system. Harrington's reading of history was influenced not by a belief in providence, as was the case for several of the translators considered in this study, but by the central role that landownership played in his conception of political authority and legitimacy.[12] His modification of the classical tripartite taxonomy of power – rule by the one, the few and the many – was that each of these systems was only viable when the individual or group in question possessed the majority of the polity's land. For Harrington the balance of possession in England had passed out of the monarchy (the one) into the aristocracy (the few) during the period of Plantagenet rule, and under the Tudors had passed from the aristocracy to the people (the many). Whatever Harrington thought of Charles I as an individual, he believed that, whilst his actions may not have single-handedly caused the crisis in royal authority, they had helped exacerbate it. By ruling without Parliament for an extended period Charles had undermined his power by excluding the many from government. Harrington mourned the fact and manner of Charles I's death, but he did not advocate for the return of Stuart rule either under the Prince of Wales as Charles II or any other member of the dynasty. Harrington's opposition to the restoration of the Stuarts to their former kingdoms came from a belief that, due to the current balance of property, the type of monarchical rule that they had practised and hoped to restore was no longer sustainable.

Harrington held that securing long-term rule by the many that was focused on the common interest involved establishing the correct institutional *'superstructions'* (*Oceana*, p. 22). This attitude was one of the major ways in which Harrington's autocratic republicanism differed from that of his contemporaries who favoured oligarchic or monarchical rule. In addition to the royalists (and certain supporters of Cromwell) who were concerned with the rights of a dynasty, similar attitudes existed amongst a subset of republicans, the 'godly republicans', who wished to entrust power to those they felt possessed the necessary godly virtues.[13] For Harrington no individual or group of individuals could be relied upon to privilege the common good over private interest at all times, but establishing the right superstructions allowed the harnessing of self-interest to serve the interests of the state. Harrington argues that two superstructions are required to guarantee an equal commonwealth. The first is the law of an *'equal Agrarian'* that acts as 'a perpetuall Law establishing and preserving the ballance of *dominion*, by such a distribution, that no one man or number of men within the compasse of the *Few* or *Aristocracy*, can come to overpower the whole people by their possessions in Lands' (*Oceana*, p. 22). The equal Agrarian should be supported by an *'Equal Rotation'*, an 'equall *vicissitude* in Government, or *Succession* unto *Magistracy* conferred for such convenient *terms*, enjoying equall *vacations*, as take in the whole body by parts, succeeding others through the free *election* or *suffrage* of the *People*' (*Oceana*, pp. 22–3). Harrington advocates this equal rotation across three branches of government, with '*the Senate debating and proposing, the people resolving, and the Magistracy executing*' (*Oceana*, p. 23).

Harrington uses quotations from Virgil to underline the value of these superstructions. He has Megaletor claim:

the depth of a Common-wealth is the just height of it.

Ipsa hæret Scopulis et tantum vertice ad auras
Æthereas, quantum Radice ad Tartara, tendit.[14]

She raises up her head unto the Skies,
Neer as her Root unto the center lies.

(*Oceana*, p. 63)

The quotation comes from a passage where Aeneas' ability to withstand Anna's entreaties that he remain in Carthage is compared to an oak tree being buffeted by the winds (*A* 4.445–6; 'the oak clings to the crag, and as far as it lifts its top to the lofty skies, so far it strikes its roots down towards Tartarus'). This is the only occasion in *Oceana* when Harrington provides a translation for his quotations from Virgil, which suggests that he took particular pains to make the resonance of the comparison available to readers of *Oceana* who had no Latin. The translation's equivalent moment in his *Æneis* reads 'Yet with his head exalted will he dwell / As near to Heav'n, as go his roots to hell' (p. 37). The different gendering of the two translations is in accordance with the fact that Virgil uses the feminine noun 'quercus' to denote the oak tree of the simile. This allows Harrington in *Oceana* to invoke the tradition of personifying commonwealths as female, but in his *Aeneid* translation he wished to underline the connection between the oak tree and Aeneas' conduct.

It is not necessary to know the Virgilian origin of the Latin quotation to appreciate its application in *Oceana* – and although the passage from *Aeneid* 4 is translated Harrington retains his usual practice of not acknowledging the source of his quotations – but it forms part of a larger pattern in *Oceana* where Harrington adapts or repurposes Virgilian depictions of trees. Such moments serve the same purpose in *Oceana* as they do in the *Aeneid*: to discuss anxieties regarding a society's longevity and stability. In Virgil, these descriptions are largely concerned with questions of political succession and the transferral of power.[15] Such issues also inform Harrington's quotation of another Virgilian arboreal passage when arguing that an equal agrarian and equal rotation create a society that acts in the public interest and according to ancient prudence. *Oceana* states that, when they are implemented together, they provide the ideal combination of innovation and continuity:

> as a *Common-wealth* is a Government of *Lawes* and not of *Men*; so is this the *Principality* of the *Virtue*, and not of the *Man*; if that fail or set in one, it riseth in another, which is created his immediate Successour.
> (– *Uno avulso non deficit alter,*
> *Aureus et simili frondescit virga metallo.*)
> And this taketh away that vanity from under the Sun, which is an errour proceeding more or less from all other Rulers under heaven but an equal *Common-wealth*.
>
> (*Oceana*, p. 24)

The quotation slightly adapts the Sibyl's account of the self-regenerating Golden Bough that Aeneas must present to secure his passage into the Underworld (*A* 6.143–4; 'primo avulso non deficit alter / aureus, et simili frondescit virga metallo'; 'when the first is torn away, a second fails not, golden too, and the spray bears a leaf of the same metal'). The adaptation supports Norbrook's contention that the quotation 'harnesses the magical mystique of monarchy to a demystified republican order' as it preserves and adapts Virgil's emphasis on continuity.[16] By changing 'primo' ('first') to 'uno' ('one') he makes the meaning less hierarchical or dynastic: one replaces another, rather than a second bough replacing the original. Office holders in an equal commonwealth are, like the Golden Bough, self-regenerating. The production of successors is uncontested, possesses political legitimacy, and does not engender any dispute or suffering. An equal rotation would avert the succession crises that affect systems of government based on wholesale change, such as the accession of a monarch or the advent of a new parliament. Removing these pressure points on governmental institutions also secures rule for the common good over rule that serves the interests of an individual or faction.

The society that Harrington advocates in *Oceana* ensures that his reference to the Golden Bough critiques the contemporary political situation. The succession from Stuart monarchy to Cromwellian Protectorate via the Commonwealth was anything but immediate and painless, and so did not follow the precedent of a self-regenerating polity. Each of those changes was largely instigated through military force on Cromwell's directive, but Harrington's criticism was not directed at Cromwell as the commander of an army, even though he associated such power with monarchical authority. The presence of a chief magistrate means that Oceana has the potential to be governed under a figure with the powers and authority of a monarch, but this magistrate would have this status only if the Senate proposed that he be awarded it, and the decision was resolved (that is, passed) by the Popular Assembly. This situation reversed the means by which Cromwell came to hold supreme military power in the Interregnum and his own relationship with successive Parliaments by the mid-1650s; they largely derived their authority from Cromwell, not the other way round. The first half of that decade saw the most destabilising aspects of innovation, through wholesale changes in the structure of government, and of continuity, through Cromwell's ability to abolish and establish these structures.

Oceana's discussion of political succession recognises that, even though by the mid-1650s Cromwell (with the army) was capable of providing some form of stable rule, the emphasis remained on the individual over the institution. To use Harrington's own terminology, the necessary superstructions had not been put in place. Blair Worden has established that Harrington began work on *Oceana* in 1651–2,[17] so the text's origins indicate that Harrington initially concerned himself with the succession of Parliaments during the Commonwealth (1649–53), not the Protectorate (1653–8). By the time of the text's publication in 1656, though, such observations could easily apply to the question of

Cromwell's successor, either as Protector or as the head of an alternative form of government. The question of the succession was a renewed area of concern at the moment of *Oceana*'s publication, due to the preparation in the same period of the Humble Petition and Advice that granted Cromwell the power to name his own successor.[18] As this was another right usually associated with monarchy, *Oceana* acknowledges that the foundation of a dynastic House of Cromwell seemed increasingly likely.

Harrington's system allows for the succession of the chief magistrate to proceed on the grounds of primogeniture, but, as with the command of the army, it would have to be both proposed and resolved by the legislature. It could not be decreed by the magistrate himself. Nor could any new chief magistrate assume that he would inherit the same powers that his predecessor held; he would need to have any supreme power granted by the governmental superstructions. Although Harrington refers to Cromwell as 'His Highnesse' on the title page of *Oceana* his thinking was distinct from the Virgilian-infused Protectoral Augustanism represented by Waller's optative celebration of Cromwell as the first of a new monarchical dynasty.[19] For Harrington the chances that the Cromwellian succession would possess the necessary legitimacy, privilege public over private interest and imitate the self-replenishing quality of the Golden Bough seemed remote. The utopia established by Cromwell's proxy in *Oceana*, by contrast, had no such concerns, or the potential for such, in either the short or long term.

Further anxieties about the legitimacy of the Protectorate emerge in *Oceana* when Harrington has Megaletor, on establishing the equal agrarian and equal rotation, immediately resign his position as Lord Archon. Megaletor's initial surrender of power to a Parliamentary body inverts Cromwell's use of military force in 1653 to dissolve the Rump Parliament and the Nominated Assembly (the 'Barebones Parliament') that was intended to replace it, and his installation as Lord Protector later that same year. Megaletor is only persuaded to resume his powers once the Senate advocates that he do so, and following the approval of this policy in the Popular Assembly (*Oceana*, sigs Pp2v–Qq3v). The final section of *Oceana*, the Corollary, states that after Megaletor was recalled to the position of Chief Archon he held that office for fifty years. As the necessary superstructions were in place there was no anxiety over the succession on Megaletor's death, since his achievements in founding an equal commonwealth had made his role obsolete. Where Megaletor was memorialised with a colossal equestrian statue by a grateful nation, Cromwell could not be said to have commanded the same universal respect and love in Protectorate England (to say nothing of Scotland or Ireland). J. C. Davis has read the shift in focus in the Corollary from past to future as part of Harrington's engagement with the prose romance tradition,[20] but it is also helpful to see this section of the text as Harrington's engagement with the tradition of the *vates*-cum-counsellor and with the optative practices of his Virgilian contemporaries discussed in previous chapters. He outlines the version of the future that he would like to come to pass in a way that acknowledges that the present circumstances make it extremely unlikely.

Such discrepancies between Cromwell and Megaletor, and between the likely futures of Britain and Oceana, support Worden's argument that Megaletor 'is an anti-Cromwell, whose creation opposes fiction to fact' and that 'The Archon may be Cromwell as Cromwell, the arch-hypocrite, represents himself, but he is the reverse of what Cromwell is'.[21] For Worden, the dedication of *Oceana* to Cromwell as Lord Protector is 'an anti-dedication, as the Archon is an anti-Cromwell'.[22] There is, no doubt, a satirical aspect to Harrington's Megaletor, but he is not only a means of indicating that Cromwell's installation as Lord Protector and the country's drift towards monarchical rule represents thwarted utopian hopes and republican disillusion. Jonathan Scott finds *Oceana* 'furnishing Cromwell with the means for fulfilment of his own frequently stated ambitions' and reads it as a 'republican act of Protectoral counsel'.[23] It is possible to combine Worden and Scott's approaches, since Harrington's Megaletor combines satire with both encouragement and optative moral instruction. As Harrington frequently cites Francis Bacon in *Oceana* he would likely have been familiar with Bacon's 'On Praise'.[24] His citations indicate that he used the 1625 edition of Bacon's *Essays*, and the version of 'On Praise' in that volume claims:

> Some *Praises* come of good Wishes, and Respects, which is a Forme due in Civilitie to Kings, and Great Persons, *Laudando præcipere* ['praising in advance']; When by telling Men, what they are, they represent to them, what they should be.[25]

Harrington's dedication of *Oceana* to Cromwell and his use of Megaletor as a Cromwellian avatar make most sense as examples of *laudando praecipere*. He praises Cromwell for what he hopes he will achieve in order to prompt him into validating that praise. The technique thus parallels Fanshawe's practice of providing the Prince of Wales with contingent panegyric and prophecy during the civil wars and Interregnum.[26] But where Fanshawe largely emphasises the Prince's potential to secure a national revival, Harrington's focus is on Cromwell's squandering of his potential and the opportunities that he has missed to establish an equal commonwealth. 'Praecipere' can mean 'to instruct' and 'to admonish' as well as 'to receive in advance',[27] and Harrington's praise of Cromwell/Megaletor is more censorious than laudatory. Nonetheless, the use of *laudando praecipere* in *Oceana* intimates that Cromwell still has the potential to emulate Megaletor, even if his chance of doing so was becoming increasingly unlikely on account of the re-establishment of autocratic, dynastic monarchical rule. What in the mid-1650s reads as satire still had the chance to become panegyric.

Within the context of Virgil's early modern reception, the most Virgilian aspect of *Oceana* lies in its evocation of precedents that should be followed and avoided as part of the advice the text proffers to a head of state. Like the work of his contemporary Virgilians, Harrington engages with the tradition that Virgil used Aeneas as a touchstone for Augustus to test himself against to provide him with this advice. Hammersley has noted that 'most of the citations from the *Aeneid* in *Oceana* are placed in the mouth of the Lord Archon, perhaps deliberately implying a parallel between him and Virgil's Augustus and between England and Rome'.[28] Again, the use of Augustus as a point of comparison for a contemporary head of state has parallels in the writings of Harrington's contemporaries, particularly the works of Fanshawe, but for Harrington Augustus was not as unequivocally positive a figure or example to follow as he was in those works. Where Fanshawe presents an idealised Augustus, Harrington acknowledges the more problematic aspects of Augustus' reputation. Nor does Harrington compare Cromwell to Augustus via Aeneas in the way that several of his royalist contemporaries do when hailing either Charles I or his son as a second or potential Augustus; his comparisons are more direct.

Oceana is influenced by Harrington's sense that in the 1650s Cromwell was someone who, like Augustus at the end of the Roman civil wars, had come to hold (by various and not necessarily admirable means) sufficient power to enact the social reforms that could lead to the foundation of a permanent ideal society. That is precisely what Virgil's Jupiter states he has granted to the Romans under Augustus: 'his ego nec metas rerum nec tempora pono; / imperium sine fine dedi' (*A* 1.278–9; 'for these I set no bounds in space or time; but have given empire without end'). Yet (for reasons discussed later in this chapter) Harrington felt that the flaws in Augustus' policies, principally his land resettlement programme, meant that, although the Principate's superstructions were able to last for centuries, it ultimately found itself as time-bound and subject to decay as other imperfect societies. Harrington intimates that, unless Cromwell heeds his advice, the Protectorate will experience the same decline. *Oceana* quotes from the arboreal passages of the *Aeneid* to acknowledge the Protectorate's shallow roots.

In *Oceana* Harrington sees himself as providing Cromwell with the chance to learn from Augustus' failed opportunity, and advising him on how to make amends for errors made at the start of the Interregnum. He has Megaletor draw on another part of Jupiter's prophecy of Roman greatness to express the potential his utopian society has in terms of expansion and longevity. Megaletor tells the members of the consulting assembly:

> You cannot plant an Oak in a flowerpot: She must have earth for her root, and heaven for her branches.
> *Imperium Oceano famam quæ terminet astris.*
>
> (*Oceana*, p. 255)

The choice of metaphor links the quotation to his use of arboreal terminology in his other Virgil quotations. Here, however, the Virgilian line refers not to parts of a tree but to Augustus' achievements as emperor. Harrington slightly adapts Jupiter's prediction that Augustus is one 'imperium Oceano, famam qui terminet astris' (*A* 1.287; 'who shall extend his empire to the ocean, his glory to the stars'). As in his translation of the tree simile from *Aeneid* 4, 'Quæ' for 'qui' regenders the subject from male to female in accordance with the tenor and vehicle of the metaphor, but it also makes a more subtly republican point. In Virgil the Roman empire extends to the boundaries of the known world on account of a heroic individual, Augustus. In Megaletor's speech this expansion is the result of a heroic institution, the equal commonwealth of Oceana, whose name Harrington is able to recall via the presence of 'Oceano' in the quotation. The comparisons between Augustus, Megaletor and Cromwell that are the result of a repurposing of Virgilian panegyric allow Harrington to stress a continuity between Augustus and Cromwell, only this continuity is their shared status as leaders who did not capitalise on their chance to instigate and propagate an equal commonwealth founded on ancient prudence.

As mentioned above, Harrington saw Augustus' consolidation of a land redistribution programme that had begun in the final period of the Roman Republic, and that was subsequently propagated by Augustus' successors, as having laid the conditions for the power imbalance between the one and the many in seventeenth-century England. Harrington's translations of Virgil's *Eclogues* 1 and 9 (1658), which form the focus of the following section, reflect his interest in an equal agrarian, as these two poems have long been read as commentaries on this programme. In the translations, Harrington preserves his interest in the original historical context of the *Eclogues*, but also includes details which point to the England of the civil wars and Interregnum to examine his long-standing interest in the relationship between landownership and power. As was the case for the other translators considered in this study, Harrington signals his political interests through his interpolations in the Virgilian original and the translation's paratextual material.

Two of Virgil's Eclogues

The 'Argument' that prefaces Harrington's translations of *Eclogues* 1 and 9 foregrounds the poems' relevance to his interests in the Augustan land programme:

> The occasion of writing this Eclogue and the next was this, When after the death of *Julius Cæsar*, slain in the Senate, *Augustus* his son, by a war against them that slew him, and against *Anthony*, had obtained the victory of them all, he divided the lands of the inhabitants of *Cremona* among his souldiers, meerly because they had quarterd his enemies, whom they were not able to resist, and the lands of *Cremona* not sufficing for this use, he also divided those of *Mantua* after the same manner, for no other reason then that *Mantua* was neerest *Cremona*. *Virgil* being an inhabitant of *Mantua*, and coming by this means to lose his patrimony, repaired unto *Rome*, and there by the favour of the great ones, obtained such particular respect, that he alone continu'd his ancient possession; which nevertheless was siezed by *Arius* the Centurion, who took it so ill to be removed, that if *Virgil* had not escaped his fury by plunging himself into the river *Mincius*, the Centurion had kill'd him.
> (*Essay*, sig. A4r)

This biographical reading of the two poems is recorded in most contemporary critical editions of Virgil, and in other translations of the period.[29] That said, many of the additions that Harrington includes in the translations themselves challenge a straightforwardly historicist reading. In *Eclogue* 1 Tityrus states, with no prompt from the Latin, that he travelled from the countryside to Rome 'when I saw the souldiers come, / And here misuse us so' (*Essay*, sig. A5r). Although the Argument provides a historical interpretation of this addition Harrington's first readers were still likely to have read it through more recent events. They would have found close resonances between the events described in the two poems and the programme of renewed sequestrations and confiscations of land from the royalists that was coordinated by Cromwell's military government under the major generals (1655–7). Such policies, largely a response to the royalist uprisings of 1655, also represented an attempt to acquire the assets necessary to finance the army.[30] Cromwell, like Augustus, redistributed land that he had taken from those who had quartered his enemies to prevent his supporters turning against him.

Harrington also encourages a contemporary application of his *Eclogues* through their setting. At points Harrington includes more specific references to the Italian countryside than are present in the Virgilian original: when in *Eclogue* 9 Virgil's Lycidas refers to his and Moeris' arrival 'in urbem' (*E* 9.62; 'in the city'), Harrington's claims 'We shall be time enough at *Mantua*' (*Essay*, sig. A8v). Elsewhere, however, he combines Italian with English pastoral by translating 'undique' (*E* 1.11; 'everywhere') as 'throughout the shire' (*Essay*, sig. A5v). Harrington's Lycidas uses the language of 1630s English court panegyric to refer to the shepherd Menalcas beseeching 'the gallant Courtiers' (*Essay*, sig. A6r) in vain to prevent his lands from being dispossessed.[31] The reference to gallantry occurs only in passing, but it nonetheless reaffirms Harrington's position as someone who was not hostile to courtiers and people in royal service, even if he held that their lack of landownership had left them politically impotent. In Harrington's *Eclogues*, as in Protectorate England under the rule of the major generals, it is the army commanders, not the aristocracy, who can effect change.

Other changes that Harrington makes to the *Eclogues* to forge further links between Augustan Italy and the Cromwellian Protectorate show the influence of his political theories. They suggest that the contemporary balance of landownership in England has its origins in the Augustan land confiscations. Virgil's Meliboeus congratulates Tityrus for having his farm restored to him by saying 'tua rura manebunt' (*E* 1.46; 'these lands will be yours'). Harrington translates this as 'thy land / Remains for ever at thy blest command' (*Essay*, sigs A5r–A6v), which adds the concept of permanent ownership. Harrington devotes especial attention to the policy in the 'A Note upon the fore-going *Eclogues*' that is printed after his translation of *Eclogue* 9 (*Essay*, sigs A8r–B1v). The note also stresses the continuity between Virgil's Rome and Harrington's England that the interpolated material in the translations had already highlighted. In accordance with the belief he had previously expressed in *Oceana* that Augustus' rule instigated the decline from ancient to modern prudence, Harrington claims that the redistribution of land amongst the veterans of Augustus' army ensured that 'the *Roman* Empire was never founded upon a sufficient ballance of absolute Monarchy' (sig. A8r). Successive rulers made these tracts of confiscated land hereditary instead of being in the gift of the emperor. Not only did this shift the balance of power from the one to the many, it also made the emperor dependent on the needs and demands of the army, placing 'the ballance or foundation of the *Roman* Empire in a matter of eight or ten thousand Prætorians [the emperor's personal bodyguard]' (sig. A8r). Attempts by later emperors to overcome this dependence by employing the Goths and Vandals as mercenaries precipitated the empire's fall, and were the origins of 'government by King, Lords, and Commons, throughout Christendom' (sig.

B1v). Harrington uses the *Eclogues* translations and their accompanying material to show that the fall of the Roman empire was seeded at its foundation, and that its lack of the necessary superstructions later birthed England's system of government.

Harrington's account of the relationship between the head of state and the army in 'A Note upon the fore-going *Eclogues*' reflects his reading of recent events through the prism of antiquity. The Roman praetorians were, like Cromwell's army, primarily loyal to an individual rather than the state, and so were liable to act according to private interest (first the emperor's, then subsequently their own) instead of the common good. Harrington translates these *Eclogues* as a reminder of the difficulty of demobilising an army without fomenting discord in either the civilian or military population. The same issue dominated English politics during the 1650s: many of the key events of that decade can be seen as the result of an army looking for a state that could pay it off.

Harrington preserves Virgil's emphasis on the arbitrariness of the land redistribution and the suffering that it causes. Reading *Eclogue* 9 immediately after *Eclogue* 1, the poem with which it is paired in 'ring-composition' readings of the collection,[32] also indicates that the confidence the fortunate shepherd Tityrus expresses in *Eclogue* 1 regarding the preservation of his patrimony may be misplaced. *Eclogue* 9 tells how Menalcas – who like Tityrus has traditionally been interpreted as a proxy for Virgil – had his lands preserved at the orders of the emperor but still ended up having them confiscated by one of the emperor's former soldiers. Between the end of *Eclogue* 1 and the start of *Eclogue* 9 power has shifted from the emperor to the army. As in *Oceana*, Harrington uses Virgil both to look back to the transition from monarchy to republic and to look forward to the possible collapse of the Protectorate. The likeliest causes of such a collapse, for Harrington, seem to be Cromwell losing the support of the army, or Cromwell's death leading to the succession of a new individual as head of state, who lacked Cromwell's capacity to keep the army under control and have them accept the political status quo. Harrington's *Eclogues* were published in 1658, but even though Cromwell died in September of that year and his health had been in decline for a number of months Harrington's anticipation of the event seems more speculative than a response to specific circumstances.[33] It transpired that, although the succession from Oliver to Richard Cromwell initially appeared to bypass the concerns about stable transferrals of power that Harrington had raised in *Oceana*, the collapse of the Protectorate soon afterwards was to a large degree the result of Richard Cromwell's inability to command the loyalty of the army.[34]

What took centuries in the Roman Principate took only months in the Cromwellian Protectorate.

Harrington's *Eclogues* are clearly influenced by his theories regarding the connection between landownership and political power and the recent period of direct military rule in England. Yet, where *Oceana* uses Virgil to outline the changes that were possible to his present society, Harrington's *Eclogues* are more concerned with investigating the factors that caused that society to come into being. His translations from the *Aeneid* (1658; 1659) continue this use of Virgil for the purposes of historical retrospection, but they contain significantly fewer examples of engagement with political matters. In fact, as the following section demonstrates, the trajectory of Harrington's reception of Virgil reverses that of an author considered earlier in this study, Sir John Denham. In Denham's Virgilian works an interest in aesthetics is displaced by a desire to provide political commentary. Harrington's initial encounters with Virgil are highly politically engaged and are addressed to a head of state, but his subsequent engagement with Virgil's poetry concerns itself primarily with literary, scholarly and purely historical matters.

Virgil's Æneis

As with the *Eclogues*, the most distinctive elements of Harrington's *Aeneid* translations can be discerned through their interpolated and paratextual material. The longest individual expansion in Harrington's *Aeneid* translation comes in the passage from *Aeneid* 2 which occurs immediately after the murder of Priam discussed at the beginning of this chapter:

> Which words by <u>unrelenting</u> *Pyrrhus* said,
> The other hand <u>strikes off old *Priam*'s head</u>.
> <u>The sons of *Atreus* with equal rage</u>
> <u>Succeeding *Pyrrhus* spare nor sex, nor age,</u>
> <u>Till in their blood upon the altar lay</u>
> <u>By thoughtless *Priam* willing *Hecuba*,</u>
> <u>Extinguishing the flames they us'd to feed,</u>
> <u>By these an hundred of their off-spring bleed</u>.
> Such was the end of *Priamus*, when he
> The ruine of his realm had liv'd to see;
> The potent Prince to whom all *Asia* gave
> Obedience <u>is not allow'd a grave</u>;
> His mighty trunk upon the shore <u>is thrown</u>
> A <u>common</u> carkass, <u>and a corse unknown</u>.

(*Essay*, p. 38)

Given the broader tradition in seventeenth-century translations of Virgil of adapted and interpolated material representing interventions in contemporary political debates, and Harrington making decapitation the cause of Priam's demise to remind readers of Charles I's death, it would be reasonable to assume that the rest of this passage was also intended as political commentary. It is precisely the lack of application to recent events that makes the remainder of this passage so striking. The references to the fates of the House of Priam depart significantly from the experiences of Charles I's family in the aftermath of his execution. Not only that, they have no prompt in the Virgilian narrative or the broader classical tradition of the post-Trojan fates of the House of Priam. In Virgil, Polites is the only child of Priam and Hecuba to die at the altar. In Harrington it is the entire dynasty that is destroyed. The reference to their hundred offspring seems inspired by an earlier reference to 'Hecubam centumque nurus' (*A* 2.501; 'Hecuba and her hundred daughters') which lacks a translation at the equivalent moment in Harrington's version, but the deaths of these individuals do not form part of the Virgilian narrative. Harrington's decision to have Hecuba die, not (as was usual) survive the fall of Troy, represents an even greater rewriting of the established tradition.

The nature of Harrington's interpolation lends credence to his claim in the 'Preface to the Reader' in his 1659 *Aeneid* 3–6 translation that translating Virgil '*hath not been my Work, but my Play*' (*Æneis*, sig. A3r), and a move away from his political concerns. In fact, of all the other additions to the original text across the two volumes of his Virgil not already discussed in this chapter, only one contains political commentary. It comes in his account of Dido and Anna sacrificing to 'legiferae Cereri' (*A* 4.58; 'Ceres the law-giver') at the beginning of *Aeneid* 4. In Harrington's version this becomes

> Lawgiving Ceres *that inventing corn*
> *Is she, of whom bright Empire first was born,*
> *While men, for Acorns tasting bread, began*
> *To parcel fields by Laws Agrarian,*
> *And thence (as lots have chanc'd to rise or fall)*
> *Become the prize of One, or Few, or All.*
>
> (*Æneis*, p. 21)

Harrington draws attention to this passage in his preface: 'For the Verses in the fourth Book, concerning the *Agrarian*, they are according to *Servius* upon the place, without whose Commentary it is not rightly to be understood, so at least by other translators it should seem.'[35] Harrington also adds a marginal gloss 'Servius' to the passage in question to connect it to his preface and uses italics to indicate its status as an interpolation. Harrington, in fact, expands Servius' text:

> leges enim ipsa dicitur invenisse, nam et sacra 'thesmophoria vocantur'. sed hoc ideo fingitur quia, ante inventum frumentum a Cerere, passim homines sine lege vagabantur; quae feritas interrupta est invento usu frumentorum, postquam ex agrorum divisione nata sunt iura.

> ('she [Ceres] herself is said to have invented laws and her sacred rites are called *thesmophoria*. But this is supposed to have happened because, before grain was invented by Ceres, men wandered far and wide without laws; this savagery was broken off when the cultivation of grain was acquired, and after that laws arose from the division of fields.')[36]

Servius does not make any connection between the agrarian law and the shift in power between the one, the few and the many that is the subject of the extract's final couplet. The references in Harrington's translation are clearly inspired by the theories that underpin his political convictions. In addition, although Servius does refer to land distribution, the cornerstone of Harrington's political thinking, his commentary lacks the reference to the arbitrariness of this process that is present in Harrington's translation. The addition is poised to invite a parallel with the political situation in 1650s England, but unlike Harrington's references in his *Eclogues* to Augustus' agrarian laws and the arbitrary manner in which land was redistributed, the Ceres passage in his *Aeneid* makes no connection between the classical past and the Cromwellian present. Harrington here reminds readers of his political opinions, but does not then apply them to his own present moment.

The only other addition to the narrative outside of the Ceres passage to which Harrington draws his reader's attention in his preface is more concerned with aesthetics than politics. There Harrington claims 'I have added out of *Ronsard* the famous similitude of the Caterpillar, both to set it by those of *Virgil*, which *Paquier* saith it excels, and to enrich our Language with it.'[37] The similitude in question comes as the Trojan fleet leaves Actium:

> linquere tum portus iubeo et considere transtris;
> certatim socii feriunt mare et aequora verrunt.
>
> (*A* 3.289–90)

('Then I bid them leave the harbour and man the benches; with rival strokes my comrades lash the sea and sweep the waters.')

> Then with <u>the milder season</u> quit the shores,
> Salute the <u>easier</u> furrow with our Oares,

> *As Caterpillars with a thousand feet,*
> *The pleated bark of trees in Summer greet.*
>
> (*Æneis*, p. 8)

As in the Ceres passage Harrington italicises the lines of non-Virgilian origin and adds the name of this material's author in a marginal note. Harrington's use of Ronsard has previously been recorded,[38] but there has been no attempt until now to trace it to its source. The reference to 'Paquier' in the preface establishes its provenance. Étienne Pasquier (1529–1615) was a legal theorist and literary critic, and in a passage added to a posthumously published (1621) edition of his *Les Recherches de La France* he considers Virgil and Ronsard's respective depictions of the natural world. He quotes the aforementioned lines from the *Aeneid* alongside the following passage from Ronsard's *La Franciade* (pub. 1572), a Virgilian epic on the founding of the French nation by Hector's son Astyanax (to whom Ronsard gives the name Francus), to establish Ronsard's superiority over Virgil:

> Ceste Navire également tiree,
> S'alloit trainant dessus l'onde azuree
> A dos rompu, ainsi que par les bois,
> Sur le printemps au retour des beaux mois,
> Va la chenille, errante à toute force
> Avec cent pieds sur le plis d'une escorce.[39]

('This ship, drawing steadily along, made its way over the blue waves and their broken backs, as in the woods, in spring, when the fine months return, and the caterpillar goes along, in brave wandering, with a hundred feet on the folds of the bark.')

The incorporation of this reference suggests that Harrington had devoted at least some time to the study of poetry and poetics, although this study may not have been that extensive. I have not found any further quotations or imitations of Ronsard in Harrington's writing, and he may only have known the parts of Ronsard that were quoted by Pasquier. He only needed to have read *Recherches* to include this reference in his translation.

Pasquier's *Recherches* is primarily a work of history, and the remainder of Harrington's interpolations are more concerned with antiquarian matters than with literature or aesthetics. Harrington, like other early modern translators, incorporates material from scholarly commentaries on Virgil into his translation to fill out somewhat exiguous references in the text to historical or mythological events with which seventeenth-century readers would not necessarily have been as familiar as their Roman counterparts. These references, like the imitation of Ronsard via Pasquier, help to establish the books that Harrington consulted in the course of preparing his translation, or rather those that he had used when writing his political tracts, which he then capitalised on in a largely apolitical manner when translating Virgil. This tendency can be seen in the reference to 'Tarquinios reges', (*A* 6.817; 'the Tarquinian kings'), who feature in the Parade of Heroes in the Underworld. The kings in question are Tarquinius Priscus and Tarquinius Superbus, the fifth and seventh kings of Rome. Harrington's translation gives more extensive details about these figures than are present in the original, and also names the monarch who followed Priscus and preceded Superbus, Servius Tullius:

> Then *Priscus*, by the Eagle taught his fate,
> Then *Servius*, second Founder of the State;
> And last of all comes *Tarquin*.
>
> (*Æneis*, p. 84)

One of Harrington's political tracts shows how he came to be aware of the myth that an eagle told Priscus that he would become king of Rome:

> We find it recorded by *Livy*, of *Tarquinius Priscus*, and of *Servius Tullius*, that before either of them was King, the one had his hat taken off, and carried up by an Eagle; the other a flame sitting upon his forehead: by which it was firmly believed, that each of them was designed of the Gods to be King.[40]

Quotations from Livy are second in frequency only to those from Virgil in Harrington's writings, and they often serve to advance his political attitudes, but in this instance he uses his knowledge of the author only for exegetical purposes.[41] Virgil's reference to the last kings of Rome provided a clear opportunity for Harrington to articulate his views regarding kingship, governance and the origins of political structures, especially with the reference to Servius Tullius as a founder of a state, but in this instance it was an opportunity that he chose to forego.

The interpolations in Harrington's *Aeneid* have drawn less critical attention than the passages in his source material that he chose not to translate.[42] Like the interpolations, however, the omissions shed little light on his political status as an autocratic republican who was frustrated by Cromwell's failure to found an equal commonwealth. The prefatory poem 'The Translator to the Reader' draws attention to several moments that Harrington has omitted:

> Thou never shalt perswade me to inform
> Our Age, *Æneas* in thy greatest storm
> Could raise both palmes, though to the Gods; one hand
> At last had hold, or there he could not stand.

> Nor is it in a Picture to devise
> How *Hector* round his *Troy* should be dragg'd thrice.[43]

Here and in the rest of 'The Translator to the Reader' Harrington focuses on moments in the narrative that take up very little space in the text, sometimes no more than a single word. Such omissions are commonplace in the other Virgil translations in this period, but no other translator draws attention to them in the manner that Harrington does here. Although some of the excisions to which Harrington refers in the poem are minor they nonetheless hint at more substantial interpretative issues. Harrington's reference to Hector is to one of the images that tell of the 'Iliacas ... pugnas' (*A* 1.456; 'the battles of Ilium') that decorate the doors of Juno's Carthaginian temple: 'ter circum Iliacos raptaverat Hectora muros ... Achilles' (*A* 1.483–4; 'three times had Achilles dragged Hector around the walls of Troy'). The qualms about the limits of artistic representation that he expresses in his prefatory poem correlate to his claim '*For Life unto a Picture to derive / Is hard, but harder from a Picture Life*' (*Æneis*, p. 48), which has no prompt in Virgil's Latin.

Harrington's concern with plausibility and accuracy may illuminate why he makes his most extensive cuts during moments in the *Aeneid* which involve non-human agents. He expresses a noticeable scepticism towards dream visions, supernatural forces and episodes where divinities disguise themselves as humans in order to influence mortals' behaviour. He cuts in their entirety Mercury's second speech to Aeneas telling him to flee Carthage (*A* 4.556–83; Mercury's earlier speech is also significantly abbreviated); Dido's protracted death and Juno sending Iris down to earth to relieve her suffering (*A* 4.672–705); Iris disguising herself as the matron Beroe to exhort the Trojan women to set fire to the fleet (*A* 5.641–53); the spirit of Anchises visiting Aeneas in a dream to give him his instructions on how to enter the Underworld (*A* 5.721–49); and Somnus disguising himself as Phorbus to encourage Palinurus to sleep (*A* 5.840–51). Such cuts may also respond to the discussion regarding what constituted the fittest subject for modern epic in Davenant's preface to *Gondibert*. Harrington's excisions chime with Davenant's reference in his survey of epic poetry at the beginning of the *Gondibert* preface to those who have criticised Virgil for his use of 'conversation with Gods and Ghosts' in the *Aeneid*, which 'sometimes deprives us of those naturall probabilities in Story, which are instructive to humane life'.[44] Harrington may also have been influenced by the response to Davenant by Thomas Hobbes that was often published alongside the *Gondibert* preface. The influence of Hobbes's political thought on

Harrington is now well established;[45] the material Harrington chose not to include in his *Æneis* suggests that Hobbes may have helped to shape his approach towards literature too, since in his response to the *Gondibert* preface Hobbes praised Davenant's decision to write an epic without any supernatural machinery.[46] Lucan's republican epic the *Pharsalia* also provided a precedent for a classical text that lacks this feature, so the extensive cuts that Harrington makes to the supernatural elements of his *Aeneid* tradition could additionally represent his reading of Virgil's poem through a republican lens.

Harrington could not, of course, remove the supernatural machinery of the *Aeneid* altogether without fatally compromising his translation; the gods play too significant a role in the narrative to allow that. At certain points when he retains (rather than removes) the moments when mortal characters are speaking to a disguised divinity, however, Harrington omits the moments of foreshadowing in Virgil's narrative that reveal this to be the case. When Aeneas and Achates encounter a nymph on the Carthaginian shore who says she is a member of Diana's hunting party (*A* 1.314–401) readers of Virgil's *Aeneid* know that the nymph is Venus in disguise. Yet, in Harrington's translation, Venus' identity is only made clear on her departure (*Essay*, p. 13). This makes the encounter a supernatural one only retrospectively, so readers are more likely to experience the events of the poem according to the sensibilities of the mortal protagonists than those of the narrator.

Harrington also has Aeneas himself adopt this strategy of not disclosing important information to his interlocutors, which gives a greater immediacy to his narrative. When telling Dido about Sinon's role in the fall of Troy Virgil's Aeneas says 'accipe nunc Danaum insidias et crimine ab uno / disce omnis' (*A* 2.65–6; 'Hear now the treachery of the Greeks and from a single crime learn the wickedness of all'). Harrington's translation lacks this address. Harrington also omits Aeneas' reference to Sinon speaking 'ficto pectore' (*A* 2.107; 'with feigned emotion'). Sinon's true status is thus delayed until the later reference to 'the fraud and perjuries of Sinon' (*Essay*, p. 29, translating 'talibus insidiis periurique arte Sinonis' (*A* 2.195; 'through such snares and craft of forsworn Sinon')).

An exception to this practice of withholding information comes in a foreshadowing of Priam's death in Harrington's translation of *Aeneid* 1. Whilst he removes the description of Hector's death on the temple doors at Carthage, Harrington retains the reference in the same passage to 'Atriadas Priamumque et saevum ambobus Achillem' (*A* 1.458; 'the sons of Atreus, and Priam, and Achilles, fierce in his anger against both'). But Harrington translates the line as 'Here *Agamemnon*, there *Achilles* stood; / Here Priam sacrificed in his blood' (*Essay*, p. 15). It is unclear in Virgil's *Aeneid* how Priam is depicted on the temple doors, but the references to sacrifice and bloodshed in Harrington's *Aeneid* anticipate Priam's death on his ancestral altar at the hands of Pyrrhus. There is nothing here that connects the Priam of Harrington's *Aeneid* 1 to the Charles-as-Priam of his *Aeneid* 2, so if the interpolation was intended to function as a means of commemorating the king it could have been recognised as such only by Harrington himself, or by somebody reading the translation for the second time.

Few people, however, have read Harrington's Virgil even once. His translations have never attracted a wide readership: neither the 1658 nor the 1659 volume has ever been reprinted. Harrington initially planned to translate the *Aeneid* in its entirety: the full title of the 1658 edition is *An Essay Upon two of Virgil's Eclogues, and Two Books of his Æneis (If this be not enough) Towards the Translation of the whole*. The lack of a version of *Aeneid* 7–12 by Harrington has not generally been considered a source of regret. His translation is an uneven one, in large part because of the sharp discrepancies in tone, which do not always appear deliberate or controlled. Harrington transposes certain words or phrases as literally as possible: 'denounced ire' for 'denuntiat iras', 'obscurer fame' for 'fama obscura', 'inextricable errour' for 'inextricabilis error'.[47] This can lead to infelicities of expression, such as when Harrington translates a reference to the Golden Bough as 'auricomos ... fetus' (*A* 6.141; 'golden-haired fruitage') as 'goldy-locked sprout' (*Æneis*, p. 65). Other passages use a noticeably more paraphrastic and informal mode of expression. At the fall of Troy the Greek soldier Androgeos, mistaking Aeneas and his band of soldiers for Greeks, rebukes them for what he interprets as hesitancy: 'You creep out of your wooden shells like snails!' (*Essay*, p. 34, translating 'festinate, viri! nam quae tam sera moratur / segnities?' (*A* 2.373–4; 'Hurry, men; what sloth keeps you back so long?')). Such diction is far removed from the 'Thunder-thumping way of Grandsire *Virgil*' that Harrington refers to in one of his political tracts,[48] but it does introduce an element of pathos, since Androgeos' casual attitude is quickly revealed to be misplaced. At other points, though, the looser form of expression is inappropriate or gratuitous, such as when Juno's reference to Dido and Aeneas' plan to go hunting 'ubi primos crastinus ortus / extulerit Titan radiisque retexerit orbem' (*A* 4.118–19; 'as soon as tomorrow's sun shows his rising and with his rays unveils the world') becomes 'ere the Sun have wip'd his face' (*Æneis*, p. 23).

Possible factors behind Harrington's failure to produce a full translation of the *Aeneid* include readerly indifference, a lack of leisure time to work on the translation, caused by the high number of political pamphlets that he produced in the last years of the 1650s, and the collapse in his health that occurred in the early 1660s. Hammersley, though, finds a different reason for Harrington's *Aeneid* ending at Book 6. For Hammersley 'the idea that reason must be in control of passion' recurs across Harrington's writing, and where *Aeneid* 4 provides a successful example of reason overcoming passion the last books of the poem show Aeneas failing to achieve this control.[49] The translation may, then, imitate Harrington's practice of using Virgil for instructional purposes in his political writings. In Hammersley's reading, Harrington's Aeneas functions as a means of providing readers with a positive model of how to behave; ending the translation at the end of Book 6 allows him to present Aeneas as a type, not an antitype.

An unwillingness to articulate Aeneas' regression into passionate behaviour could lie behind Harrington's decision to excise the parts of the Sybil's prophecy to Aeneas that outline what lies in store for him in Italy (*A* 6.56–71). Yet, as discussed above, Harrington was more interested in using Augustus than Aeneas as a vehicle for moral instruction, and his use of Augustus in *Oceana* shows that he did not shy away from presenting both types and antitypes of behaviour within a single individual. If there was an element of counsel in the *Aeneis* translation it differs from the counsel of *Oceana* in that it is addressed to a general readership and not a head of state. The focus is also on moral rather than political instruction, or on investigating the Augustan origins of the political situation in 1650s England.

Harrington's *Aeneid* was one of two apolitical translations of Virgil in this period by a writer with connections to royal service whose literary output otherwise contains a high degree of political engagement. The other is a translation which has hitherto attracted almost no critical attention: *A Collection of parts of some Bookes of Virgill* by Sir William Kingsmill (the father of the more celebrated poet Anne Finch). As *A Collection* is preserved in a single manuscript now held in Lichfield Cathedral Library, was only published for the first time in 2018, and existing scholarship on Kingsmill is confined to a single journal article which refrains from discussing Kingsmill's translations from classical texts, the following section gives a brief account of the text.[50] It then considers the factors that influenced Kingsmill's composition of a non-royalist *Aeneid*, as well as his links to one of the authors who forms the subject of the next chapter, Sir Robert Howard.

Coda: Sir William Kingsmill, *A Collection of parts of some Bookes of Virgill*

A Collection translates passages from *Aeneid* 1, 2 and 4 that have been reorganised to tell Aeneas' voyage from Troy to Carthage in chronological order.[51] Kingsmill dedicates *A Collection* to Lady Catherine Sidney, and the reference to her in the full title of the translation as Lady Lisle sheds light both on the date of *A Collection*'s composition and its lack of royalist sentiment.[52] Catherine became Lady Lisle on her marriage in 1645 to Philip Sidney (later 3rd Earl of Leicester), and died in 1652, so *A Collection* must date from this seven-year period. The Sidneys were a prominent Parliamentarian family, and Kingsmill's own politics may well have been close to theirs at the time he completed *A Collection*. Although at the start of the civil wars he was appointed Sheriff of Hampshire, the king's representative in the county, he does not seem to have conducted his duties willingly or with much enthusiasm. The dates given in the titles of Kingsmill's satires and occasional poems, along with their subject matter, indicate a shift from an anti-republican and anti-Cromwellian standpoint to more overtly royalist sympathies only in the later 1650s.[53]

Kingsmill's interest in the *Aeneid* also seems to have been more in its representations of desire than the chances it offered for political commentary. The 'interpositions of the Author' that frame his translation state that the events of the poem are caused by erotic passion. In addition, the passages that Kingsmill translates are comprised of the moments when Venus herself appears to Aeneas or when the narrative is being driven by her actions, and the one interpolation in the translation (lines 289–94) is a hymn in praise of Venus' power. Despite the fact that he completed the translation after her marriage, it is likely that Kingsmill intended it as an extended love letter to Catherine Sidney. Kingsmill wrote several love lyrics to Catherine,[54] and given this context it is notable that the introduction of political commentary in his poetry occurred after her death.

Amongst Kingsmill's other literary works that appear in the same manuscript as *A Collection* is a poem to Sir Robert Howard.[55] This poem was occasioned by the publication of Howard's translation of Statius' *Achilleid*, which appeared in his 1660 collection *Poems by the Honourable Sir Robert Howard*. The appearance of this volume was almost exactly contemporaneous with the Restoration: it was entered in the Stationer's Register on 16 April 1660, and the title page of Thomason's copy is annotated 'June', the month after Charles was proclaimed king.[56] As Howard was Kingsmill's kinsman (Howard's first wife was a cousin of Kingsmill), and Howard was a prominent figure at the Restoration court, Kingsmill's poem was likely prompted more by a bid for political patronage than any appreciation for Howard's literary endeavours.

In addition to his *Achilleid* commentary, Howard's 1660 *Poems* included, amongst other texts, his translation of *Aeneid* 4. This was the first of two Virgil translations to be published in the year of the Restoration. The title page of the other, John Boys's translation of *Aeneid* 6, is dated 1661, but the flyleaf in a copy now in the British Library is inscribed 'Wm Amherst. Novemb: 1660. Pret: 3s–0d', which presumably records the name of its owner, date of acquisition and price.[57] The literary careers of both Howard and Boys began later than, but largely ended before, the other writers considered in this study. Although Howard lived until 1698, his poetic career was confined to the 1660s; Boys appears to have died around 1661/2, soon after the publication of his second published translation from Virgil. The two men's translations thus form a suitable means of bringing my account of Virgil's English translators who were active in the middle decades of the seventeenth century to a close.

Notes

1. John Ogilby, *The Works of Publius Virgilius Maro* (London, 1649), sig. ²D6v; John Ogilby, *The Works of Publius Virgilius Maro Translated, adorn'd with Sculpture, and illustrated with Annotations* (London, 1654), p. 217; Sir John Denham, *The Destruction of Troy, an Essay upon the Second Book of Virgils Æneis. Written in the year, 1636* (London, 1656), p. 28.
2. James Harrington, *An Essay Upon two of Virgil's Eclogues, and Two Books of his Æneis (If this be not enough) Towards the Translation of the whole* (London, 1658) (hereafter *Essay*), p. 38. As in my other chapters, underline indicates where the translations substantially depart from or add to the Virgilian original.
3. *Aubrey's Brief Lives*, ed. Oliver Lawson Dick (London, 1949), p. 124.
4. See *Aubrey's Brief Lives*, p. 124.
5. James Harrington, *The Common-Wealth of Oceana* (London, 1656) (hereafter *Oceana*), p. 2.
6. Rachel Hammersley, *James Harrington: An Intellectual Biography* (Oxford, 2019), p. 90.
7. James Harrington, *Virgil's Æneis: The Third, Fourth, Fifth and Sixth Books* (London, 1659) (hereafter *Æneis*), sigs A4r–A5v. I discuss the prefatory poem at greater length later in the chapter.
8. *A System of Politics*, in *The Oceana of James Harrington, and his Other Works*, ed. John Toland (London, 1700), pp. 496–514 (503).

9. See Hammersley, *Harrington: An Intellectual Biography*, pp. 86–7, 92–3.
10. David Norbrook, *Writing the English Republic: Poetry, Rhetoric and Politics, 1627–1660* (Cambridge, 1999), p. 365.
11. Hammersley, *Harrington: An Intellectual Biography*, p. 125.
12. For the intellectual background to Harrington's agrarianism, see Jonathan Scott, *Commonwealth Principles: Republican Writing of the English Revolution* (Cambridge, 2004), p. 3; Hammersley, *Harrington: An Intellectual Biography*, pp. 97–108. Harrington's influence on later debates regarding the connection between landownership and power is discussed in J. G. A. Pocock, *The Machiavellian Moment: Florentine Political Thought and the Atlantic Republican Tradition* (Oxford, 2016), pp. 417–19.
13. See Rachel Hammersley, 'James Harrington's *The Commonwealth of Oceana* and the Republican Tradition', in *The Oxford Handbook of Literature and the English Revolution*, ed. Laura Lunger Knoppers (Oxford, 2012), pp. 534–50 (543–4).
14. Harrington's quotation follows the version printed in seventeenth-century editions of Virgil; modern editions reverse the order of 'tantum' and 'quantum'.
15. See Emily Gowers, 'Trees and Family Trees in the *Aeneid*', *Classical Antiquity*, 30 (2011), 87–118 (pp. 90–1).
16. Norbrook, *Writing the English Republic*, p. 369.
17. Blair Worden, 'Harrington's *Oceana*: Origins and Aftermath, 1651–1660', in *Republicanism, Liberty, and Commercial Society, 1649–1776*, ed. David Wootton (Stanford, 1994), pp. 111–38 (113–14).
18. See Nicholas McDowell, 'Harrington, James', *The Encyclopedia of English Renaissance Literature*, ed. Garrett A. Sullivan Jr and Allen Stewart, 3 vols (Oxford, 2012), vol. 2, pp. 437–41 (p. 438).
19. As discussed on p. 16, above.
20. In J. C. Davis, 'The Prose Romance of the 1650s as a Context for *Oceana*', in *Perspectives on Revolutionary English Republicanism*, ed. Dirk Wiemann and Gaby Mahlberg (London, 2014), pp. 65–84.
21. Worden, 'Harrington's *Oceana*', p. 120.
22. Worden, 'Harrington's *Oceana*', p. 124.
23. Scott, *Commonwealth Principles*, pp. 286; 292.
24. For quotations from 'Verulamius' (Bacon), see *Oceana*, sig. B1r, pp. 143, 145, 152, 154, 219, 227–8.
25. 'On Praise', in *The Essayes or Counsels, Civill and Morall, of Francis Lo. Verulam, Viscount St. Alban* (London, 1625), pp. 304–7 (305–6).
26. For which see Chapter 5, *passim*.
27. Charlton T. Lewis and Charles Short, *A Latin Dictionary* (Oxford, 1879), s.v. 'praecipere' 2b; 1a.
28. Hammersley, *Harrington: An Intellectual Biography*, p. 133.
29. See, amongst others, Paulus Manutius and Georgius Fabricius (eds), *Opera P. Virgilii Maronis* (Cambridge, 1632), pp. 1, 23; Thomas Farnaby (ed.), *Publii Virgilii Maronis Opera* (London, 1634), pp. 1, 25; Ogilby, *The Works of Publius Virgilius Maro* (1654), pp. 1, 49.
30. See Christopher Durston, *Cromwell's Major-generals: Godly Government during the English Revolution* (Manchester, 2001), pp. 97–8.

31. For the connections between Virgil and 'gallant' Caroline literary culture, see pp. 13–15, above.
32. As outlined in Syrithe Pugh, *Spenser and Virgil: The Pastoral Poems* (Manchester, 2016), p. 160.
33. I draw here on Cromwell's biography in the *Oxford Dictionary of National Biography* (*ODNB*), www.oxforddnb.com.
34. See Rachel Foxley, 'Democracy in 1659: Harrington and the Good Old Cause', in *The Nature of the English Revolution Revisited*, ed. Stephen Taylor and Grant Tapsell (Woodbridge, 2013), pp. 175–96 (175).
35. *Æneis*, sig. A5v; roman/italic fonts reversed.
36. *Servius' Commentary on Book Four of Virgil's Aeneid*, ed. and trans. Christopher M. McDonough, Richard E. Prior and Mark Stansbury (Wauconda, IL, 2004), pp. 18–19.
37. *Æneis*, sigs A3r–A4r; roman/italic fonts reversed.
38. See L. Proudfoot, *Dryden's Aeneid and Its Seventeenth Century Predecessors* (Manchester, 1960), p. 146.
39. *Les Recherches de La France D'Estienne Pasquier* (Paris, 1621), pp. 639–40, citing Ronsard, *Franciade* 1.1229–34. Line numbers and translation are taken from Pierre Ronsard, *The Franciad (1572)*, trans. Phillip John Usher (New York, 2010). The *Franciad* simile revises a passage from Ronsard's earlier poem *Hymne de Calaïs, et de Zetes* (pub. 1556).
40. James Harrington, *The Art of Law-Giving* (London, 1659), p. 28, drawing on Livy, *History of Rome*, 1.34.
41. For quotations from Livy in *Oceana*, see *Oceana*, pp. 4, 56, 57.
42. See Joy Connolly, 'Border Wars: Literature, Politics, and the Public', *Transactions of the American Philological Association*, 135 (2005), 103–34 (pp. 122–3); Ariane Schwartz, 'A Revolutionary Vergil: James Harrington, Poetry, and Political Performance', in *Reading Poetry, Writing Genre: English Poetry and Literary Criticism in Dialogue with Classical Scholarship*, ed. Silvio Bär and Emily Hauser (London, 2018), pp. 51–65; Gordon Braden, 'The Passion of Dido: *Aeneid* 4 in English Translation to 1700', in *Virgil and His Translators*, ed. Susanna Braund and Zara Martirosova Torlone (Oxford, 2018), pp. 80–96 (86–8; 91).
43. *Æneis*, sig. A5r; roman/italic fonts reversed.
44. *A Discourse upon Gondibert. An Heroick Poem Written by S*$^{r.}$ *William D'avenant. With an Answer to it by M*$^{r.}$ *Hobbs* (Paris, 1650), p. 4.
45. See especially Arihiro Fukuda, *Sovereignty and the Sword: Harrington, Hobbes, and Mixed Government in the English Civil Wars* (Oxford, 1997).
46. See *Discourse upon Gondibert*, pp. 135–6, responding to pp. 10–11.
47. *Æneis*, pp. 10, 49, 61, translating *A* 3.366, 5.302, 6.27.
48. James Harrington, *Politicaster* (London, 1659), p. 2.
49. Hammersley, *Harrington: An Intellectual Biography*, p. 135.
50. Kingsmill's *Collection* forms part of the online annexe for *Newly Recovered English Classical Translations 1600–1800*, ed. Stuart Gillespie (Oxford, 2018) (www.nrect.gla.ac.uk), which also contains a brief account of the translation. For Kingsmill's other poetry see John Eames, 'Sir William Kingsmill (1613–1661) and His Poetry', *English Studies*, 2 (1986), 126–56.
51. The passages Kingsmill translates are, in order of appearance in the

manuscript: *A* 2.13–16, 20, 77–267, 361–9, 506–804; *A* 1.315–417, 257–304, 419–756; *A* 4.1–173, 196–330.
52. The full title of the translation reads *A Collection of parts of some Bookes of Virgill, with some interpositions of the Author, for entertainment of my Lady Lisle, begunn but left unfinisht. Partly paraphrasd, but for the most part strictly translated.*
53. See Kingmill's biography in *ODNB*, and Eames, 'Sir William Kingsmill', p. 132.
54. See Eames, 'Sir William Kingsmill', pp. 130–1, 141–5.
55. Cited in Eames, 'Sir William Kingsmill', p. 131.
56. I draw here on G. E. B. Eyre (ed.), *A Transcript of the Registers of the Worshipful Company of Stationers, From 1640–1708 AD*, 3 vols (London, 1913–14), vol. 2, p. 258, and information in the entry for Howard's *Poems* in *English Short Title Catalogue* (http://estc.bl.uk).
57. See London, British Library, 11375.c.36.

Chapter 7

Future Contingencies: Sir Robert Howard and John Boys

Introduction

This final chapter begins by examining Sir Robert Howard's and John Boys's respective declarations of royalist affinities in the year of the Restoration through their engagement with Virgil. Howard's 1660 collection *Poems by the Honourable Sir Robert Howard* includes material that compares Charles II to Aeneas; these associations, along with quotations from the *Aeneid* elsewhere in the volume, are brought to bear (albeit implicitly) on his apolitical translation of *Aeneid* 4, *Of the Loves of Dido and Æneas*. By contrast, the connections between Charles and Aeneas in Boys's translation of *Aeneid* 6, *Æneas His Descent into Hell* (1660), are more overt. Where certain poems in Howard's collection express anxieties regarding the source of Charles II's authority as monarch, but confine themselves to providing commentary rather than counsel, Boys intends parts of *Descent* to advise Charles on the best course of action against those who had taken up arms against the Stuarts. This chapter also considers Howard's and Boys's reception of the tradition which connects Virgilian poetry with prophecy. Where Howard uses retrospective prophecy to 'anticipate' the Restoration, Boys's *Descent* and, subsequently, his second translation from Virgil, *Æneas His Errours* (a 1661 translation of *Aeneid* 3) make a more genuine attempt to predict clear, specific futures. Boys held that prophecies which did otherwise indicated face-saving, even sinister, motives:

> It was the subtilty of the Devill, who could not positively affirm any thing of future contingencies, lest his Prophets and Oracles should by the non-successe of his predictions he had in disrepute, to deliver his answers in dark and obscure riddles, in intricate and involved terms, and such as might be taken two wayes; that whether they succeeded or not, his credit might not suffer.[1]

In consequence of this attitude Boys's prophecies were more vulnerable to acquiring additional or unintentional applications than the poems Howard framed as containing prophetic insights. Circumstances ultimately frustrated the events that Boys predicted from coming to pass soon after (and even, in some cases, before) his works had appeared in print.

I conclude this study with a brief sketch of Virgil's English reception from the publication of Boys's *Errours* in 1661 to the end of the century. The Virgilian writings in the later years of Charles II's rule and in the reigns of his successors continued the debates on the limits of royal power and the place of the monarch within the system of government that dominated and curtailed the reign of Charles I. The return of fears regarding the outbreak of civil war at the time of the Exclusion Crisis (1679–81), and the recognition of a contingent future following the 'Glorious Revolution' of 1688, saw Virgil's English translators of the 1680s and 1690s finding precedents for their own situation in the works of their mid-century counterparts. These Virgil translators took not just individual lines and phrases from their royalist predecessors, but also their technique of imagining a version of the nation's future that offered more stability than their current circumstances allowed and was more in accord with their political sensibilities.

Poems by the Honourable Sir Robert Howard

Howard's 1660 *Poems* is a substantial volume: in addition to *Of the Loves of Dido and Æneas* it contains his stage comedy *The Blind Lady*, several occasional poems, a collection of love lyrics and (as mentioned in the previous chapter) a translation, with extensive commentary, of Statius' *Achilleid*. Considerable as this collection is, Howard implies in a preface that the volume only represents selections from a greater body of work. Amongst the texts he hints that he has excluded is a fuller *Aeneid* translation. When discussing *Of the Loves of Dido and Æneas* Howard claims he has

> onely publish'd this one Book, that lay finished by me; not judging it convenient to perfect those other Books of his *Aeneid's*, which I have rudely gone through, having long since laid aside all designes of that nature; and this little of it rather grew publick from accident, than designe, the Mingle it had with my private Papers, was the greatest cause, that it received its share in the publick Impression.[2]

These disclaimers combine standard early modern tropes of the self-effacing author, the gentlemanly amateur poet writing purely for his private amusement, and translators confessing themselves to be incapable of equalling or accurately representing Virgil's achievement. Yet although they are generic in nature there is evidence elsewhere in *Poems* that supports Howard's claims. The *Achilleid* commentary includes a substantial number of quotations from the *Aeneid*.[3] Howard usually translates these quotations, as when he cites 'ergo Iris croceis per caelum roscida pinnis, / mille trahens varios adverso sole colores' (*A* 4.700–1; 'so Iris on dewy saffron wings flings down through the sky, trailing athwart the sun a thousand shifting tints'):

> Swift *Iris* therefore with her dewy wings,
> On which the Sun a thousand colours flings.
>
> (*Poems*, p. 208)

This couplet differs from his translation of the same lines in *Of the Loves of Dido and Æneas*:

> From heaven then, *Iris* with dewie wings,
> On which the Sun a thousand glories flings.
>
> (*Poems*, p. 169)

Similar discrepancies exist between the other translations Howard gives for quotations from *Aeneid* 4 in the *Achilleid* commentary and the equivalent lines in *Of the Loves of Dido and Æneas*.[4] In each case, the differences represent the type of aesthetic changes that suggest the revision of draft material. As the *Achilleid* commentary contains translated passages from several classical authors, its renderings from Virgil may simply have been produced ad hoc as Howard incorporated quotations from the Latin original into the notes, and thus been independent of *Of the Loves of Dido and Æneas*. But, as Virgil is the most cited author in the commentary by a considerable margin, they may well have come from a draft version of the *Aeneid* that Howard produced prior to 1660.

The translations from Virgil that appear in Howard's commentary on Statius' *Achilleid* are mostly non-political. They suggest that Howard's initial engagement with Virgil was, like that of several of the translators considered in earlier chapters, primarily intended as apprentice work for a poetic career. An exception comes as part of the gloss on the *Achilleid*'s reference to Achilles as the murderer of Hector and Priam. Howard notes 'The ruine of *Priam* is justly attributed to *Achilles*, in that he begat *Pyrrhus*, who killed him before the Altar' (*Poems*, p. 236). He then cites the relevant lines from the *Aeneid* that record this event (*A* 2.554–8), and provides a translation:

> This was of once-great *Priam* the hard fate,
> *Troy* seen on fire, and his ruin'd state;
> He who o're part of *Asia* late did reign,
> Now headlesse lies, a corps without a name.
>
> (*Poems*, p. 236)

Howard's rendering of Virgil's Latin is fairly compressed and, in keeping with the other translations in the commentary, shows little sign of being anything other than functional or illustrative. However, immediately after these lines Howard states 'We read of few examples, of so great alteration of fortune, unlesse this late age hath produced them' (*Poems*, p. 236). When taken in reference to a headless monarch the statement suggests that he is encouraging readers to find a parallel between the death of Priam and the death of Charles I. Howard extends the potential parallel, and adds an emphasis on sacred monarchy that briefly aligns his views with those of the king's most committed supporters, by saying the modern examples of individuals who have experienced a great alteration of fortune 'now perhaps, take such a prospect of their scorned bodies, as *Lucan* . . . giveth Pompey of his from Heaven'; he then cites the passage from the *Pharsalia* which charts the ascent of Pompey's spirit into the heavens.[5] This reference too can only have been inspired by a desire to commemorate Charles I as a royal martyr. Howard's implied connection between Charles and Priam (and indeed Pompey) is, however, not as explicit or as prominent as in the comparable parallels previously discussed with regard to the translations and imitations of the same *Aeneid* 2 passage by Denham, Cowley, Ogilby and Harrington. It is also Howard's gloss on the translation, rather than the translation itself, which aligns it with the royalist tradition of Interregnum-era receptions of Virgil's Priam and Lucan's Pompey to commemorate the death of Charles I.

A more overt use of Virgil by Howard to articulate royalist sentiments in *Poems* occurs in his panegyric to Charles II. The poem offers a confidently teleological reading of recent events through a comparison between Charles and Aeneas. It presents Charles's actions at the 1650 Battle of Dunbar, where his army was defeated by Cromwell, as mirroring Aeneas' return to the fighting on the last night of Troy:

> And in the Victory those *Scots* had found
> Their Crimes together with your Vertues crown'd.
> Then 'twas You did attempt your debt to pay
> To Us of Nature, by a noble way.
> The bold *Æneas* so, having left *Troy*
> In its own funerall flames, scorn'd to enjoy
> Safety alone; but, led by Vertues great

> As were the Dangers he was to repeat,
> Return'd among his ruin'd Friends and State,
> To bring them safety, or to fetch their fate.
>
> *(Poems, p. 8)*

In addition to praising Charles for his virtuousness and sense of duty to his supporters, the poem makes Charles's defeat at Dunbar akin to the fall of Troy, the lowest ebb of his fortunes from which he ultimately ascended to a throne.

As the panegyric on Charles opens *Poems*, the connection it draws between him and Aeneas helps to encourage the same application in *Of the Loves of Dido and Æneas* later in the volume. Tanya Caldwell has argued that Howard's desire to present both Aeneas and Charles as paragons of princely virtues means that he 'strives to make Aeneas appear spotless' in the translation.[6] Caldwell's claim overstates the nature of Howard's approach to the text, since *Of the Loves of Dido and Æneas* retains Aeneas' readiness when in Carthage to privilege pleasure over duty and ignore his known destiny as the founder of the Roman nation in Italy. Nonetheless, whilst the conduct of Howard's Aeneas in Carthage contains questionable elements it is true that, like some (but by no means all) of his contemporary translators, Howard reframes the relationship between Dido and Aeneas in order to make Aeneas' actions less opprobrious than is the case in Virgil. Although Howard preserves some of the references to marriage in the text, in his version when Aeneas sails from Carthage he leaves behind a lover, not a wife.[7] Howard even has Dido recognise this fact, although in both Virgil and other translations she is the figure who insists most forcefully that she and Aeneas are married. When Howard's Dido entreats Aeneas not to leave Carthage she adjures him not by 'conubia nostra' and 'inceptos hymenaeos' (*A* 4.316; 'the marriage that is ours'; 'the nuptial rites begun'), but 'By our young Loves' (*Poems*, p. 154). There are similarities here with the Godolphin/Waller *Passion of Dido for Æneas* (1658) discussed in Chapter 1.[8] Both translations change the Virgilian text to have Aeneas' behaviour reflect that of a Caroline-era courtly gallant (other works in Howard's *Poems*, especially the collection of love lyrics and the 'gallant' protagonists of *The Blind Lady*, also looked back to this tradition). Despite their use of a discourse that derived from the pre-civil-war Stuart court, the translations themselves lack any meaningful political commentary and represent an initial encounter with Virgil that was primarily focused on honing poetic skill. They only became politicised at a later date thanks to the poets' other literary activities, in which they drew on their experiences of translating Virgil, and (in the case of Howard) the publication of the translation alongside these other works.

An additional connection between Howard's and Waller's reception of Virgil comes in the last poem in Howard's collection, a panegyric to George Monck. In the poem, Howard compares Monck's role in securing the Stuart restoration to Neptune calming the storm that harried the Trojan fleet off the coast of Carthage:

> So when the Trojan Prince was almost lost
> In Storms, among ungentle billows tost,
> Displeased *Neptune* from the surges rose;
> And storms of frowns among the tempests throws.
> At which the waves no longer durst aspire,
> But to obedient calmnesse all retire.
>   At your approach, phanatique storms so shrink,
>   And factions waves to seeming quiet sink.
>
> (*Poems*, pp. 283–4)

Howard's poem makes use of the same passage from the *Aeneid* that Waller had previously evoked in one of his panegyrics to Cromwell.[9] But where Waller compares Neptune to Cromwell as England's head of state, in Howard's poem the Neptune figure is not Charles, but Monck. Charles, like Aeneas, is dependent on the power of others. Howard's use of the *Aeneid* here thus compromises the more straightforwardly encomiastic, enthusiastically royalist sentiments of other Virgilian elements in *Poems*.

Concerns about the stability and longevity of Charles II's reign also inform the poem's concluding couplet: 'You that a KING a Scepter gave to sway, / And taught rebellious Subjects to obey' (*Poems*, p. 285). These lines are highly indebted to the conclusion of the 1642 edition of Denham's *Coopers Hill*: 'And may that Law, which teaches Kings to sway / Their Scepters, teach their Subjects to obey'.[10] The shift in tense, however, between Denham's original and Howard's imitation initially suggests a different form of royalism than the constitutional royalism that pervades Denham's poem. It also connects the poem to the more absolutist and ultra-loyalist attitudes in Howard's implied presentation of Charles I as a martyr and a sacred monarch in his *Achilleid* commentary. The instruction is addressed only to the king's subjects, not the king himself, and the addition of 'rebellious' to describe these subjects also increases its royalist sentiment. In Howard's imitation of Denham the act of instructing people to become obedient has already occurred, rather than lying ahead in the future. Yet here, as in Denham, the passage expresses anxiety as well as confidence. It acknowledges that royal power is not inherent to the monarch himself, but is contingent on those who have chosen to support him. Where in Denham the 'Law' is the only authority that exists above monarchical power, in Howard that role is taken by an individual. There is a hint at the end of this panegyric that, since Monck chose to give the sceptre to Charles II, he could just as easily have chosen to bestow it on someone else, or could yet decide to do so. The poem to Monck qualifies the more positive associations between Charles and Aeneas that open the volume, and that are partially sustained through his translation of *Aeneid* 4 and the *Achilleid* commentary.

Several works in Howard's *Poems* register concerns about the stability of the restored monarchy, but they provide no advice on how Charles should rule or on how to avoid a second period of exile. Unlike in other poems on the Restoration, and indeed other works from the previous decades that were addressed to a head of state, the Virgilian references in Howard's panegyrics do not engage with the tradition of Virgil as a counsellor to a sovereign, who offered advice on good governance. The volume does, however, draw on the other strand of Virgil's reception addressed across this study, the vatic tradition that uses poetry to express desired futures. Howard's panegyric on Charles reads the events of the early 1650s in a manner which suggests its composition was influenced by the hindsight that was provided by the Restoration, but Howard claims it

> was written when the King deserved the Praise as much as now, but separated farther from the Power; which was about three years since, when I was Prisoner in *Windsor-Castle*, being the best diversion I could then find for my own condition; to think, how great his Vertues were for whom I suffered.
> (*Poems*, sig. A4v)

This claim is more self-serving than the chronological gap between composition and publication that in 1656 Denham misleadingly claimed on the title page of *The Destruction of Troy*; Denham exploited that gap for the purposes of lament and self-recrimination, not panegyric.[11] By drawing attention to the delay between the (declared) composition and publication of his poem, Howard encourages readers to find a vatic element to the text's account of the Restoration. Howard also stresses the longevity and uncompromised nature of his royalism by framing the poem in this manner. It is worth noting, however, that although Howard's status as a royalist in the 1640s is not in question – he earned his knighthood in 1644 for his military service for the royalist cause – his status and activities in the 1650s are more obscure. In *Poems* Howard gives no further details about how long he spent as a prisoner, or why he was imprisoned. The implication is that it was for royalist activities, and his modern biographer treats this as fact, but there is no evidence to support Howard's claim.[12] In fact the preface to *Poems* is the only evidence for this period of imprisonment and for dating the panegyric on Charles to the late 1650s.[13] The account of the Interregnum in that poem indicates that it was at least revised in the year of the Restoration, even if Howard had begun writing it earlier. In claiming a composition date of *c.*1657, Howard at least potentially adjusts his own history as well as the poem's origins.

Æneas His Descent into Hell

The question mark over Howard's loyalties in the 1650s may also apply to the other individual who published a translation from the *Aeneid* in the year of the Restoration, John Boys. The earliest examples of Boys's political affinities are from the Interregnum. The volume he published in 1660 included, in addition to his *Aeneid* 6 translation, a satire dated 1656 that decries the political situation in England but does not call for the monarchy's restoration (*Descent*, pp. 230–2). The other two texts in the volume date from 1660. The first of these texts is a petition that Boys wrote early in that year on behalf of the 'Nobility, Gentry, Ministry and Commonalty' of Kent (*Descent*, p. 218). As it demands the recall of the members removed from Parliament by the army in 1648, but contains no direct call for the restoration of the monarchy, its sentiments are not explicitly royalist either. The other prose work that Boys includes in *Descent*, however, indicates that by May of the Restoration year Boys had (like most of the country) aligned himself with royalism: it was a speech Boys would have delivered to Charles II on his arrival at Dover, again as a representative of the citizens of Kent, had the king remained in the city long enough to hear it. Certain additions to the text of *Aeneid* 6 in Boys's *Descent* also contain royalist attitudes, but he primarily expresses them in the volume's paratexts. This section also identifies how *Descent*, as well as celebrating the return of the Stuart monarchy, provides the earliest example of post-Restoration poems continuing the 1640s and 1650s tradition of writers quoting and imitating Virgil to lament Stuart travails.

We saw in previous chapters that royalists deployed references to the Virgilian Underworld in their writings to present those who had fought against the king as agents of Satan.[14] Boys, too, adopted this practice in *Descent*, but where other Virgil translators used it to suggest the origins of the people who were hostile to the royalist cause, Boys did so to intimate their ultimate destination. When the Sibyl informs Aeneas about the role and function of Tartarus she says it holds and punishes 'quique arma secuti / impia nec veriti dominorum fallere dextras' (*A* 6.612–13;

'those who followed the standard of treason, and feared not to break allegiance with their lords'). Boys translated these lines in notably royalist terms:

> *who have deceiv'd their trust,*
> *And 'gainst their King and lawfull Soveraign*
> *(In impious broyles engag'd) their Swords have drawn.*[15]

The adaptation and expansion of the narrative to allow the expression of ultra-loyalist sentiment, when combined with the use of italics to draw the reader's attention to the passage, parallels the literary and typographical practice previously considered in relation to John Ogilby's 1649 *Works of Publius Virgilius Maro*.[16] Although this line is not one that Ogilby himself italicised, his *Aeneid* is the only other translation that makes a royalist intervention at this point in the text. Ogilby's version reads 'who impious arms persu'd, / Nor fear'd the trust of *Princes* to delude'; his revised version of 1654 reads 'those *rebell* / And did their *native Prince to Traitors sell*'.[17] Given this overlap between Boys's and Ogilby's political outlook as well as their techniques as translators, Boys may well have been directly inspired by Ogilby.

Although it is likely that Boys did know Ogilby's Virgil, he need not have done to capitalise on the value of using italics to express royalist sentiment. In *Descent* Boys states that his interpretation of one passage follows 'the exposition of our Country-man, the learned Mr. *Farnaby*' (*Descent*, p. 115). His italicised lines in *Descent* are, as is the case for Ogilby, thus probably inspired by the typography in that particular scholarly edition of Virgil. As in the 1649 Ogilby Virgil, there is a significant crossover between the lines Farnaby and Boys print in a different typeface to grant them a greater prominence. Many of them provide general moral points,[18] but, again like Ogilby, Boys suffuses his didacticism with ultra-loyalism. In addition to the account of Tartarus, this technique can be seen in his translation of Anchises's exhortation that the Romans should 'parcere subiectis et debellare superbos' (*A* 6.853) as '*The loyall cherish*, the *Rebellious Crush*' (*Descent*, p. 31). The only precedent for this emphasis on achieving violent retribution against forces hostile to the Crown is Ogilby's 'Subjects to spare, and Rebels to destroy'.[19] Boys and Ogilby are the only translators who exhort Aeneas to defeat the 'rebellious' at this point in the translation.[20] In Ogilby's 1649 *Works of Publius Virgilius Maro* this line is also italicised for additional royalist emphasis.

In *Descent* Boys was able to capitalise on the hindsight that the early Restoration provided to offer an even more emphatically ultra-loyalist interpretation than is present in Ogilby's Interregnum-era translations.

Where in Ogilby the call to destroy and crush the rebellious represents extremely wishful thinking and, at most, an instruction for a future date, the publication of *Descent* in 1660 brought such an attitude closer to a potential course of action. The line also provides an example of Boys not limiting himself to political commentary, but offering royalist counsel. It reflects an attitude towards those who had fought against and/or advocated the abolition of the monarchy that many royalists in 1660 did hope would occur, although the Act of Indemnity and Oblivion of August 1660 ultimately extended a pardon to all but the regicides. Boys's interpolated exhortation in '*the loyall cherish*' also reflects the royalists' hopes that their service would be rewarded that the Restoration made it possible to fulfil, but which newly ratified legislation curtailed.

The ultra-loyalist sentiments that inform the passages of *Descent* so far discussed are, however, uncharacteristic of the translation as a whole. It contains few other directly royalist interventions in Virgil's text. The most extensive examples of strategically deployed royalist statements instead come in the commentary that Boys includes in the volume. On the title page of the volume this commentary is called '*ample and learned*': the translation itself takes up just over thirty pages, the annotations nearly two hundred. This commentary is mostly concerned, again as the title page claims, with ensuring that 'all passages criticall, mythological, philosophical and historical, are fully and clearly explained'. Nonetheless, on a few key occasions, as in Howard's *Achilleid* commentary in *Poems*, Boys's notes are prompted more by his royalism than his knowledge of Roman myth and history. One of the creatures that Aeneas encounters in the vestibule to the Underworld is the Hydra, and Boys's remarks on this passage make use of the long-standing allegorical reading of this creature as a metaphor for mob rule to issue a warning against populist uprisings.[21] For Boys, it represents

> a type of popular sedition, and a National revolt, which is no sooner quelled in one place, but that it breaks out with triplicated rage and fury in another; whence the Vulgar is significantly denominated *Bellua multorum capitum*, that many-headed beast, as was this *Bellua Lernae*.
>
> (*Descent*, p. 81)

He also reads other passages in a similar vein as 'Fables . . . invented to keep Subjects in their due obedience' (*Descent*, p. 122), and as warnings against mutiny, revolt and sedition.

Boys's commentary also actively praises monarchy as well as denigrating forces that were hostile to it. The passage that describes Brutus' overthrow of Tarquinius Superbus and installation of a republic (*A* 6.817–18) prompts a lengthy discussion by Boys on the inaccuracy of calling Tarquinius a tyrannical king and on the associated tradition of portraying Brutus as an exemplary figure.[22] A much more idiosyncratic royalist reading comes in the note that Boys supplies for Virgil's reference to 'forma tricorporis umbrae' (*A* 6.289; 'the shape of a three-bodied shade'). The shade in question is of the triple-bodied giant Geryon, the stealing of whose cattle comprised Hercules' tenth labour. Boys uses the notion of an entity with three bodies to praise the three sons of Charles I: Charles II, James, Duke of York and Henry, Duke of Gloucester:

> And may not this Fable be verified in this our age? have not we our *Geryon*? ... when we consider in what amity and love, how united and linked together our gracious Soveraign and his two Royal Brethren live, we cannot but affirm that (according to the mythologie of this Fable) they seem to have but one soul to actuate their three bodies.
>
> (*Descent*, p. 87)

The comparison can succeed as praise only if it remains largely uninterrogated and unpursued, and Boys himself acknowledges that Geryon 'was said to be a most merciless Tyrant' (*Descent*, p. 88). Despite these limitations, Boys states that this comparison compels him to make 'a short Poeticall rapture' comparing Geryon and the three Stuart princes to various spiritual, mythological and theological triads, which culminates in a reference to the Holy Trinity.[23] Like Ogilby, then, Boys aligns himself in *Descent* with the tradition of royalism that stresses the sacred nature of monarchy.

Boys was subsequently compelled to lament that the panegyrical quality of his rapture on the Stuart princes was compromised for reasons other than its origins in Virgil's account of a mythical tyrant. The passage on Geryon must have been printed before Gloucester's death in September 1660. Boys mourns at the end of the volume that

> Since these last sheets were sent to the Press, it hath pleased the al-governing *Providence* to make a sad *Interlude* amidst our pomps and triumphs, by taking away that as highly-meriting as highly-born *Prince*, the illustrious *Duke of Glocester*. The precedent discourse leading us so naturally to it, we could not but subjoyn these following verses, and cast in our *Mire*, not of *sorrow*, (for in that we share as deeply as any) but of *expressing* the same, wherein we shall easily give place even to the meanest.[24]

A verse elegy for Gloucester immediately follows this passage. As Boys notes, this final section is also the most appropriate place for the poem to appear since it follows on from his commentary on the passage in the *Aeneid* that is dedicated to mourning the premature demise of Augustus' heir apparent, Marcellus; in a further unhappy parallel, Gloucester was only a few months older than Marcellus had been when he died. Boys makes use of this connection in the poem by presenting Gloucester as the equal of Marcellus, although he laments his lack of Virgil's talent to mourn this second Marcellus' passing with the necessary eloquence.[25] Boys had intended his annotations to *Aeneid* 6 to function as a prophecy of future glories under the restored Stuarts but, like the parade of Rome's future heroes in that book which ends with the description of Marcellus, his triumphalism was displaced by lamentation. The poem on Gloucester's death records that events had unfolded in such a way as to elicit the worst possible parallels between Virgil's society and Boys's own.

Boys subsequently attempted to reassert the more positive and hopeful associations between the Stuart monarchy and the *Aeneid* that his poem on Gloucester as a second Marcellus had compromised. At the end of *Descent* he prints, with an accompanying translation, Latin verses of his own composition that outline his desire to praise Charles as a second Aeneas:

Si dives, Rex magne, *esset mihi vena* Marônis,
    Si fœlix vatum principis ingenium,
Ipse fores meus Æneas, titulisque superbis
    Te ornarem, Herôi *quos dedit ille suo.*

Had I, *Great Monarch,* Maro's divine spirit,
Or did the Prince of Poets wit inherit,
You should be my *Æneas,* and what He
His *Heroe* gave, to you ascrib'd should be.

(*Descent,* p. 229)

The poem recognises a degree of contingency, but as in Boys's elegy for Gloucester it is confined to Boys's own poetic capabilities. That Charles II had the potential to become a second Aeneas was, for Boys, self-evident.

This connection between Charles and Aeneas is reaffirmed in Boys's second translation from Virgil, *Æneas His Errours* (1661). Boys's status as a royalist would suggest that the decision to publish a translation of the book that was dedicated to Aeneas' exile was motivated by a desire to mark Charles's own exile of the 1640s and 1650s. However, the political aspects of *Errours* have more in common with Howard's *Of the Loves of Dido and Æneas* than *Descent*'s isolated but explicit moments of royalist sentiment. The translation itself is largely apolitical, but the other material in the volume politicises it, reaffirms a connection between Charles and Aeneas and ensures that it contains moments of royalist panegyric. The paratextual material uses Virgil to praise not only Charles himself, but also his main counsellors. As well as praising

Monck (as Howard does in *Poems*), Boys also celebrates the achievements of Charles's chief minister, the Earl of Clarendon. However, as with the praise of Gloucester in *Descent*, Boys's praise of Clarendon ultimately ended up accruing resonances that were both all too appropriate and unintentionally elegiac.

Æneas His Errours

In the preface to *Errours* Boys aligns his translation with the work of several near-contemporaries. He draws attention to the 'Great wits' who

> have not blush'd to undertake and publish one single piece of this excellent *Author*, of whom every book indeed is of it self a compleat *Poem*: Hence we have Mr. *Sandys* his *Essay* upon the first; Sir *John Denhams* upon the second, and the united studies of Mr. *Waller* and Mr. *Godolphin* upon the fourth of the *Æneis*.[26]

As we saw in Chapter 1, these poets sought to refine English verse by making it emulate the qualities of Virgilian Latin.[27] By translating *Aeneid* 3 and 6 in separate volumes Boys is able to both work within and fill in some of the gaps within the tradition of aesthetic Augustan translations of Virgil, since no one else had previously published standalone versions of these books.[28]

The translations that Boys refers to in this passage frequently combine an interest in aesthetics with commentary on political matters, often through the use of terms which had particular seventeenth-century resonances and by making modern substitutions for certain details that were present in the Virgilian original.[29] This practice, however, is largely absent from *Errours*. Although the translation contains certain phrases that are more reminiscent of seventeenth-century England than the ancient Mediterranean, they are used to describe a geographical, not a political, landscape. On their arrival in Crete, for example, the Trojans build, not a citadel (as in Virgil), but a 'Castle' (*Errours*, p. 11; translating *A* 3.134). When sailing away from the Cyclops' island, Aeneas compares its inhabitants to 'spire-like Cypresse-trees' (*Errours*, p. 49), when in Virgil they stand 'caelo capita alta ferentis' (*A* 3.678; 'their heads towering to the sky').

The political elements of *Errours* and the continuation of Boys's practice of hailing Charles as a second Aeneas appear not in the translation itself, but in the 'Few Hasty Reflections' at the end of the volume. There Boys praises Charles for 'your *Æneas*-like reverence to your *Royal Father* both living and dead' (*Errours*, p. 58). Where *Descent* hails the sons of Charles I, in *Errours*'s 'Reflections' Boys adapts a speech of Apollo's prophet Anius (*A* 3.97–8) to anticipate the sons of Charles II:

> Here then as the same Poet speaks ... concerning his *Æneas* in this very book, let us, as *prophetically*, I hope affirm and conclude, (changing one word) concerning your Sacred *Majesty*.
>
> *Hic* Carolina *domus Cunctis dominabitur [o]ris,*
> *Et nati natorum, & qui nascentur ab illis*:
> Great *Charles* his house, with those who thence descend,
> Here far and near its Empire shall extend.
>
> (*Errours*, pp. 60–1)

Boys substitutes 'Carolina *domus*' for 'domus Aeneae' to make the prophecy's references to Aeneas' offspring represent Charles's own. *Errours* was published before Charles's 1662 marriage to Catherine of Braganza, but the need to secure the succession was such a fundamental aspect of monarchy that it was inevitable commentators would anticipate Charles's future heirs before any marriage that he did enter into, irrespective of his bride. The John Boys who is the author of a panegyric on the occasion of Charles's marriage may be the same John Boys of *Descent* and *Errours* (or potentially the father after whom he was named).[30] This poem too contains a prophecy of a new generation of Stuart princes. By celebrating individuals who had not yet been born, but who people were confident soon would be, both this panegyric and *Errours* continue Boys's practice of leaving his prophecies open to becoming compromised by events. As discussed at the end of Chapter 5, Charles's lack of legitimate children meant that this prophecy was never fulfilled.[31]

Even when the connections that Boys makes between events and characters in the *Aeneid* and the Stuart Restoration were fulfilled, they still ended up being a source of melancholy. Boys praises Charles II for sharing Aeneas' '*readiness* in taking, and an *ability* in giving good Councel' (*Errours*, p. 59). Boys himself provides counsel for Charles in his Virgil only rarely, but his published volumes give a clear indication of who he felt should advise the king. In his 'Reflections' Boys outlines a reading of *Aeneid* 3 as an allegory for 'a well-order'd *Common-wealth*' (*Errours*, p. 52), where Aeneas' ship represents the ship of state, and Aeneas the monarch. For Boys the king's counsellors are represented by Aeneas' friend Achates and two prophets, the Sibyl and Helenus (a son of Priam). Boys completes the analogy by stating the ship's helmsman Palinurus represents a 'great *Minister* of *State*' (*Errours*, p. 62).

The beginnings of this attitude are present in *Descent*. In the supplementary speeches and public addresses of that volume Boys praises both

Charles and Monck as a second Palinurus,[32] but in the preface to *Descent* itself he calls Clarendon the nation's helmsman. He asks Clarendon, to whom *Descent* was dedicated, 'How happy then is the *Prince* where so prudent and trusty a Minister hath the chief management of affairs? and how secure the *People* where so experienc'd and watchfull a Pilot sits at the helm?' (*Descent*, sig. a3v). In *Errours* Boys extends this comparison between the helmsman of a ship and a monarch's chief minister:

> And should I, Reader, say that our gracious Soveraign is blessed in such a *Minister*, in the *Right Honourable*, the *Earl* of *Clarendon*, the present *Lord High Chancellour* of *England*, I should say no more, then what is evident by those daily dispatches, which passe through his hands, and that weight of affairs which presse, but cannot oppresse him.
>
> (p. 64)

The early 1660s marked the height of Clarendon's influence, since he was instrumental in drafting and enacting the key policies of that decade. Clarendon's removal from office in 1667 ensured that a comparison to Palinurus would prove all too appropriate for certain royalists. In *Aeneid* 5 Neptune tells Venus that he will secure the safe passage of the Trojan fleet from Sicily to Italy if one of the Trojans dies on the voyage, and Palinurus serves as this sacrifice (*A* 5.779–871). Clarendon's supporters read his fall in similarly sacrificial, scapegoating terms: the anti-Clarendon faction at Charles's court (which included Howard amongst its members) capitalised on the disastrous outcome of the 1665–7 war with the Dutch to impeach him, although Clarendon had always opposed the war and was not responsible for its outcome.[33]

Boys can only have intended to draw positive associations between Clarendon and Palinurus, yet Clarendon invited a closer parallel with Palinurus than Boys could have anticipated. It is nonetheless fitting that Boys's praise of Clarendon as a Palinurus ended up having a different outcome to the one he originally intended, since in the *Aeneid* Palinurus himself is the subject of a prophecy that is fulfilled in an unexpected manner. When Aeneas encounters Palinurus' shade in the Underworld he states that Apollo told him Palinurus would arrive safe in Italy, and that he had interpreted this to mean that Palinurus would not be lost on the voyage. Palinurus states that, after he fell overboard, he arrived on the coast of Italy before being killed by a group of native Italians (*A* 6.337–83). Clarendon ultimately emulated the elements of Virgil's Palinurus that were aligned with lament rather than panegyric.

Conclusion: Virgil's English Translators in the Later Stuart Period

Virgil remained an important presence in both epic and political poetry in the 1660s, but his influence was less strong in the decade that followed the fall of Clarendon, the event which is often held to have brought the first phase of restored Stuart rule to an end. Several of the translations considered across this study were republished during this period, but the only new versions of Virgil that appeared in print were a 1670 imitation of *Eclogue* 10 and translations of brief passages from *Georgics* 2 and 4, all of which were by Charles's ambassador to the Netherlands, Sir William Temple. From the late 1670s to the end of the century, however, there was a renewed engagement with Virgil, first through imitation, and subsequently through direct translation. It is not a coincidence that this period was also one of intense political uncertainty, the origins of which lay in the failure of the very future that Boys (and other writers) had optatively prophesied in their Virgilian writings: the birth of a legitimate male heir to Charles II. The events of the Exclusion Crisis (1679–81) had suggested an alternative to the expected future of the dynasty by excluding from the succession Charles II's legitimate (but Catholic) heir presumptive, his brother the Duke of York, in favour of the king's illegitimate (but Protestant) son the Duke of Monmouth. The Exclusion Crisis threatened to precipitate armed conflict, and the political convulsions it prompted were often seen as a repetition of the debates regarding royal power at the start of the 1640s. Even the names that emerged to describe the two major factions, the Whigs and the Tories, resurrected terms of abuse that originated in the civil wars.

Where the start of the Exclusion Crisis was compared to the civil wars, its conclusion in 1681 with royal power reasserted and a newly confident Stuart monarchy saw comparisons with 1660. Stuart loyalists attempted to grant royal authority a greater stability than it truly possessed in the early 1680s by portraying this conclusion as the only possible outcome. Chief among these loyalists was the Poet Laureate, John Dryden. The Virgilian elements of Dryden's most extensive poem on the Exclusion Crisis, *Absalom and Achitophel* (1681), have been acknowledged,[34] but less attention has been paid to the extent to which the poem's content and technique is also indebted to the works of Virgil's mid-seventeenth-century English translators. Dryden's use of the Books of Samuel to reflect on the Crisis, where King David represents Charles and Absalom the Duke of Monmouth, is indebted to Cowley's use of biblical material in *Davideis* (1656). The Charles/David association in

Absalom, however, is shorn of the latent contingencies regarding the prospect of Stuart rule that inform Cowley's poem.[35] Dryden's removal of these contingencies shows the influence of Denham as well as Cowley on *Absalom*. The speech which reaffirms David's power imitates a couplet from the 1642 edition of *Coopers Hill*:

> The Law shall still direct my peacefull Sway,
> And the same Law teach Rebels to Obey.[36]

Here Dryden draws on the same couplet from Denham's poem that Howard imitates in the 1660 panegyric to Monck discussed earlier in this chapter. Where Howard's version places the act of obedience in the immediate past, Dryden's looks with confidence to the future. Dryden adopts Denham's Virgilian technique in *Coopers Hill* and *The Destruction of Troy* of using retrospective prophecy, but where Denham uses it to 'foretell' royalist catastrophe, in Dryden it serves to 'predict' royalist successes that had already occurred by the time of the poem's composition.

This couplet is taken from Denham, but the attitude towards monarchy that Dryden expresses in *Absalom* and the function of prophecy within the poem are more reminiscent of the confident, ultra-loyalist prophecies that are present in Ogilby's Virgil. Charles-as-David is not a king who is under the law; the king's will is the law. A further parallel between *Absalom* and Ogilby's ultra-loyalism comes in the prophecy that ends the poem and which connects heavenly and kingly power:

> Henceforth a Series of new time began,
> The mighty Years in long Procession ran:
> Once more the Godlike *David* was Restor'd,
> And willing Nations knew their Lawfull Lord.
> (Dryden, *Absalom and Achitophel*, p. 32)

John McTague has outlined how in this passage Dryden seeks to occlude historical contingencies and to present the Tory triumph of the Exclusion Crisis as a second Stuart Restoration.[37] McTague's discussion focuses on the passage's connections to biblical prophecy, and its recycling of Dryden's own conclusion to his poem on the Restoration itself, *Astræa Redux*. Yet the lines are (as in *Astræa Redux*) Virgilian as well as biblical in their content and tone: they imitate lines from Virgil's fourth *Eclogue* on the imminent return of the Golden Age. Dryden's Virgilian allusions in this passage were recognised by Francis Atterbury when he translated *Absalom* into Latin, since he directly quotes from *Eclogue* 4 in his rendering of *Absalom*'s conclusion.[38] Atterbury also renders the couplet immediately prior to this passage, 'Th' Almighty, nodding, gave Consent; / And Peals of Thunder shook the Firmament' (*Absalom*, p. 32), with a direct transcription of Virgil's Jupiter's assenting to a fellow god's request (*A* 9.106).[39] Again, the Virgilian references underline the poem's presentation of sacred monarchy and the celebration of renewed Stuart authority.

For all its official rhetoric of security and confidence, in the intersection of the Virgilian with the biblical in *Absalom* Dryden acknowledges and anticipates various possible futures. As in Virgil, and the works of many of his mid-seventeenth-century English translators, the *post eventum* prophecy registers anxieties for the future. In ending the poem where he does, Dryden is also able to engage with the tradition of the Virgilian poet–counsellor, but rather than directing his advice to the sovereign, Dryden intends Monmouth as the recipient of his counsel. He warns Monmouth (and his followers) against continuing or extending the parallel between his situation and Absalom's, since in the Books of Samuel Absalom dies in an unsuccessful rebellion against his father. *Absalom* thus represents a noticeably Virgilian approach to the poem's biblical subject matter. Here too Dryden follows in the footsteps of Cowley's *Davideis*. Dryden stops his poetic retelling of the life of King David at a specific point in order to register two versions of the future, one that he hopes will be averted, and another that he hopes will come to pass. *Absalom* is, therefore, unlike the attempts at prophecy by Dryden's fellow Restoration-era Stuart loyalist Boys, able to accommodate alternative outcomes. It is consequently less prone to being undermined or nullified by subsequent events, even if Monmouth's rebellion and execution in 1685 would, for certain readers, have vindicated and validated the prophetic qualities of Dryden's implied counsel to Monmouth at *Absalom*'s conclusion.

The hopes of stable Stuart rule that Dryden expressed in *Absalom* proved short-lived thanks to Charles II's death soon after the Exclusion Crisis and the renewed tensions between king and Parliament in the reign of his brother as James VII and II. These tensions precipitated the 'Glorious Revolution' of 1688 that exiled James and enthroned as co-monarchs his son-in-law William of Orange and his daughter Mary, the eldest child of his marriage to Clarendon's daughter, Anne Hyde. It was in this period that Dryden went from imitating and quoting Virgil to translating him directly: first in the partial translations from the *Miscellany Poems* of 1684 and its 1685 sequel *Sylvae*, and the wholesale translation that he published in 1697. As in the middle decades of the seventeenth century, the most extensive translations from Virgil after 1688 were produced by supporters of dispossessed Stuarts. Dryden was removed from the Laureateship in 1688 because his sense of obligation to James prevented him from swearing the Oath of Allegiance to William and Mary that was a prerequisite for holding public office. The other complete rendering of Virgil that was completed in the 1690s was by Richard Maitland, 4th Earl of Lauderdale; this translation helped shape Dryden's, as he had access to it in manuscript.[40] Lauderdale's Jacobite sympathies were such that he followed James into exile, where he presented a partial translation of his *Aeneid* to James's second wife, Mary of Modena. In the preface to this translation, also addressed to Mary, Lauderdale reads several passages in the *Aeneid* as prophecies for recent events, including the fall of Strafford, the outbreak of civil war, and the Stuarts' experience of exile.[41]

This is not to say that Virgil remained the sole preserve of the Jacobites. William's supporters sought to co-opt the cultural legitimation that Virgil could bring to their own cause, albeit more through imitation than direct translation and in noticeably less accomplished verse than Dryden's. In his 1695 epic *Prince Arthur* the Williamite poet Sir Richard Blackmore imitates the Parade of Heroes from *Aeneid* 6 to include a passage where Arthur is presented with a vision of his descendants. Blackmore makes particularly heavy use of Anchises' encomium of Augustus in his description of William, who like Augustus also holds the place of honour in the parade.[42] For all its attempt to reapply the rhetoric of security and inevitability to William's reign, however, Blackmore's imitation of the Parade of Heroes in *Prince Arthur* unwillingly preserves the anxieties about the longevity of Aeneas' and Augustus' reign that inform the Virgilian original. William's dynastic claim to the throne rested on insecure foundations, and his lack of a biological heir raised issues regarding the succession.

Dryden sought to delay publication of his *Works of Virgil* in the hopes that William would be deposed and he would thus be able to dedicate the volume to a restored King James.[43] This was wishful thinking on his part. Nonetheless, a Jacobite restoration remained an active possibility during the last decade of the seventeenth century. The reasserted associations with Aeneas and Augustus for both the Williamite and Jacobite branches of the House of Stuart, which included claims of direct lineal Romano-Trojan descent, represented attempts to mitigate concerns regarding their longer-term dynastic prospects. The sources of this uncertainty took different forms: James had several Catholic heirs – indeed, the birth of a male heir in 1688 had precipitated the end of his reign – but those who sought a Protestant succession had to rest their hopes on James's younger daughter from his marriage to Anne Hyde, Princess Anne, and her son Prince William, Duke of Gloucester. Like Prince Henry, the previous holder of the dukedom, Gloucester gained the status of a second Marcellus: he died at the age of eleven in 1700. Parliament was only able to secure a Protestant royal succession via the Act of Settlement that was passed in the wake of Gloucester's death by excluding over fifty individuals to favour James VI and I's granddaughter, the Electress Sophia of Hanover, and her descendants. The two lines of descent from James's respective marriages, one Protestant, the other Catholic, offered alternative political futures for the nation, which fostered tensions that were not resolved until the defeat of the Jacobites at Culloden in 1746.

Irrespective of their political affinities Virgil's English translators after 1688 imitated their mid-seventeenth-century predecessors in their use of Virgil to display and interrogate their political loyalties, articulate personal responses to past traumas, acknowledge competing accounts of the recent past and express their sometimes confident, but frequently anxious, hopes for the future. What distinguishes the works of Dryden and his contemporaries from their mid-seventeenth-century counterparts is that the range of possible futures they anticipated was narrower. Monarchical rule was often the desired future that Virgil's translators articulated during the period considered in this book, but it was only one of the possible futures that they contemplated. The ability to apply to an English context Virgil's recognition that his own historical moment had made a plurality of futures possible, but that, however much individual futures could be anticipated or desired, securing them was ultimately at the mercy of chance events, was the product of the unstable, contingent and (despite the efforts of certain translators) unpredictable years of the civil wars, Interregnum and early Restoration.

Notes

1. John Boys, *Æneas His Descent into Hell* (London, 1661 [for 1660]) (hereafter *Descent*), p. 50.
2. *Poems by the Honourable Sir Robert Howard* (London, 1660) (hereafter Howard, *Poems*), sig. A4r.
3. See Howard, *Poems*, pp. 181, 188, 190, 195, 232, 234, 236, 263, 264, 277–8.
4. Cf. the translations from *Aeneid* 4 at Howard, *Poems*, pp. 160 and 198 (*A* 4.474–91); pp. 143 and 249 (*A* 4.59); pp. 149 and 216 (*A* 4.203–4).
5. *Poems*, pp. 236–7, citing *Pharsalia* 9.11–14.
6. Tanya Caldwell, *Virgil Made English: The Decline of Classical Authority* (Basingstoke, 2008), p. 40.
7. At Howard, *Poems*, p. 148.
8. See pp. 13–14, above.

9. For a discussion of which, see p. 16, above.
10. Sir John Denham, *Coopers Hill. A Poëme* (London, 1642), p. 19.
11. See pp. 35–6, above.
12. See H. J. Oliver, *Sir Robert Howard (1626–1698): A Critical Biography* (Durham, NC, 1963), pp. 11–12.
13. See James A. Winn, *John Dryden and His World* (London, 1987), p. 559.
14. See pp. 60–1, 83, above.
15. *Descent*, p. 23. As in my other chapters, underline indicates where the translations substantially depart from or add to the Virgilian original.
16. See pp. 87–90, above.
17. John Ogilby, *The Works of Publius Virgilius Maro* (London, 1649), sig. L1v; John Ogilby, *The Works of Publius Virgilius Maro Translated, adorn'd with Sculpture, and illustrated with Annotations* (London, 1654), p. 354.
18. See *Descent*, p. 23 (A 6.620) and John Boys, *Æneas His Errours, or His Voyage from Troy into Italy* (London, 1661) (hereafter *Errours*), p. 5 (A 3.56–7), p. 30 (A 3.415).
19. Ogilby, *Works of Publius Virgilius Maro* (1649), sig. L4r; *Works of Publius Virgilius Maro* (1654), p. 363.
20. I discussed Fanshawe's more eirenic translation of this line on p. 123, above.
21. For examples contemporary with *Descent*, see David Norbrook, *Writing the English Republic: Poetry, Rhetoric and Politics, 1627–1660* (Cambridge, 1999), pp. 182–4.
22. See *Descent*, pp. 155–61.
23. See *Descent*, pp. 87–8.
24. *Descent*, p. 214; roman/italic fonts reversed.
25. See *Descent*, pp. 214–15.
26. *Errours*, sig. A4r; roman/italic fonts reversed.
27. See pp. 10, 20, above.
28. In 1604 Sir John Harington (a distant kinsman of James Harrington) had produced a stand-alone translation of *Aeneid* 6, but as it had only a very limited circulation and remained in manuscript until 1991 Boys is unlikely to have known of its existence.
29. As discussed above on pp. 13–14 (Godolphin/Waller), pp. 20–1 (Sandys), p. 30 (Denham).
30. John Boys, *A Panegyrick to His Sacred Majesty Upon the Conclusion of the auspicious Marriage Between the two Crowns of England and Portugal* (London, 1662).
31. See p. 133, above.
32. In *Descent*, p. 225 (Monck), p. 227 (Charles).
33. I draw here on Ronald Hutton, *Charles the Second: King of England, Scotland and Ireland* (Oxford, 1989), pp. 214–53.
34. See Paul Hammond, *Dryden and the Traces of Classical Rome* (Oxford, 1999), pp. 105–16.
35. As discussed on pp. 65–7, above.
36. John Dryden, *Absalom and Achitophel. A Poem* (London, 1681), p. 31.
37. John McTague, *Things That Didn't Happen: Writing, Politics and the Counterhistorical, 1678–1743* (Woodbridge, 2019), p. 74.

38. The borrowing is noted in Hammond, *Traces of Classical Rome*, p. 113.
39. See Francis Atterbury, *Absalon et Achitophel. Poema Latino Carmine Donatum* (Oxford, 1682), p. 29 (for 39).
40. For a summary of the relationship between Dryden and Lauderdale, their respective translations, and previous scholarship on this topic, see Arthur Sherbo, 'Dryden and the Fourth Earl of Lauderdale', *Studies in Bibliography*, 39 (1986), 199–210.
41. I draw here on Murray Pittock, *Poetry and Jacobite Politics in Eighteenth-Century Britain and Ireland* (Cambridge, 1994), pp. 38–9.
42. Cf. *A* 6.756–886 (791–7) with Sir Richard Blackmore, *Prince Arthur* (London, 1695), pp. 145–55 (152–3).
43. As outlined in a letter to the Earl of Chesterfield: see *The Letters of John Dryden with Letters Addressed to Him*, ed. Charles E. Ward (Durham, NC, 1942), pp. 85–6.

Bibliography

Primary Sources

Manuscripts

Los Angeles, William Andrews Clark Memorial Library, MS.1946.007.

Printed Books with Marginalia

Boys, John, *Æneas His Descent into Hell* (London, 1661 [for 1660]). London, British Library, 11375.c.36.
Denham, Sir John, *Poems and Translations, with The Sophy* (London, 1668). New Haven, Beinecke Rare Book and Manuscript Library, Osborn MS pb53.

Early Modern Editions of Virgil

Farnaby, Thomas (ed.), *Publii Virgilii Maronis Opera* (London, 1634).
Germanus [Germain Vaillant de Guélis] (ed.), *P. Virgilius Maro* (Antwerp, 1575).
La Cerda, Juan Luis de (ed.), *P. Virgilii Maronis Opera Omnia*, 3 vols (Cologne, 1642–7).
Manutius, Paulus [Paolo Manuzio], and Georgius Fabricius [Georg Goldschmidt] (eds), *Opera P. Virgilii Maronis* (Cambridge, 1632).
Ogilby, John (ed.), *Publii Virgilii Maronis Opera* (London, 1658).
Pontanus, Jacobus [Jakob Spanmüller] (ed.), *Symbolarum Libri XVII Virgilii* (Augsburg, 1599).
Schrevelius, Theodore, and Cornelius Schrevelius (eds), *P. Virgilii Maronis* (Leiden, 1646).
Stephanus, Henricus [Henri Estienne] (ed.), *Publii Virgilii Maronis poemata* (London, 1593).
Taubmann, Friedrich, and Christian Taubmann (eds), *P. Virgilii Maronis Opera Omnia* (Wittenberg, 1618).

Printed

Atterbury, Francis, *Absalon et Achitophel. Poema Latino Carmine Donatum* (Oxford, 1682).
Aubrey, John, *Aubrey's Brief Lives*, ed. Oliver Lawson Dick (London, 1949).

Bacon, Francis, *The Essayes or Counsels, Civill and Morall, of Francis Lo. Verulam, Viscount St. Alban* (London, 1625).
Barbauld, Anna Letitia, *The Poems of Anna Letitia Barbauld*, ed. William McCarthy and Elizabeth Kraft (Athens, GA, 1994).
Blackmore, Sir Richard, *Prince Arthur* (London, 1695).
Bowman, Henry, *Songs for 1, 2, & 3 Voyces* (Oxford, 1677).
Bowman, Henry, *Songs, for One, Two, & Three Voyces to the Thorow-Bass* (Oxford, 1679).
Boys, John, *Æneas His Descent into Hell* (London, 1661 [for 1660]).
Boys, John, *Æneas His Errours, or His Voyage from Troy into Italy* (London, 1661).
Boys, John, *A Panegyrick to His Sacred Majesty Upon the Conclusion of the auspicious Marriage Between the two Crowns of England and Portugal* (London, 1662).
Brome, Richard (ed.), *Lachrymæ Musarum* (London, 1649).
Camdeni Insignia (Oxford, 1624).
Camões, Luís Vaz de, *Os Lusíadas*, ed. Álvaro Júlio da Costa Pimpão, 4th edn (Lisbon, 2000).
Camões, Luís Vaz de, *The Lusíads*, trans. Landeg White (Oxford, 2008).
Carolus Redux (Oxford, 1623).
Corneille, Pierre, *Horace, Tragedie* (Paris, 1641).
Cowley, Abraham, *Abraham Cowley: The Civil War*, ed. Allan Pritchard (Toronto, 1973).
Cowley, Abraham, *Abrahami Couleii Angli, Poemata Latina* (London, 1668).
Cowley, Abraham, *A Critical Edition of Abraham Cowley's Davideis*, ed. Gayle Shadduck (New York, 1987).
Cowley, Abraham, *Cutter of Coleman-Street* (London, 1663).
Cowley, Abraham, '*De Plantis Libri Sex* (1668): A Hypertext Critical Edition', ed. Dana Sutton, in *The Philological Museum* (2006/7), www.philological.bham.ac.uk/plants/
Cowley, Abraham(?), *The Foure Ages of England: Or, The Iron Age. With Other Select Poems* (London, 1648).
Cowley, Abraham, '*Naufragium Joculare* (1638): A Hypertext Critical Edition', ed. Dana Sutton, in *The Philological Museum* (2001/2), www.philological.bham.ac.uk/cowley/
Cowley, Abraham, *Naufragium Joculare Comædia* (London, 1638).
Cowley, Abraham, *Ode, Upon The Blessed Restoration and Returne of His Sacred Majestie, Charls the Second* (London, 1660).
Cowley, Abraham, *Poems Written by A. Cowley* (London, 1656).
Cowley, Abraham, *Verses, Lately Written Upon Several Occasions* (London, 1663).
Cowley, Abraham, *A Vision, Concerning his late Pretended Highnesse, Cromwell, the Wicked* (London, 1661).
Cowley, Abraham, *The Visions and Prophecies Concerning England, Scotland, and Ireland* (London, 1660).
Cowley, Abraham, *The Works of Mr Abraham Cowley* (London, 1668).
Crashaw, Richard, *Steps to the Temple* (London, 1646).
Davenant, Sir William, and Thomas Hobbes, *A Discourse upon Gondibert. An Heroick Poem Written by S^r· William D'avenant. With an Answer to it by M^r· Hobbs* (Paris, 1650).

Davies, Sir John, *The Poems of Sir John Davies*, ed. Robert Krueger and Ruby Nemser (Oxford, 1975).
Denham, Sir John, *Aeneid 2–6*, in *Early Augustan Virgil: Translations by Denham, Godolphin, and Waller*, ed. Robin Sowerby (Lewisburg, PA, 2010).
Denham, Sir John, *Cato Major of Old Age. A Poem* (London, 1669).
Denham, Sir John, *Coopers Hill. A Poëme* (London, 1642).
Denham, Sir John, *Coopers Hill. A Poëme* (Oxford, 1643).
Denham, Sir John, *Coopers Hill. Written in the yeare 1640. Now Printed from a perfect Copy; And a Corrected Impression* (London, 1653).
Denham, Sir John, *Coopers Hill. Written in the yeare 1640. Now Printed from a perfect Copy; And A Corrected Impression* (London, 1655).
Denham, Sir John, *The Destruction of Troy, an Essay upon the Second Book of Virgils Æneis. Written in the year, 1636* (London, 1656).
Denham, Sir John, *Expans'd Hieroglyphicks: A Critical Edition of Sir John Denham's Coopers Hill*, ed. Brendan O Hehir (Berkeley, 1969).
Denham, Sir John, *Poems and Translations, with The Sophy* (London, 1668).
Denham, Sir John, *The Poetical Works of Sir John Denham*, ed. Theodore Howard Banks, 2nd edn (Hamden, CT, 1969).
Denham, Sir John, *The Sophy* (London, 1642).
Dryden, John, *Absalom and Achitophel. A Poem* (London, 1681).
Dryden, John, *Astræa Redux* (London, 1660).
Dryden, John, *The Letters of John Dryden with Letters Addressed to Him*, ed. Charles E. Ward (Durham, NC, 1942).
Duppa, Brian (ed.), *Jonsonus Virbius* (London, 1638).
Fanshawe, Sir Richard, *Il Pastor Fido, The Faithfull Shepherd* (London, 1647).
Fanshawe, Sir Richard, *Il Pastor Fido The Faithfull Shepheard with an Addition of divers other Poems Concluding with a short Discourse of the Long Civill Warres of Rome. To His Highnesse the Prince of Wales* (London, 1648).
Fanshawe, Sir Richard, *The Lusiad, or Portugals Historicall Poem* (London, 1655).
Fanshawe, Sir Richard, *The Poems and Translations of Sir Richard Fanshawe*, ed. Peter Davidson, 2 vols (Oxford, 1997).
Fanshawe, Sir Richard, *Selected Parts of Horace, Prince of Lyricks; and of all the Latin Poets the fullest fraught with Excellent Morality* (London, 1652).
Godolphin, Sidney, *The Poems of Sidney Godolphin*, ed. William Dighton (Oxford, 1931).
Godolphin, Sidney and Edmund Waller, *The Passion of Dido for Aeneas*, in *Early Augustan Virgil: Translations by Denham, Godolphin, and Waller*, ed. Robin Sowerby (Lewisburg, PA, 2010).
Harrington, James, *The Art of Law-Giving* (London, 1659).
Harrington, James, *The Common-Wealth of Oceana* (London, 1656).
Harrington, James, *An Essay Upon two of Virgil's Eclogues, and Two Books of his Æneis (If this be not enough) Towards the Translation of the whole* (London, 1658).
Harrington, James, *The Oceana of James Harrington, and his Other Works*, ed. John Toland (London, 1700).
Harrington, James, *Politicaster* (London, 1659).
Harrington, James, *Virgil's Æneis: The Third, Fourth, Fifth and Sixth Books* (London, 1659).
Heath, Robert, *Clarastella* (London, 1650).

Heath, Robert, *Paradoxical Assertions and Philosophical Problems* (London, 1659).
Herrick, Robert, *The Complete Poetry of Robert Herrick*, ed. Tom Cain and Ruth Connolly, 2 vols (Oxford, 2013).
Holyday, Barten, *Horace. The best of Lyrick Poets. Containing much morality, and Sweetnesse* (London, 1652).
Homer, *Iliad*, ed. and trans. A. T. Murray, rev. William F. Wyatt, 2 vols (London, 1999).
Homer, *Odyssey*, ed. and trans. A. T. Murray, rev. George E. Dimock, 2 vols (London, 1995).
Horace, *Odes and Epodes*, ed. and trans. Niall Rudd (London, 2004).
Howard, Sir Robert, *Poems by the Honourable Sir Robert Howard* (London, 1660).
Jevon, Rachel, *Exultationis Carmen* (London, 1660).
Jonson, Ben, *The Complete Poems*, ed. George Parfitt (London, 1988).
Kingsmill, Sir William, *A Collection of parts of some Bookes of Virgill*, in *Newly Recovered English Classical Translations 1600–1800*, ed. Stuart Gillespie (Oxford, 2018), www.nrect.gla.ac.uk.
Lake, Edward, *Diary of Dr. Edward Lake*, ed. George Percy Elliot (London, 1846).
Livy, *History of Rome, Books I–II*, ed. and trans. B. O. Foster (London, 1919).
Loftis, John (ed.), *The Memoirs of Anne, Lady Halkett and Ann, Lady Fanshawe* (Oxford, 1979).
Lucan, *The Civil War*, ed. and trans. J. H. Duff (London, 1928).
Matthew, Edward, *The Most Glorious Star, or, Celestial Constellation of the Pleiades, or Charles Waine* (London, 1660).
Mendoza, Antonio Hurtado de, *Querer por Solo Querer* (Lisbon, 1639).
Ogilby, John, *Africa* (London, 1670).
Ogilby, John, *The Entertainment of His Most Excellent Majesty Charles II: A Facsimile*, ed. Ronald Knowles (Binghamton, NY, 1988).
Ogilby, John, *The Fables of Æsop* (London, 1651).
Ogilby, John, *Homer his Iliads Translated, adorn'd with Sculpture, and illustrated with Annotations* (London, 1660).
Ogilby, John, *Homer his Odysses Translated, adorn'd with Sculpture, and illustrated with Annotations* (London, 1665).
Ogilby, John, *The Relation of His Majestie's Entertainment Passing through the City of London, To His Coronation: with a Description of the Triumphal Arches, and Solemnity* (London, 1661).
Ogilby, John, *The Translation of Homers Works into English Verse being Undertaken by John Ogilby* (London, 1660).
Ogilby, John, *The Works of Publius Virgilius Maro* (London, 1649).
Ogilby, John, *The Works of Publius Virgilius Maro* (London, 1650).
Ogilby, John, *The Works of Publius Virgilius Maro Translated, adorn'd with Sculpture, and illustrated with Annotations* (London, 1654).
Ovid, *Metamorphoses*, ed. and trans. Frank Justus Miller, rev. G. P. Goold, 2 vols (London, 1977).
Pasquier, Etienne, *Les Recherches de La France D'Estienne Pasquier* (Paris, 1621).
Philips, Katherine, *Poems By the most deservedly Admired Mrs Katherine Philips* (London, 1669).

Ronsard, Pierre, *The Franciad (1572)*, trans. Phillip John Usher (New York, 2010).
Sadler, Anthony, *The Loyall Mourner* (London, 1660).
Sandys, George, *A Paraphrase upon the Divine Poems* (London, 1638).
Servius, *Servii Grammatici qui feruntur in Vergilii Carmina Commentarii*, ed. Georg Thilo and Hermann Hagen, 3 vols (Leipzig, 1878–1902).
Servius, *Servius' Commentary on Book Four of Virgil's Aeneid*, ed. and trans. Christopher M. McDonough, Richard E. Prior and Mark Stansbury (Wauconda, IL, 2004).
Sidney, Sir Philip, *An Apologie for Poetrie* (London, 1595).
Stapylton, Robert, *Dido and Aeneas The Fourth Booke of Virgils Æneis Now Englished By Robert Stapylton Esqr* (London, 1634).
Statius, *Thebaid*, ed. and trans. D. R. Shackleton Bailey, 2 vols (London, 2004).
Vaughan, Henry, *The Mount of Olives* (London, 1652).
Vicars, John, *The XII Aeneids of Virgil* (London, 1632).
Virgil, *Eclogues, Georgics, Aeneid*, ed. and trans. H. Rushton Fairclough, rev. G. P. Goold, 2 vols (London, 1999).
Virgil, *Georgics*, ed. Richard Thomas, 2 vols (Cambridge, 1988).
Waller, Edmund, *A Panegyrick to my Lord Protector* (London, 1655).
Waller, Edmund, *Poems, &c. Written by Mr. Ed. Waller of Beckonsfield, Esquire* (London, 1645).
Waller, Edmund, *Poems &c. Written upon several Occasions, and to several Persons* (London, 1711).
Waller, Edmund, *The Poems of Edmund Waller*, ed. George Thorn Drury, 2 vols (London, 1904).
Waller, Edmund, *Upon the late storme, and of the death of His Highnesse ensuing the same* (London, 1658).
Waller, Edmund, and Sidney Godolphin, *The Passion of Dido for Æneas. As it is Incomparably exprest in the Fourth Book of Virgil* (London, 1658).
Ziolkowski, Jan M., and Michael C. J. Putnam (eds), *The Virgilian Tradition: The First Fifteen Hundred Years* (New Haven, CT, 2008).

Secondary Sources

Allsopp, Niall, *Poetry and Sovereignty in the English Revolution* (Oxford, 2020).
Archer, Ian W., 'Royal Entries, the City of London, and the Politics of Stuart Successions', in *Stuart Succession Literature: Moments and Transformations*, ed. Paulina Kewes and Andrew McRae (Oxford, 2019), pp. 257–81.
Bowie, A. M. 'The Death of Priam: Allegory and History in the *Aeneid*', *Classical Quarterly*, 40 (1990), 470–81.
Braden, Gordon, 'The Passion of Dido: *Aeneid* 4 in English Translation to 1700', in *Virgil and His Translators*, ed. Susanna Braund and Zara Martirosova Torlone (Oxford, 2018), pp. 80–96.
Brammall, Sheldon, *The English Aeneid: Translations of Virgil, 1555–1646* (Edinburgh, 2015).
Burrow, Colin, 'Virgil in English Translation', in *The Cambridge Companion to Virgil*, ed. Fiachra Mac Góráin and Charles Martindale, 2nd edn (Cambridge, 2019), pp. 109–27.

Caldwell, Tanya, 'Translation', in *The Oxford Handbook of British Poetry, 1660–1800*, ed. Jack Lynch (Oxford, 2016), pp. 596–614.

Caldwell, Tanya, *Virgil Made English: The Decline of Classical Authority* (Basingstoke, 2008).

Calvert, Ian, 'Augustan Allusion: Quotation and Self-Quotation in Pope's *Odyssey*', *Review of English Studies*, 297 (2019), 869–89.

Calvert, Ian, 'Hindsight as Foresight: Virgilian Retrospective Prophecy in *Coopers Hill* and *The Destruction of Troy*', *International Journal of the Classical Tradition*, 26 (2019), 150–74.

Calvert, Ian, 'Slanted Histories, Hesperian Fables: Material Form and Royalist Prophecy in John Ogilby's *The Works of Publius Virgilius Maro*', *The Seventeenth Century*, 33 (2018), 531–55.

Chernaik, Warren L., *The Poetry of Limitation: A Study of Edmund Waller* (London, 1968).

Connolly, Joy, 'Border Wars: Literature, Politics, and the Public', *Transactions of the American Philological Association*, 135 (2005), 103–34.

Corns, Thomas, *Uncloistered Virtue: English Political Literature, 1640–1660* (Oxford, 1992).

Crowther, Stefania, '"An Old and Unfashionable Building": Cowley's Dramatic Writing and Rewriting', in *Royalists and Royalism in 17th-Century Literature: Exploring Abraham Cowley*, ed. Philip Major (Abingdon, 2020), pp. 229–50.

Davis, J. C., 'The Prose Romance of the 1650s as a Context for *Oceana*', in *Perspectives on Revolutionary English Republicanism*, ed. Dirk Wiemann and Gaby Mahlberg (London, 2014), pp. 65–84.

Davis, Paul, *Translation and the Poet's Life: The Ethics of Translating in English Culture, 1646–1726* (Oxford, 2008).

De Groot, Jerome, 'John Denham and Lucy Hutchinson's Commonplace Book', *Studies in English Literature*, 48 (2008), 147–63.

De Groot, Jerome, *Royalist Identities* (Basingstoke, 2004).

Durston, Christopher, *Cromwell's Major-generals: Godly Government during the English Revolution* (Manchester, 2001).

Eames, John, 'Sir William Kingsmill (1613–1661) and His Poetry', *English Studies*, 2 (1986), 126–56.

Ereira, Alan, *The Nine Lives of John Ogilby: Britain's Master Map Maker and His Secrets* (London, 2016).

Eyre, G. E. B. (ed.), *A Transcript of the Registers of the Worshipful Company of Stationers, From 1640–1708 AD*, 3 vols (London, 1913–14).

Foxley, Rachel, 'Democracy in 1659: Harrington and the Good Old Cause', in *The Nature of the English Revolution Revisited*, ed. Stephen Taylor and Grant Tapsell (Woodbridge, 2013), pp. 175–96.

Foy, Anna, 'Epic', in *The Oxford Handbook of English Poetry, 1660–1800*, ed. Jack Lynch (Oxford, 2016), pp. 473–94.

Fraser, Antonia, *King Charles II* (London, 1979).

Fukuda, Arihiro, *Sovereignty and the Sword: Harrington, Hobbes, and Mixed Government in the English Civil Wars* (Oxford, 1997).

Gowers, Emily, 'Trees and Family Trees in the *Aeneid*', *Classical Antiquity*, 30 (2011), 87–118.

Hammersley, Rachel, *James Harrington: An Intellectual Biography* (Oxford, 2019).

Hammersley, Rachel, 'James Harrington's *The Commonwealth of Oceana* and

the Republican Tradition', in *The Oxford Handbook of Literature and the English Revolution*, ed. Laura Lunger Knoppers (Oxford, 2012), pp. 534–50.
Hammond, Paul, *Dryden and the Traces of Classical Rome* (Oxford, 1999).
Hardie, Philip, 'Abraham Cowley, *Davideis. Sacri poematis operis imperfecti liber unus*', in *Neo-Latin Poetry in the British Isles*, ed. L. B. T. Houghton and Gesine Manuwald (London, 2012), pp. 69–86.
Harrison, T. W., 'English Vergil: The *Aeneid* in the XVIII Century', *Philologica Pragensia*, 10 (1967), 1–11, 80–91.
Hopper, Andrew, *Turncoats and Renegadoes: Changing Sides during the English Civil Wars* (Oxford, 2012).
Hutton, Ronald, *Charles the Second: King of England, Scotland and Ireland* (Oxford, 1989).
Jenkinson, Matthew, *Culture and Politics at the Court of Charles II, 1660–1685* (Woodbridge, 2010).
Kilgour, Maggie, 'Cowley's Epic Experiments', in *Royalists and Royalism in 17th-Century Literature: Exploring Abraham Cowley*, ed. Philip Major (Abingdon, 2020), pp. 93–123.
Lewis, Charlton T., and Charles Short, *A Latin Dictionary* (London, 1879).
Lloyd, Robert B., 'Superbus in the *Aeneid*', *American Journal of Philology*, 93 (1972), 125–32.
Lockey, Brian C., *Early Modern Catholics, Royalists, and Cosmopolitans: English Transnationalism and the Christian Commonwealth* (Abingdon, 2015).
Løsnes, Arvid, *'Arms, and the Man I sing . . .': A Preface to Dryden's Æneis* (Newark, DE, 2011).
Loxley, James, *Royalism and Poetry in the English Civil Wars: The Drawn Sword* (Basingstoke, 1997).
Lynch, Jack, 'Political Ideology in Translations of the *Iliad*, 1660–1715', *Translation and Literature*, 7 (1998), 23–41.
McDowell, Nicholas, 'Harrington, James', *The Encyclopedia of English Renaissance Literature*, ed. Garrett A. Sullivan Jr and Allen Stewart, 3 vols (Oxford, 2012), vol. 2, pp. 437–41.
McDowell, Nicholas, 'Herrick and the Order of the Black Riband: Literary Community in Civil-War London and the Publication of *Hesperides* (1648)', in *'Lords of Wine and Oile': Community and Conviviality in the Poetry of Robert Herrick*, ed. Ruth Connolly and Tom Cain (Oxford, 2011), pp. 106–26.
McElligott, Jason, and David L. Smith (eds), *Royalists and Royalism during the English Civil Wars* (Cambridge, 2007).
McElligott, Jason, and David L. Smith (eds), *Royalists and Royalism during the Interregnum* (Manchester, 2010).
MacLean, Gerald M., *Time's Witness: Historical Representation in English Poetry, 1603–1660* (Madison, WI, 1990).
McTague, John, *Things That Didn't Happen: Writing, Politics and the Counterhistorical, 1678–1743* (Woodbridge, 2019).
Major, Philip (ed.), *Sir John Denham (1614/15–1669) Reassessed: The State's Poet* (London, 2016).
Miner, Earl, *The Cavalier Mode from Jonson to Cotton* (Princeton, 1971).
Momeni, Amin, 'John Denham's *The Sophy* and Anglo-Persian Political Parallels', in *Sir John Denham (1614/15–1669) Reassessed: The State's Poet*, ed. Philip Major (London, 2016), pp. 75–87.

Moore, Lucy, *Lady Fanshawe's Receipt Book: The Life and Times of a Civil War Heroine* (London, 2017).
Nethercot, Arthur H., *Abraham Cowley: The Muse's Hannibal* (Oxford, 1931).
Newman, J. K., *The Concept of Vates in Augustan Poetry* (Brussels, 1967).
Norbrook, David, 'Lucy Hutchinson versus Edmund Waller: An Unpublished Reply to Waller's *A Panegyrick to My Lord Protector*', *The Seventeenth Century*, 11 (1996), 61–86.
Norbrook, David, 'An Unpublished Poem by Sidney Godolphin', *Review of English Studies*, 192 (1997), 498–500.
Norbrook, David, *Writing the English Republic: Poetry, Rhetoric and Politics, 1627–1660* (Cambridge, 1999).
O'Hara, James J., *Death and the Optimistic Prophecy in Vergil's Aeneid* (Princeton, 1990).
O Hehir, Brendan, *Harmony from Discords: A Life of Sir John Denham* (Berkeley, 1968).
Oliver, H. J., *Sir Robert Howard (1626–1698): A Critical Biography* (Durham, NC, 1963).
O'Sullivan, Timothy M., 'Death *ante ora parentum* in Virgil's *Aeneid*', *Transactions of the American Philological Association*, 139 (2009), 447–86.
Parry, Graham, 'A Troubled Arcadia', in *Literature and the English Civil War*, ed. Thomas Healy and Jonathan Sawday (Cambridge, 1990), pp. 38–55.
Patterson, Annabel, *Pastoral and Ideology: Virgil to Valéry* (Oxford, 1988).
Pittock, Murray, *Poetry and Jacobite Politics in Eighteenth-Century Britain and Ireland* (Cambridge, 1994).
Pocock, J. G. A., *The Machiavellian Moment: Florentine Political Thought and the Atlantic Republican Tradition* (Oxford, 2016).
Potter, Lois, *Secret Rites and Secret Writing: Royalist Literature, 1641–1660* (Cambridge, 1989).
Power, Henry, 'The *Aeneid* in the Age of Milton', in *A Companion to Vergil's Aeneid and Its Tradition*, ed. Joseph Farrell and Michael C. J. Putnam (Chichester, 2010), pp. 186–202.
Power, Henry, '"Teares breake off my Verse": The Virgilian Incompleteness of Abraham Cowley's *The Civil War*', *Translation and Literature*, 16 (2007), pp. 141–59.
Power, Henry, 'Virgil's *Georgics* and the Poetic Landscape of the English Civil War', in *Interlacing Words and Things: Bridging the Nature–Culture Opposition in Gardens and Landscapes*, ed. Stephen Bann (Washington, DC, 2012), pp. 51–63.
Proudfoot, L., *Dryden's Aeneid and Its Seventeenth Century Predecessors* (Manchester, 1960).
Pugh, Syrithe, *Herrick, Fanshawe and the Politics of Intertextuality: Classical Literature and Seventeenth-Century Royalism* (Farnham, 2010).
Pugh, Syrithe, *Spenser and Virgil: The Pastoral Poems* (Manchester, 2016).
Raylor, Timothy, 'The Early Poetic Career of Edmund Waller', *Huntington Library Quarterly*, 69 (2006), 239–66.
Reynolds, Matthew, *The Poetry of Translation: From Chaucer and Petrarch to Homer and Logue* (Oxford, 2011).
Robertson, Barry, *Royalists at War in Scotland and Ireland, 1638–1650* (Farnham, 2014).
Rogerson, Anne, *Virgil's Ascanius: Imagining the Future in the Aeneid* (Cambridge, 2017).

Schoenberger, Melissa, *Cultivating Peace: The Virgilian Georgic in English, 1650–1750* (Lewisburg, PA, 2019).
Schwartz, Ariane, 'A Revolutionary Vergil: James Harrington, Poetry, and Political Performance', in *Reading Poetry, Writing Genre: English Poetry and Literary Criticism in Dialogue with Classical Scholarship*, ed. Silvio Bär and Emily Hauser (London, 2018), pp. 51–65.
Scodel, Joshua, *Excess and the Mean in Early Modern English Literature* (Princeton, 2002).
Scott, Jonathan, *Commonwealth Principles: Republican Writing of the English Revolution* (Cambridge, 2004).
Sherbo, Arthur, 'Dryden and the Fourth Earl of Lauderdale', *Studies in Bibliography*, 39 (1986), 199–210.
Smith, David L., *Constitutional Royalism and the Search for Settlement, c.1640–1649* (Cambridge, 1994).
Smith, Geoffrey, *The Cavaliers in Exile, 1640–1660* (Basingstoke, 2003).
Sousa Garcia, Tiago, 'How *The Lusiad* Got English'd: Manuel Faria y Sousa, Richard Fanshawe and the First English Translation of *Os Lusíadas*', *Literature Compass*, 14 (2017), 1–18.
Sowerby, Robin, *The Augustan Art of Poetry: Augustan Translation of the Classics* (Oxford, 2006).
Spearing, Caroline, *Abraham Cowley's Plantarum Libri Sex: A Cavalier Poet and the Classical Canon* (unpublished doctoral thesis, King's College London, 2017).
Spearing, Caroline, 'The Fruits of Retirement: Political Engagement in the *Plantarum Libri Sex*', in *Royalists and Royalism in 17th-Century Literature: Exploring Abraham Cowley*, ed. Philip Major (Abingdon, 2020), pp. 180–201.
Starke, Sue, '"The Eternal Now": Virgilian Echoes and Miltonic Premonitions in Cowley's *Davideis*', *Christianity and Literature*, 55 (2006), 195–219.
Thomas, P. W., *Sir John Berkenhead 1617–1679: A Royalist Career in Politics and Polemics* (Oxford, 1969).
Van Eerde, Katherine S., *John Ogilby and the Taste of His Times* (Folkestone, 1976).
Venuti, Lawrence, *The Translator's Invisibility: A History of Translation* (London, 1995).
Walker, Roger, with W. H. Liddell, 'A Commentary by Sir Richard Fanshawe on the Royal Arms of Portugal', in *Studies in Portuguese Literature and History in Honour of Luís de Sousa Rebelo*, ed. Helder Macedo (London, 1992), pp. 155–70.
Wilcher, Robert, *The Writing of Royalism, 1628–1660* (Cambridge, 2001).
Winn, James A., *John Dryden and His World* (London, 1987).
Worden, Blair, 'Harrington's *Oceana*: Origins and Aftermath, 1651–1660', in *Republicanism, Liberty, and Commercial Society, 1649–1776*, ed. David Wootton (Stanford, 1994), pp. 111–38.

Index

Absalom and Achitophel (Dryden), 180–2
Achilleid (Statius [Howard]), 160–1, 166, 167, 170, 171
Act of Indemnity and Oblivion, 71, 174
Æneas His Descent into Hell (Boys), 165, 172–7, 178–9
Æneas His Errours (Boys), 165, 176–9
Aeneid (Virgil), 5–6, 7–8
   Book 1, 63, 64, 77, 79, 94, 146, 147, 156, 157
   Book 2, 6, 29, 31, 34, 66, 76, 92–3, 100, 152, 157, 158
   Book 3, 106, 152, 153, 177
   Book 4, 6, 13, 14, 18, 44, 45–6, 118, 119–20, 121, 141, 142, 156, 158, 161, 167, 169
   Book 5, 88, 156, 179
   Book 6, 3, 6, 53, 65, 104, 122–3, 155, 158, 159, 172, 173, 175
   Book 7, 4, 37–8, 39, 60–1
   Book 9, 103
   Book 11, 62, 89
Aeneid 2–6 (Denham), 20–1
aesthetics, 153–4, 177
   Augustan, 10
Allsopp, Niall, 8, 66
America *see* New World
Apollo, 33, 53, 54, 77–8, 179
Apsley, *Sir* Allen, 20
Astraea, 45
Astræa Redux (Dryden), 45, 103, 181
Atterbury, Francis, 181
Aubrey, John, 8, 53, 55, 104, 122, 137, 138
Augustan aesthetic, 10
Augustus
   Aeneid (Virgil), 3–4, 5, 7–8
   The Commonwealth of Oceana (Harrington), 146, 147, 159
   An Essay Upon two of Virgil's Eclogues (Harrington), 149
   On His Majesties Great Shippe (Fanshawe), 113, 114
   Os Lusíadas (Camões), 130
   Presented to His Highnesse the Prince of Wales (Fanshawe), 115
   Prince Arthur (Blackmore), 183
   Selected Parts of Horace (Fanshawe), 125
   A Summary Discourse of the Civil Warres in Rome (Fanshawe), 122
autocratic republicanism, 139, 141, 155

Bacon, Francis, 145
Barbauld, Anna Letitia, 78
Battle of Dunbar, 168–9
Battle of Lowestoft, 77
Battle of Worcester, 42, 128–9
Berkenhead, *Sir* John, 39
Blackmore, *Sir* Richard, 183
Bowie, A.M., 7, 31
Boys, John, 1, 161, 180
   Æneas His Descent into Hell, 165, 172–7, 178–9
   Æneas His Errours, 165, 176–9
Brammall, Sheldon, 35, 105
British imperial power, 76–9

Caesar, Julius, 87, 114–15
Caldwell, Tanya, 83, 169
Camden, William, 11
Canto of the Progresse of Learning, A (Fanshawe), 118
Carew, Thomas, 20
Carolies (Ogilby), 84, 107n
Cary, Lucius *see* Falkland, *Viscount*
Catherine of Braganza, 129, 132, 133, 178
Cato Major of Old Age (Denham), 30
Cavendish, Charles, 61–2
Cavendish, *Lady* Anne (*Lady* Rich), 11, 134
Cecil, *Lady* Anne, *Countess of Northumberland*, 11
Charles, *Prince of Wales*, 2, 55
Davideis (Cowley), 64–5, 67
The Faithfull Shepherd (Fanshawe), 117
The Lusiad, or Portugals Historicall Poem (Fanshawe), 129, 130, 131–2
On the Loves of Dido and Æneas (Fanshawe), 117–18, 121
Presented to His Highnesse poems (Fanshawe), 114–16
Selected Parts of Horace (Fanshawe), 124, 125
A Summary Discourse of the Civil Warres in Rome (Fanshawe), 122
Virgil's Bull (Fanshawe), 127

The Works of Publius Virgilius Maro
    (Ogilby), 90, 92
  see also Charles II
Charles his Wain, 98–9, 112
Charles I, 2, 6, 7, 38, 55, 137, 138
  Carolies (Ogilby), 84, 107n
  The Commonwealth of Oceana
    (Harrington), 140
  Coopers Hill (Denham), 37, 39, 40
  The Destruction of Troy (Denham), 26,
    27–30, 32, 35, 36
  An Essay Upon two of Virgil's Eclogues
    (Harrington), 152
  Fanshawe's criticism of, 111, 112–14
  Homer his Iliads Translated (Ogilby), 96
  Homer his Odysses Translated (Ogilby), 98,
    100
  *Of the danger his Majestie (being Prince)
    escaped at the rode at St. Andere* (Waller),
    11–13
  On the Loves of Dido and Æneas
    (Fanshawe), 121
  The Passion of Dido (Denham), 46–8
  *Poems by the Honourable Sir Robert
    Howard*, 168
  The Relation of His Majestie's Entertainment
    (Ogilby), 104
  Sex Libri Plantarum (Cowley), 75, 76
  Virgil's Bull (Fanshawe), 128
  The Works of Publius Virgilius Maro
    (Ogilby), 34, 84, 86, 87, 92
Charles II, 2, 8, 45
  Æneas His Descent into Hell (Boys), 176–7
  Æneas His Errours (Boys), 177–8
  coronation procession, 102
  death, 182
  Homer his Iliads Translated (Ogilby), 94
  Homer his Odysses Translated (Ogilby), 98,
    99, 101
  *Poems by the Honourable Sir Robert
    Howard*, 165, 168–9, 170, 171
  The Relation of His Majestie's Entertainment
    (Ogilby), 103–4
  Sex Libri Plantarum (Cowley), 77
  Specimen Rerum a Lusitanis (Fanshawe),
    133
  Verses (Cowley), 70, 71
  Visions and Prophecies (Cowley), 72
  The Works of Publius Virgilius Maro
    (Ogilby), 85
  see also Charles, Prince of Wales
Chernaik, Warren L., 11
Cicero, 30
Civil War, The (Cowley), 56, 58, 60–3, 64, 90,
  112, 113
Clarastella (Heath), 106
Clarendon, Earl of (Edward Hyde), 46, 179,
  180
classical republicanism, 138
Cleveland, John, 20
Collection of parts of some Bookes of Virgill, A
  (Kingsmill), 159, 160–1
Commonwealth, The, 7, 87, 143
Commonwealth of Oceana, The (Harrington),
  138, 139–47, 159
constitutional royalism, 26, 40, 46, 48, 57,
  105–6, 111

Coopers Hill (Denham), 21, 36, 37–44, 62, 97,
  170, 181
Corns, Thomas, 42, 65
Covenanters, 83
Cowley, Abraham, 1, 49, 53–79
  The Civil War, 56, 58, 60–3, 64, 90, 112,
    113
  Cutter of Coleman-Street, 73–4
  Davideis, 56, 60, 63–7
  Duo Libri Plantarum, 74
  The Foure Ages of England, 57
  The Guardian, 73
  A Letter to a Friend, 57
  The Mistress, 59
  Naufragium Joculare (The Jolly Shipwreck),
    53
  Poems, 59, 63, 69
  The Puritan and the Papist, 58
  royalism, 57–60
  Sex Libri Plantarum, 56, 60, 74–9
  To the Lord Falkland, 57
  *Verses, Lately Written Upon Several
    Occasions*, 56, 67–72
  Visions and Prophecies, 72–3
Crashaw, Richard, 1, 126
Cresswell, Robert, 57
Croke, Sir George, 41
Cromwell, Oliver
  Battle of Dunbar, 168
  The Commonwealth of Oceana
    (Harrington), 139–40, 143–4, 145–7
  Edmund Waller, 16, 18, 19
  An Essay Upon two of Virgil's Eclogues
    (Harrington), 148, 150
  Penruddock uprising, 42
  *Poems by the Honourable Sir Robert
    Howard*, 170
  Virgil's Æneis (Harrington), 155
Cromwell, Richard, 72
Cromwellian Protectorate, 7, 72, 143, 144,
  146, 149, 150–1
Crowther, Stefania, 73
Cutter of Coleman-Street (Cowley), 73–4

Davenant, Sir William, 73, 95, 156–7
Davideis (Cowley), 56, 60, 63–7
Davidson, Peter, 118
Davis, J.C., 144
Davis, Paul, 36, 68
de factoist thought, 95
De Groot, Jerome, 20, 33
death *see mors immatura*; Priam's death
Delights of the Muses, The (Crashaw), 126
Denham, Sir John, 1, 26–49
  Abraham Cowley, 58
  Aeneid 2–6, 20–1
  aesthetics, 151
  Cato Major of Old Age, 30
  Coopers Hill, 21, 36, 36–44, 62, 97, 170,
    181
  The Destruction of Troy, 21, 26–36, 42, 66,
    137, 171
  Horace (Corneille/Philips/Denham), 48–9
  The Passion of Dido, 21, 44–8
  Poems and Translations, 26, 32, 43–4, 47
  The Progress of Learning, 32
  The Sophy, 21, 29, 43

Destruction of Troy, The (Denham), 21, 26–36, 42, 66, 137, 171
Digges, *Sir* Dudley, 31
domestication (translation theory), 30
Dryad of the Oak, 75–8
Dryden, John, 45, 103, 180–3
Dunbar, Battle of, 168–9
Duo Libri Plantarum (Cowley), 74
Dutch naval power, 76–7
Dyer, John, 78

Eclogues (Virgil)
  in *The Civil War* (Cowley), 60
  in *An Essay Upon two of Virgil's Eclogues* (Harrington), 147–51
  in *An Ode Upon occasion of His Majesties Proclamation* (Fanshawe), 112
  in *The Works of Publius Virgilius Maro* (Ogilby), 85–7, 89, 91
Edward III, 40
Eighteen Hundred and Eleven (Barbauld), 78
empire *see* imperium
engravings, 92, 96, 106, 130
Ereira, Alan, 83, 92
Essay Upon two of Virgil's Eclogues, An (Harrington), 148–51, 157–8
Exclusion Crisis, 166, 180, 181

Faithfull Shepherd, The (Fanshawe), 106, 111, 115, 116–18
Falkland, *Viscount*, 10, 16, 20, 57, 58, 62, 64
Fanshawe, *Sir* Richard, 1, 15, 31, 111–34
  A Canto of the Progresse of Learning, 118
  The Faithfull Shepherd, 106, 111, 115, 116–18
  The Lusiad, or Portugals Historicall Poem, 111, 129–33
  An Ode Upon occasion of His Majesties Proclamation, 60, 112–13, 114
  On His Majesties Great Shippe, 112, 113–14, 116
  On the Loves of Dido and Æneas, 118–21
  Presented to His Highnesse, In the West, Ann. Dom. 1646., 114, 115
  Presented to His Highnesse the Prince of Wales, 114–15
  Selected Parts of Horace, 111, 123–5:
    Virgil's Bull, 123–4, 125–9
  Specimen Rerum a Lusitanis, 129, 132, 133–4
  A Summary Discourse of the Civil Warres in Rome, 122–4
Farnaby, Thomas, 87–8
Foure Ages of England, The (Cowley), 57

Georgics (Virgil), 7, 68, 87, 91, 104, 123, 126, 127, 128, 180
Gloucester, *Duke of* (*Prince* Henry), 175–6
Gloucester, *Duke of* (*Prince* William), 183–4
Godolphin, Sidney, 1, 21
  death, 10, 61
  Lady Rich, 134
  Passion of Dido for Æneas, The, 9–10
  poetry, 10–11, 14
  royalism, 17–18
Golden Age, 45, 70–1

Great Tew Circle, 10, 20, 21, 57
Guardian, The (Cowley), 73

Hammersley, Rachel, 138–9, 146, 159
Harrington, James, 1, 8, 18, 137–59
  The Commonwealth of Oceana, 138, 139–47, 159
  An Essay Upon two of Virgil's Eclogues, 148–51, 157–8
  'The Translator to the Reader', 155–6
  Virgil's Æneis, 151–9
Harrington, *Sir* James (cousin of J.H.), 138
Hastings, *Lord* Henry, 37
Heath, Robert, 1, 105–6
Henrietta Maria, *Queen*, 2, 12–13, 58, 59
Henrique of Portugal, *Dom*, 130
Henry VIII, 40
Herrick, Robert, 88
Hesperus, 93–4
Hobbes, Thomas, 156–7
Homer, 85, 94–5
  Iliad, 95, 96, 97
  Odyssey, 98, 99–100, 101
Homer his Iliads Translated (Ogilby), 94–8
Homer his Odysses Translated (Ogilby), 98–102
Horace *see Selected Parts of Horace* (Fanshawe)
Horace (Corneille/Philips/Denham), 48–9
Howard, *Sir* Robert, 1, 159, 160–1
  Poems by the Honourable Sir Robert Howard, 160, 165, 166–72
hunting *see* stag-hunts
Hutchinson, Lucy, 19–20
Hyde, Anne, 182, 183
  Anne, *Princess*, 183
Hyde, Edward *see* Clarendon, *Earl of* (Edward Hyde)

Il Pastor Fido (Guarini), 4, 15, 106, 111, 116; *see also Faithfull Shepherd, The* (Fanshawe)
Iliad (Homer), 95, 96, 97
illustrations, 92, 130; *see also* engravings
imperium, 76–7, 78, 79
Interregnum, 8, 59, 143
italicisation, 87–8, 89, 91, 103, 104, 154, 173

James VII and II, 182, 183
Jenkinson, Matthew, 92
Jermyn, Henry, 58
João I (*King of Portugal*), 130, 132
Jolly Shipwreck, The (*Naufragium Joculare*) (Cowley), 53
Jonson, Ben, 10, 11

Kilgour, Maggie, 77
Kingsmill, *Sir* William, 1, 159, 160–1
Knowles, Ronald, 102

La Franciade (Ronsard), 154
Lachrymæ Musarum (Brome, ed.), 37
Lake, Edward, 55, 58
land confiscation/distribution, 91, 139, 147, 148, 149, 150, 153
landownership, 140, 141, 149
Les Recherches de La France (Pasquier), 154
Letter to a Friend, A (Cowley), 57

Lockey, Brian, 131
Løsnes, Arvid, 93
Louvre faction, 58
Lowestoft, Battle of, 77
Loxley, James, 69
Lucan, 33, 60, 157
Lusiad, or Portugals Historicall Poem, The (Fanshawe), 111, 129–33

McElligott, Jason, 59
MacLean, Gerald M., 61
McTague, John, 181
Maitland, Richard, *Earl of Lauderdale*, 183
'Man in Darkness' (Vaughan), 126
Marcellus, 8
Maria Anna, 11; *see also* Spanish Infanta, The
Maria Theresa, 116; *see also* Spanish Infanta, The
Megaletor, Olphaeus, 139, 141, 144–6, 147
Miscellany Poems (Dryden), 182
Mistress, The (Cowley), 59
Momeni, Amin, 29
Monck, George, 170, 171
mors immatura, 6, 61, 62, 64
Moseley, Humphrey, 15

Naufragium Joculare (*The Jolly Shipwreck*) (Cowley), 53
naval powers, 76–7, 78, 79
New World, 77–8
Norbrook, David, 11, 33, 139, 142–3
Northumberland, Countess of (*Lady* Cecil), 11

O Hehir, Brendan, 27
Ode Upon occasion of His Majesties Proclamation (Fanshawe), 60, 112–13, 114
Odyssey (Homer), 98, 99–100, 101
Of the danger his Majestie (being Prince) escaped at the rode at St. Andere (Waller), 11–13, 14–15, 16
'Of the Fox and the Lyon' (Ogilby), 92
Of the Loves of Dido and Æneas (Howard), 166, 167, 169
Ogilby, John, 1, 17, 34, 68, 79, 83–104
  Carolies, 84, 107n
  Homer his Iliads Translated, 94–8
  Homer his Odysses Translated, 98–102
  'Of the Fox and the Lyon', 92
  The Relation of His Majestie's Entertainment, 103–4
  The Works of Publius Virgilius Maro, 83–5: 1649 edition, 85–90, 173; 1654 edition, 90–4, 99
O'Hara, James J., 5
On His Majesties Great Shippe (Fanshawe), 112, 113–14, 116
'On Praise' (Bacon), 145
On the Loves of Dido and Æneas (Fanshawe), 118–21
Order of the Black Riband, 88
Order of the Garter, 130–1
Os Lusíadas (Camões), 129, 130, 136n; *see also Lusiad, or Portugals Historicall Poem, The* (Fanshawe)

Panegyrick to my Lord Protector, A (Waller), 16, 19

Paradoxical Assertions (Heath), 106
Parliament, 105–6, 144
parliamentary royalism *see* constitutional royalism
Parry, Graham, 117
Pasquier, Étienne, 154
Passion of Dido (Denham), 21, 44–8
Passion of Dido for Æneas, The (Godolphin and Waller), 9–19, 169
  and *Of the danger his Majestie (being Prince) escaped at the rode at St. Andere* (Waller), 11–15
Patterson, Annabel, 86
Penruddock uprising, 42
Pharsalia (Lucan), 33, 157
Philip II (*King of Spain*), 116
Philippa of Lancaster, 130, 132
Poems (Cowley), 59, 63, 69
Poems and Translations (Denham), 26, 32, 43–4, 47
Poems by the Honourable Sir Robert Howard, 160, 165, 166–72
poeta, 4
political allegiances, 105
Portuguese Infanta, The, 131–2; *see also* Catherine of Braganza
post eventum prophecies, 5–6
  Absalom and Achitophel (Dryden), 182
  Cutter of Coleman-Street (Cowley), 74
  Davideis (Cowley), 65
  The Destruction of Troy (Denham), 33
  Of the danger his Majestie (being Prince) escaped at the rode at St. Andere (Waller), 16
  The Passion of Dido (Denham), 47
  Sex Libri Plantarum (Cowley), 74, 78
  Specimen Rerum a Lusitanis (Fanshawe), 133
  Verses (Cowley), 56
  see also prophecies; retrospective prophecies
Power, Henry, 62, 122
Presented to His Highnesse, In the West, Ann. Dom. 1646 (Fanshawe), 114, 115
Presented to His Highnesse the Prince of Wales (Fanshawe), 114–15
Priam's death
  Aeneid (Virgil), 6
  The Destruction of Troy (Denham), 26, 27–31, 32–3, 35
  An Essay Upon two of Virgil's Eclogues (Harrington), 157–8
  Homer his Odysses Translated (Ogilby), 100
  Poems by the Honourable Sir Robert Howard, 167, 168
  Sex Libri Plantarum (Cowley), 76
  Virgil's Æneis (Harrington), 137, 152
  The Works of Publius Virgilius Maro (Ogilby), 34, 84
Prince Arthur (Blackmore), 183
Prince's Party royalism, 111
Pritchard, Allan, 60, 62
Progress of Learning, The (Denham), 32
prophecies, 4–7
  Cutter of Coleman-Street (Cowley), 73
  Davideis (Cowley), 63
  The Faithfull Shepherd (Fanshawe), 116
  John Boys, 165–6, 180

prophecies (cont.)
  The Relation of His Majestie's Entertainment (Ogilby), 104
  retrospective, 181
  Sex Libri Plantarum (Cowley), 75–8
  Verses (Cowley), 70
  see also post eventum prophecies; *Visions and Prophecies* (Cowley)
prophets see vates
providence, 66, 85
Pugh, Syrithe, 112, 113, 121
Puritan and the Papist, The (Cowley), 58

Queen's Party royalism, 58–9

Raylor, Timothy, 12, 14
Relation of His Majestie's Entertainment (Ogilby), 103–4
republicanism
  autocratic, 139, 141, 155
  classical, 138
retrospective prophecy, 181; see also post eventum prophecies; prophecies
Rich, *Lady* Anne (*Lady* Cavendish), 11, 134
Rogerson, Anne, 5, 37
Ronsard, Pierre, 154
royalism, 2
  Abraham Cowley, 57–60, 64, 66–7, 69–70
  Henry Vaughan, 126
  John Boys, 172–3, 174–5
  John Denham, 26, 34, 42–3; see also constitutional royalism
  John Ogilby, 84–5, 87–9, 90–1, 92, 94, 95–7, 100–2
  The Passion of Dido for Æneas (Godolphin and Waller), 15
  Richard Crashaw, 126
  Richard Fanshawe, 111
  Robert Howard, 170, 171
  Sidney Godolphin, 17–18
Ruins of Rome, The (Dyer), 78

St Edward's Crown, 92
St Giles Riots, 33–4
Sandys, George, 11, 20, 21, 31
Schoenberger, Melissa, 7
Scott, Jonathan, 145
sculptures, 92; see also engravings; illustrations
Sebastião I (*King of Portugal*), 130
Selected Parts of Horace (Fanshawe), 111, 123–5
  Virgil's Bull, 123–4, 125–9
Sequestration Committee, 91
Sex Libri Plantarum (Cowley), 56, 60, 74–9
Seymour, William, *Earl of Hertford*, 86
Sherburne, Edward, 88
Ship Money levy, 41, 113
Shirley, James, 88
Sidney, *Lady* Catherine, 160
Sidney, Philip, *Earl of Leicester*, 160
Sidney, *Sir* Philip, 5
Smith, David L., 40, 59
'Sons of Ben', 10
Sophia of Hanover, 184
Sophy, The (Denham), 21, 29, 43
Soveraigne of the Seas, The (Fanshawe)
  see *On His Majesties Great Shippe* (Fanshawe)
Sowerby, Robin, 9, 10, 13, 20, 32, 44
Spanish Infanta, The, 12, 14, 116, 117, 129, 131
Spanish Match, The, 11, 12, 13, 14
Spearing, Caroline, 69, 70
Specimen Rerum a Lusitanis (Fanshawe), 132, 133–4
Spenserian stanza, 118–19
Sprat, Thomas, 58
stag-hunts, 37–8, 39, 43
Stanley, Thomas, 88
Stapylton, *Sir* Robert, 31
Strafford, 1st Earl of see Wentworth, Thomas, 1st Earl of Strafford
Strafford, 2nd Earl of see Wentworth, William, 2nd Earl of Strafford
Stuart monarchy, 7
Summary Discourse of the Civil Warres in Rome, A (Fanshawe), 122–4
superstructions, 141, 143
Sylvae (Dryden), 182

Temple, *Sir* William, 180
Thomas, Richard, 70
To the Lord Falkland (Cowley), 57
translatio imperii, 77, 78
translation, 30
'Translator to the Reader, The' (Harrington), 155–6
typography, 87–8, 173; see also italicisation

Van Eerde, Katherine S., 96
vates, 4–5, 40, 104, 113
Vaughan, Henry, 1, 126
Verses, Lately Written Upon Several Occasions (Cowley), 56, 67–72
Vicars, John, 90, 105
Virgil's Æneis (Harrington), 151–9
Virgil's Æneis Translated in English Heroick Verse (Heath), 105–6
Virgil's Bull (Fanshawe), 123–4, 125–9
Visions and Prophecies (Cowley), 72–3

Waller, Edmund, 1
  A Panegyrick to my Lord Protector, 16, 19
  Passion of Dido for Æneas, The, 9–11: and *Of the danger his Majestie (being Prince) escaped at the rode at St. Andere*, 11–15; and political allegiances, 15–19
Wentworth, Thomas, *1st Earl of Strafford*, 38, 39, 41, 43, 47, 96
Wentworth, William, *2nd Earl of Strafford*, 129, 129–30
William of Orange, 182, 183
Worcester, Battle of, 42, 128–9
Worden, Blair, 143, 145
Works of Publius Virgilius Maro, The (Ogilby), 83–5
  1649 edition, 85–90, 173
  1654 edition, 90–5, 99
Wroth, *Sir* Thomas, 31

XII Aeneids of Virgil (Vicars), 90, 105

Young, Edward, 77

EU representative:
Easy Access System Europe
Mustamäe tee 50, 10621 Tallinn, Estonia
Gpsr.requests@easproject.com

www.ingramcontent.com/pod-product-compliance
Lightning Source LLC
Chambersburg PA
CBHW070356240426
43671CB00013BA/2524